GEORGE

WASHINGTON

ARCHITECT

GEORGE WASHINGTON

ARCHITECT

ALLAN GREENBERG

FOREWORD BY VINCENT SCULLY
SELECTED PHOTOGRAPHS BY TIM BUCHMAN

ANDREAS PAPADAKIS PUBLISHER

DEDICATED TO THE MEMORY

OF MY MOTHER,

SYBIL GREENBERG (1915 - 1998)

———————◆———————

AND MY FRIEND AND MENTOR,

ARTHUR DREXLER (1925 - 1987)

ARLY VERSIONS OF BOTH PAPERS HAVE BEEN PUBLISHED. A PAPER ON WASHINGTON AND L'ENFANT WAS PRESENTED AT THE symposium *The Mall in Washington 1791–1986* held at the National Gallery of Art, Washington, D.C., in 1987. My text was not included in the publication of the conference proceedings because of a misunderstanding with the book's editors. A shorter version of the section on symbolism, "L'Enfant, Washington, and the Plan of the Capital," was published in *The Magazine Antiques*, July 1991, 112–123. The volume, *George Washington's Mount Vernon*, published last year by The Monacelli Press, included a chapter entitled "Architecture," that explored some of the design challenges of the Mansion House. I am grateful to the publisher of *The Magazine Antiques* and to The Monacelli Press for permission to reuse parts of these two papers.

In writing these essays, I am indebted to many people without whose help and advice I would still be floundering. In particular, I am grateful to Barbara A. McMillan, Librarian of the Ladies' Association of Mount Vernon, who read and commented on numerous drafts of the Mount Vernon paper and generously shared her vast knowledge of Washington and Mount Vernon with me. The staff at Mount Vernon, including Dennis J. Pogue, Director of Restoration, and John Riley, Assistant to the Director, read and commented on the paper, corrected errors of fact, and patiently answered all my queries; Marc A. Le François, Architectural Conservator, thoughtfully initiated me into the details of his current study of the fabric of the house; and King Laughlin, Associate Curator, provided invaluable assistance and information. Professor Charles Brownell of Virginia Commonwealth University and Calder C. Loth, Senior Architectural Historian, Department of Historic Resources, Commonwealth of Virginia, read the Mount Vernon paper and generously shared their unpublished material and ideas; Professor Pamela Scott of Cornell University and Professor Richard Longstreth of George Washington University helped me with advice and criticism of the Washington, D.C., paper. Professor James Kornwolf of the College of William and Mary, Professor Carroll William Westfall of the University of Virginia, William C. Allen, Architectural Historian of the U. S. Capitol, and William L. MacDonald, my teacher at Yale in the 1960s and friend of thirty years, all read early versions of the paper and generously assisted me with their criticism and advice.

To Louise Fili and Mary Jane Callister, whose eloquent design graces the pages of this book, to Tim Buchman, whose photographs portray Mount Vernon in new ways, and to Vincent Scully, who generously consented to write the foreword, I can only say thank you. I am also indebted to Slade Elkins, William Bourque, Bob Colarusso, Michael Callison, Katherine Flanigan, and Robert McClennan, of my office, who were responsible for the drawings specially prepared for this book; Karen Lee and Kathryn McCutchen Mirabella who helped with editorial and picture research; Lynn Goldberg and Mark Fortier for their advice on publication of the book and their help arranging lectures and publicity; and my wonderful editors, Sara Blackburn and Julie Lasky, who meticulously guided both papers through numerous drafts. Finally, I owe a special debt of gratitude to Beth Saidel who provided salutary doses of common sense, organizational genius, and drive that ultimately moved this project off the shoals of preparation and into the arena of publication.

I am grateful to Andreas Papadakis, my friend of long standing, for publishing this book and to my wife, Judith Seligson, for her incisive criticism and support of this venture.

All errors, unproven inferences, and inaccuracies are, of course, my own.

CONTENTS

IN THE 1960'S, ALLAN GREENBERG EMIGRATED FROM SOUTH AFRICA TO THE UNITED STATES AFTER A PERIOD OF STUDY AT THE ARCHITECTURAL association in London. During his years as a graduate student in the Yale School of Architecture he put his interest in the social and political meanings of architecture to direct use by working for New Haven's Redevelopment Agency, which was at that time at the height of its destructive powers. I think it is fair to say that he was the only member of its staff to concern himself with fundamental issues of historic preservation, and his efforts in that direction helped save a number of distinguished government buildings in New Haven, the United States Post Office most of all.

During those years, Greenberg might best have been described as an idealistic liberal, with the vaguely Marxist orientation of the European intellectual of that period. His point of view was, however, essentially practical and pragmatic. As the father of a young family, he induced other parents in the New Haven community to set up a multiracial school in which Yale graduate students and parents were the teachers and saw to it that their children learned to read. For a few years he was also employed by Yale to teach the undergraduate major in architecture. In that role he took the first decisive step in what has turned out to be his lifelong search for classical architecture and toward a political orientation much closer to the *Federalist Papers* than to *Das Kapital*. Modernist opponents of classicism are fond of claiming that its practitioners are all politically conservative or even reactionary and that classical architecture is the same. That generalization is of course wholly ridiculous. Jefferson, our first and greatest architectural classicist, himself gives it the lie. For Greenberg, too, the embrace of classical architecture involved a kind of radical politics. It expressed his outrage at the blight of urban renewal and the social and architectural

premises upon which it was based. To his eye, the modernist academy was the source of the trouble and had indeed become a conservative bastion. In his teaching at Yale he threw out the inane folded-paper exercises of the Bauhaus system, still mistakenly regarded at that time as a revolutionary one, and dared to reinstate, with enormous success, many of the old, supposedly conservative, Beaux-Arts methods of instruction. His students read books, learned history, traced the plans of famous buildings, learned to draw those buildings as they looked and with all their difficult details, and studied not only traditional urban spaces like New Haven's incomparable Green, but also the contemporary misuse of zoning to create neighborhoods excluding blacks and the poor. As a professor of history much younger than I am now, I was struck by the feeling of liberation which those actions of Greenberg's generated. Like Andres Duany and Elizabeth Plater-Zyberk a few years later, he restored forbidden things, made lost experiences accessible once more, and in general broke the conceptual limitations within which modernism had bound us. In fact, Duany and Plater-Zyberk were students in Greenberg's classes and served as teaching assistants in his undergraduate program.

At the same time Greenberg, who had been trained in classical design in South Africa, began to execute overtly classical architectural commissions, among the earliest of a new classical revival and, as always, he was working with government where he could. In the seventies he executed a series of designs for courthouses in Connecticut that seemed enormously daring at the time, groping their way back toward classicism step by step, as they were all trying to do. It is difficult to express now how revolutionary they seemed to those of us who, however historical in approach, had been prevented by modernist proscription from perceiving that the past could indeed be reused, not metaphorically but straight. Now, of course, neo-modernist architectural theory does its best to make all that look timid and regressive — even, in accordance with modernism's inveterate paranoia — traitorous to some aesthetic or moral ideal. But that is not the way it was; it was fresh, releasing, and new, and it has since proved itself by producing, in concert with other movements, a new urbanism which is capable of putting decent communities together once again.

In fact, Greenberg's methods were too revolutionary for the architecture school, and his success with students much too marked. In consequence, he soon felt compelled to resign from the school, but he has always had his own students since that time. He and they together have continued to study the language of Classicism in his offices in Washington and Greenwich, and their practice is now large and varied and has included some important government work. Greenberg himself has gone on to develop his historical interest in the relationship between government and architecture. Out of that concern has grown his conviction that American classicism has always been the fundamental expression of the special qualities of American democracy and of its governmental forms. Indeed, he identifies Classicism with the United States, for which he seems to feel a special architect's version of the immigrant's patriotic fervor. It is Republicanism that moves him with its checks and balances, its measured ways. He is most of all a Federalist, believing in the primacy of the Federal government, not in states' rights. Therefore his political hero is Washington, not Jefferson, and though he passionately admires Jefferson's architecture, once saying that "God's Finger touched earth at the University of Virginia, the 'Academical Village'," he is clearly impatient with him on most other grounds.

That understood, what he does for Washington as an architect and urban planner is surely quite wonderful. He studies his achievements at Mount Vernon and in the planning of Washington, D.C., as no other historian has yet done. His conclusions are original and may well become the subject of debate. He regards the curious asymmetries of Mount Vernon as intentional (though in an ambitious design of his own for a house in Greenwich he once straightened them all out). Far beyond that, he regards the thousands of acres of the Mount Vernon farm as having been shaped by Washington into one grand ecological design, combining landscape devices both classical and romantic in origin. Monticello tends to dwindle in comparison, though Greenberg never quite says so.

Much the same happens with the nation's capital. Jefferson's original, beautifully sited little grid plan for it is made to seem small in conception, his view of the country's destiny unduly restricted. How did he ever come to purchase Louisiana, one rather irritably wonders? By contrast, Washington and his Major L'Enfant, heroes and comrades in arms, confer grandly together over their mighty vision. The big city — Greenberg makes us realize just how big it was for its time — takes form under their hands. The country's expansive future is secured. It is stirring mythography, worthy of its great subject and documented with meticulous care.

It is challenging history, and I personally, though disagreeing with some of it, find it exciting to read. It is history written by a committed architect who is trying to do the same kinds of things that the heroic precursors he writes about did. In that attempt, Greenberg is staking out a position as architect and historian that is at the very center of the American classical tradition. It recalls the stance of Fiske Kimball, a fine classical architect of the first half of this century, who was for a long time the only American art historian whose name was known in Europe. Kimball, too, wrote about American architecture from a classicist's point of view, but he taught and built at the University of Virginia so that his primary interest was in Jefferson and his works. Greenberg, no less directed by classical enthusiasms, turns to Washington to redress the balance. In so doing, he brings a new focus to the study of those years when uncommon human beings, with markedly different points of view but all believing in Reason, were doing their best to shape a stable political and architectural structure for their newly united states.

As an architect who loves to study and write about architectural history, my approach to the subject is sometimes a little different from that of bona fide architectural historians. It grows out of concerns that are part of the day-to-day activity in an architectural office. I tend to be preoccupied with particular buildings, to spend more time on a formal analysis of the work of architecture and its relationship to its surroundings. I am naturally attuned to the relationship of client and architect in order to reconstruct the process by which key decisions were made. This difference of approach proved helpful in trying to highlight George Washington's two forays into architecture: the design of the house, gardens, and farms of Mount Vernon and his collaboration with Peter Charles L'Enfant in the creation of Washington, D.C.

In both ventures, we have little or no information about Washington's design ideas. His comments on architecture are rare and guarded. With Mount Vernon, I have tried to bridge the gulf between the paucity of data and the architectonic authority of the home Washington created by undertaking a detailed formal analysis of the Mansion House in order to isolate its unusual design characteristics; relating the one extant elevation drawing of Mount Vernon in Washington's hand to the house he built; and studying Washington's 1793 survey map of the property for its documentation of the landscape and architectural relationships between farm buildings, roads, and the main house. Using topographic surveys made in the 1930s and 1950s of the land occupied by the five farms at Mount Vernon, I obtained some sense of the approximate contours and land forms. These maps were prepared by the United States Geodetic Survey and the Commonwealth of Virginia and show the area before it was developed as a suburb after 1960.

Although erosion may have altered it, no major construction, development, or other intervention appears to have occurred between 1793 and the time of these surveys that would radically change the land forms. Many roads created by Washington and his predecessors still survive on these maps. While nothing definitive may be concluded, I have used these maps to hypothesize some of the relationships between different parts of the five farms that Washington may have had in mind, as drawn on the 1793 survey. Scrutinizing Washington's correspondence and diaries, I located clues about his plans and intentions. Further information was obtained through careful reviewing of accounts of the house, gardens, and farms made in the diaries and letters of visitors to the estate and through comparisons with other houses and circumstances of the period.

I have also tried to confront the enigmatic design qualities of the house. For example, some writers have postulated that Washington was hampered with the asymmetry of the front elevation of Mount Vernon when he inherited the small house from his elder brother. As one of the wealthiest men in Virginia, he could easily have corrected the deficiency by moving four windows, a minor operation in a building program that almost trebled the house's area. It is more likely that Washington prized the asymmetry, for each of the three other elevations are also asymmetrical. Unlike Thomas Jefferson's house at Monticello, which is self-evidently a powerful work of architecture, the Mansion at Mount Vernon is difficult to come to terms with. Nonetheless, I believe that there is nothing accidental about the architecture Washington created as he completed his building program. The first expansion of the house in 1758 was an expression of the young owner's growing status in Virginia; the post-1774 construction transformed the house into something quite different—a rare combination of monumental forms that are offset by vernacular elements.

Our knowledge of George Washington's career as an amateur architect is limited to his home and the surrounding farms and gardens at Mount Vernon. He also built two townhouses in the federal city, but they have disappeared and we have no idea what they looked like or how they were planned. To compound the challenge, this unusual farmhouse at Mount Vernon is set in what must have been one of the most beautiful gardens in North America, for Washington was one of the finest landscape architects of the eighteenth century. Yet, while there is considerable data relating to gardening, farming, and horticulture in his letters, little of it actually deals directly with design. This becomes particularly frustrating when Washington describes design plans, such as his instructions to create numerous vistas to connect different parts of the property, and we are unable to relate his words to precise locations.

We can also only speculate about Washington's ideas for building a capital city. As the first president of a new nation, he dreamed of embodying republican values in its plan and public buildings. The data at hand provides a chronological outline of events but we know almost nothing about the genesis of the design or the exchange of ideas that occurred between Washington and L'Enfant. Again, a close reading of the available material led to some new thoughts. Often, these were achieved by looking at the problem from another point of view, substituting one question for another. For example, instead of speculating about why something was done, I asked what were the alternatives and why were they rejected? In particular, why did Washington reject the obvious and expeditious solution of using Jefferson's grid plan proposals or the opportunity to design such a plan himself? This question led me to scan the correspondence for references to a special type of plan, study the text of L'Enfant's plan for answers, and search for L'Enfant's own sources.

Writing about the past, of necessity, is a process of searching for new evidence, restudying original sources, and reassessing the thoughts of other writers on the subject. This may be why the second part of the word history is story. Some speculation is inevitable. These two papers are essays, attempts to improve our understanding, on aspects of Washington's architecture, landscape design, and city planning. My deductions may sometimes stray beyond a strict reading of the evidence. In such cases, the speculation is merely posited and should be challenged with superior interpretations.

There are important areas I have not addressed. Perhaps the most significant one is the question of slavery. Without understanding the role of slavery in the agricultural and social life of the times, we cannot begin to understand the daily routines of life at Mount Vernon and the other farms and plantations of Virginia. Slave labor also built the house and had direct impact on the organization of the building site, the manufacture of materials, and the quality and methods of construction. How did building with slave labor differ from construction based on salaried artisans and laborers? What were the routines of life in the house? How were the various rooms used? How did life in the houses of small farmers differ from that in the mansions of large farms and plantations? How did the society of the time use its public buildings? These matters are of fundamental importance if we are to understand the role of buildings, both in the past and present, as being worthy of more than just aesthetic speculation.

Additional chapters addressing such questions would have been the perfect conclusion to this volume. I wish I had sufficient knowledge of slavery and of the overlap of social, economic, agronomic, and cultural history to begin to study these questions. Sadly, my ignorance in these areas is so profound as to preclude even attempting to venture into this largely uncharted territory. I hope that others blessed with more knowledge than I will explore this wilderness with the same passion that Washington himself devoted to his exploration of the uncharted West. I look forward to reading the work of experts in all these areas in the future.

GEORGE WASHINGTON ARCHITECT

PART ONE

DIVINING THE BEAUTIFUL WITHOUT EVER HAVING SEEN THE MODEL

GEORGE WASHINGTON'S

ARCHITECTURE AND LANDSCAPE

FOR MOUNT VERNON

GEORGE WASHINGTON DESIGNED THE HOUSE AND GARDENS OF HIS HOME AT MOUNT VERNON. ALTHOUGH THE ESTATE IS VISITED BY NEARLY ONE MILLION PEOPLE EVERY YEAR, LITTLE RECOGNITION HAS BEEN ACCORDED TO WASHINGTON, THE INNOVATIVE architect and brilliant landscape architect (fig. 1). Perhaps Washington's achievements as a military commander and President are so significant that his buildings and gardens are seen as appendages of lesser cultural significance. Yet Washington was a genuinely inventive designer. The house and gardens at Mount Vernon are a rare and uncanny combination of high architecture and vernacular design, of formal elements and the picturesque. The garden was unusual, beautiful, and dramatic. It differed from most late-eighteenth-century estates in North America and England in two aspects. First, Washington integrated his farms into the garden, creating a vast landscape composition covering twelve square miles. While plans of great estates in the eighteenth century typically don't show the farms, he was not content to conceive of his house and gardens in isolation. Second, Washington's landscape design is a combination of existing natural features and new formal and picturesque elements. Mount Vernon may have been his subconscious paradigm for the future development of North America as a series of houses, farms, towns, and cities seamlessly woven into the virgin landscape by their beautiful gardens and garden-like farms.

The great challenge facing anyone writing about Mount Vernon is that Washington's creation is only partially available to us. The property was sub-divided among his heirs. Over the nineteenth and twentieth centuries parts were sold, and much of this land has been developed for suburban housing in the last thirty years (fig. 2).[1] Today, the grounds of Mount Vernon are only 5–6% of the area of the estate in the 1790s. Further, the gardens exist in an abbreviated form. Not only has much of the dense plantings of flowering shrubs and trees been lost, but the amazing approach to the house, one of the most innovative aspects of Washington's landscape, is now used as a service road. Visitors enter by a new, more direct, route to the house. This means that anyone wishing to write about George Washington, architect and landscape architect, has to recreate a "virtual" Mount Vernon, as it was in 1790s, for the reader to ponder. This is one of the goals of part one, with the aid of Washington's letters and diaries as well as those of visitors to the estate, survey maps, plans, and analysis of the exisiting house and grounds. What follows is an analysis of the exterior of the house, focusing on the most inventive aspects of Washington's architecture; Washington's own 1793 survey of the estate to better elucidate the organization of the farms; an analysis of the interior, including its unusual combination of formal and informal design elements; and, in conclusion, a look at

FIG. 1 *The east façade of Mount Vernon as it appears today.*

Washington as an exemplary form-giver.

Although Mount Vernon may be the most famous house in the United States, it is not clear why so many people visit it each year. Do they wish to pay tribute to a pivotal figure in the founding of a new nation, America's first President? Or, as I suspect, do they also hope to learn something about the man himself? In the case of Washington this is not easy to do. It is singularly difficult to see beyond his awesome achievements and the somewhat inert effigies of him in history books and biographies. Contemporary portraits capture something of the military and political leader, but reveal little of the man's human side. By visiting the home George and Martha Washington, created by contemplating the inti-

macy of the rooms in which the family lived and entertained, and by visiting the surrounding gardens that framed their daily routines, something of the character and personality of this couple may be gleaned. Many visitors to Mount Vernon want to learn about the George Washington who was a devoted husband and doting step-grandparent; a man who loved to listen to music, to dance, and to converse with women; a passionate farmer and gardener; and an innovative architect who built his own house.

Mount Vernon fascinates for other reasons. The nobility of the architecture and the remarkable interdependent relationship of the house to its gardens, to the river on which it fronts, and to the surrounding farmland, resonate with enduring ideals of American life. The unusual, and some-what elusive, character of the house and the magnificent twelve square miles of farms and gardens balance pragmatism, informality, and individualism; embody a reverence for gardening, horticulture, and farming; and render palpable some of the aspirations of the early American republic. These attributes of Mount Vernon focus on hitherto unexplored recesses of Washington's private world; his vision of human beings living harmoniously with nature is especially pertinent today because of our concern about ecology and preservation of the environment. Thus, the grail that visitors seek as they stream through the portals of Mount Vernon may be knowledge of the Washingtons' personal lives, experience of the ethos of the late eighteenth century, and renewed contact with an almost lost segment of the American dream.

Today we tend to think of Mount Vernon as a house. But Washington was first and foremost a farmer, and he planned his house as the focal point of an extensive agricultural estate. Between 1754, when he first leased Mount Vernon, and his death in 1799, Washington increased the size of the estate from 2,126 acres to more than 8,000, or twelve-and-a-half square miles. A pioneer of scientific agriculture in the new nation, he was one of the most innovative and success-

FIG. 2 *A photo taken in the 1850s showing Mount Vernon's condition when it was purchased in 1858 by the newly formed Mount Vernon Ladies' Association of the Union.*

ful farmers of his time and the house is the center of a group of farm and service buildings set in an elaborately planned picturesque garden at the east end of what Washington designated the "Mansion House farm." This, in turn, is surrounded by four other contiguous farms (fig. 3). House, garden, farm buildings, forests, and fields are all seamlessly woven together into a single composition. To accomplish this, Washington used hedges, ditches, and fences to separate the fields and meadows of the five farms as if they were the string courses and moldings that unify the façade of a building. Solid and void are set out by buildings, alone or in composed clusters, and by trees en-masse or as sculptural groups. Washington carefully cloaked the house in a modest architectural garb. He purposely understated his design innovations and incorporated them into the composition of house, gardens, and farms, in a manner so unpretentious that they seem almost unintentional. By the late 1790s, he had transformed his estate on the Potomac into a unique work of art, a conception of picturesque garden ideals that was profoundly American.

Washington's increasingly ambitious plans to reorganize his farms and to transform their economy was spurred initially by dissatisfaction with the fluctuating revenues generated by the annual sale of his tobacco crop in England. After he resigned from the Virginia Regiment in 1758, Washington became a tidewater farmer. He devoted himself to mastering every detail of the fifteen-month-long process of planting, nurturing, harvesting, curing, packing, shipping, and selling tobacco. Between 1759 and 1765 Washington saw his profits from the sale of tobacco decline. Successive tobacco crops also so severely depleted the soil that most planters abandoned these fields and constantly sought new land for their next crop. Despite increased investment in additional land for tobacco cultivation, he found himself forced to confront a massive and mounting burden of debt. He was determined to create a diversified agricultural base that would provide a more stable source of revenue. Thus, he initiated experiments, that would continue for three more decades, to improve the output of his fields, diversify his agricultural base, and upgrade the quality of his livestock. On April 4, 1760, he described in his diary how he experimented with alfalfa, clover, rye, grass, hops, trefoil, timothy, spelt (a type of wheat), and a number of different grasses and vegetables as well as ten varieties of compost. He also planted orchards and raised horses, dairy cows, beef cattle, hogs, chickens, turkeys, swans, and geese. He even attempted to keep sheep and golden pheasants from China. He improved his flour mill, built a sawmill, constructed a schooner to harvest shad and herring in the Potomac, and considered purchasing an iron furnace in the Shenandoah Valley.

Washington's plans were also driven by political ideals:

the protests of the American colonies against England's New Revenue Act of 1764, the Stamp Act of 1765, and other coercive legislation that would soon lead to the American Revolution.[2] The Northern Neck of Virginia was an important center of leadership in the movement to resist Parliament by boycotting the importation of British goods and encouraging local production. This resistance was all the more remarkable when we recall that many planters were so heavily in debt that Thomas Jefferson described them as "a species of property annexed to certain mercantile houses in London."[3] Washington played a critical role in drafting the county resolves that served as a model of commercial resistance for other locales and for the First Continental Congress.[4] He predicted that the financial strain imposed by

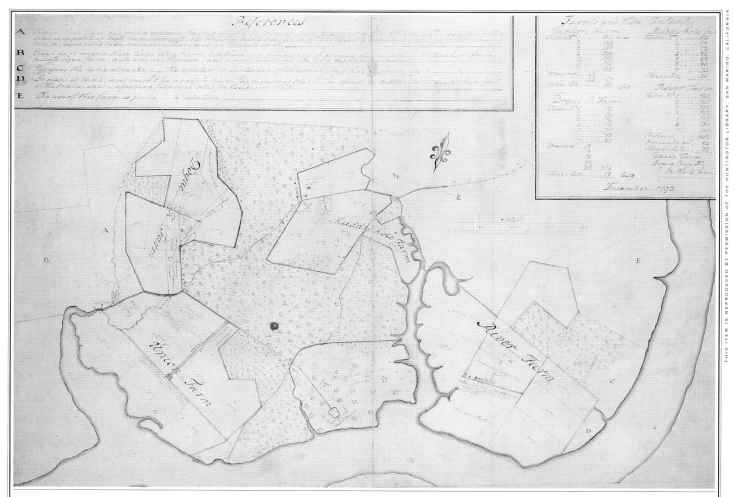

FIG. 3 *In 1793, George Washington prepared a survey map of Mount Vernon showing all five farms — River Farm, Muddy Hole Farm, Union Farm, Dogue Run Farm, and Mansion House Farm. The house appears in the center section of the map below the serpentine roadways. The area of the estate is just over 8,000 acres or twelve square miles.*

the new British taxes would encourage the colonists to lessen their importation of British goods and develop their own manufacturing capability.[5]

Washington was one of the first Virginians who understood that dependence on tobacco exports to England, without alternative crops, manufactures, or sources of credit, caused increasingly onerous colonial indebtedness. His resolve to become independent of English markets and credit, to diversify his crops, and to develop his own supplies of basic manufactured goods was so successful that he eventually became a wealthy man.[6]

Throughout his career, from the first resistance to British policy in the 1760s to the end of his two terms as president, Washington sought to realize economic independence for Virginia and the new nation. He considered economic self-sufficiency to be the basis of freedom and prosperity.[7] After the British were defeated, Washington continued to search for ways to sustain an independent economy; and by constantly improving methods of agriculture at Mount Vernon he provided a standard for innovation and diversification.[8]

THE ESTATE

Washington's father, Augustine Washington, had bought the plantation, then known as Little Hunting Creek, from his sister, Mildred, and her husband, Roger Gregory, in 1726. The land had been in the Washington family since 1674, and there is some evidence that the senior Washington may have constructed a building on the site prior to 1740, when he deeded the property to his eldest son, George Washington's half-brother, Lawrence. Sometime before he died in 1752, Lawrence Washington changed the name to Mount Vernon. The first floor of the original house on Lawrence Washington's property was 42 feet by 30 feet 6 inches, encompassing 1,280 square feet. It had four rooms, two on either side of a 13-foot-wide center passage (fig. 4). Above was a less spacious half-story, or attic floor. The house was modest by today's standards, but it was considered large at the time.

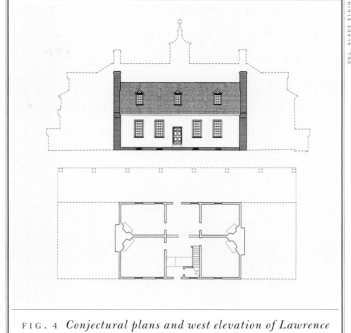

FIG. 4 *Conjectural plans and west elevation of Lawrence Washington's house in the early 1750s. The silhouette of the present Mount Vernon is indicated by the dashed line.*

Of the houses advertised for sale in the Virginia Gazette from 1736 to 1780, only 7.7% were larger than 1,216 square feet, and only 1.3% of landowners on Virginia's Northern Neck had estates of more than 2,000 acres.[9]

Visitors to Lawrence Washington's Mount Vernon may have traveled by road from Alexandria or Colchester, or by boat. The driveway to the house terminated in a circle that was contained within a forecourt. The unusual feature of this forecourt was its definition by outbuildings and wood fences that were set at angles to the house, like outstretched arms. The effect was not only to frame the view of the house's west side but also to create a more welcoming entrance court. The angled outbuildings also established a false perspective that made the house appear nearer, and more impressive, than it actually was when viewed from a distance (fig. 5). A source of this design may have been the entrance court at Belvoir, the nearby house of Col. William Fairfax, Lawrence Washington's father-in-law.[10] Documentary evidence suggests that George Washington replaced the wood fences with walls.[11]

In 1754, George Washington leased the 2,126-acre farm

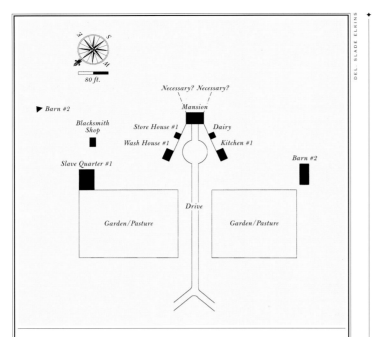

DEL. SLADE ELKINS

FIG. 5 *A conjectural site plan of Lawrence Washington's house in the early 1750s, when George Washington leased the property. The plan shows outbuildings set at an angle to the house around a centrally located driveway. Rectangular parterres enclose formal gardens on either side of it. The barn and the blacksmith's shop are the only outbuildings that are extant.*

from Lawrence's widow, Anne Fairfax Washington Lee. Upon her death, and then that of her daughter Sarah, Lawrence's only heir, George Washington inherited the estate in 1761. By that time he had purchased a number of adjacent properties, increasing the estate to 4,800 acres. He began to rebuild Mount Vernon in 1757, and shortly after commenced his courtship of Martha Dandridge Custis, whom he married on January 6, 1759. To create a full second floor and a new attic, he raised the roof and in 1760 built two "little houses," probably outhouses, on the east side of the house facing the Potomac (fig. 6). Like the outbuildings Lawrence built on the west side, these were connected to the house by fences set at an angle. In 1774 he began the second phase of construction, which would transform Mount Vernon into one of the larger houses in Virginia (fig. 7). He built extensions at each end of the house and connected larger dependencies to them with the addition of curved arcades. The piazza was constructed on the east side

of the house overlooking the river (fig. 8). The existing service and support buildings on the west side were removed and replaced with a street of others at right angles to the house, which formed a cross-axis (fig. 9). This complex of buildings became the centerpiece of the estate.

Washington also planned a completely new garden and continued to make interior improvements. After returning from the Revolutionary War, in December 1783, he completed the construction and decoration of the house and created and realized the new garden design. To implement a seven-crop rotation instead of the more typical three-crop version, he also embarked on a comprehensive reorganization of the five farms, creating larger fields and constructing new roads and farm buildings, which included three barn complexes. So it was that Washington transformed the entire estate—house, gardens, farms—into one great landscape composition. Up to the time of his fatal illness in December 1799, he would be preoccupied with perfecting his creation.

—————————◆—————————

WASHINGTON'S MANAGEMENT
OF HIS ESTATE

It is clear from Washington's voluminous correspondence that, from the time he took possession of Mount Vernon in 1754 until his death forty-five years later (in 1799), the condition of the house and surrounding farms was always in the forefront of his mind. For twenty of these years he was absent from the property, leading the Virginia Militia, commanding the Continental Army during the Revolution, acting as president of the Constitutional Convention, and serving as the first President of the United States. The extent of Washington's preoccupation with Mount Vernon, even during these years of public service, is documented in letters of instruction to his estate managers that reveal he was involved with even the smallest details of his farms. In June 1791, for example, in the midst of the awesome challenge of defining the presidency, he directed his nephew, George Augustine Washington, to repair the leaky houses on the property at

Dogue Run, build a corn house at River Farm, erect "a Necessary, with two Seats" for the New Quarter, shingle "the side of the Overseers House at the Ferry," and plant "Ivy around the Ice House."[12]

The farms are palpable in a remarkable letter he wrote to his cousin and friend Lund Washington on August 19, 1776. At the time, General Washington was preparing to confront the English forces on Long Island. He starts with an instruction to "remember that the New Chimneys are not to smoke," and then jumps to the heart of the matter, a detailed set of instructions on the location of two new groves of trees on the north and south sides of the house. Though he was

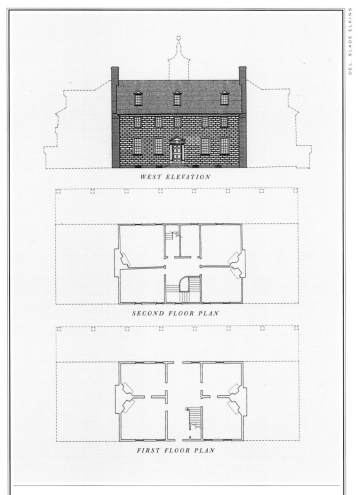

WEST ELEVATION

SECOND FLOOR PLAN

FIRST FLOOR PLAN

FIG. 6 *A conjectural plan and elevation of Mount Vernon showing the house in the 1760s, after George Washington completed the first phase of his expansion. The drawings illustrate the new second and attic floors, roof, and main staircase. The silhouette of the present house is indicated by the dashed line.*

hundreds of miles away, he seemed to be at Mount Vernon, pacing out the boundaries of the groves himself:

As I mean to have groves of Trees at each end of the dwelling House, that at the South end to range in a line from the South East Corner to Colo. Fairfax's, extending as low as another line from the Stable to the dry well, and towards the Coach House, Hen House, & Smoak House as far as it can go for a Lane to be left for Carriages to pass to, & from the Stable and Wharf.

At the other side of the house, he writes, the grove should

range so as to Shew the Barn & ca. in the Neck — from the point where the old Barn used to Stand to the No. Et. Corner of the Smiths Shop, & from thence to the Servants Hall, leaveng a passage between the Quarter & Shop, and so East of the Spinning & Weaving House [as they used to be called] *up to a Wood pile, & so into the yard between the Servts Hall & the House newly erected . . .*[13]

The letter also contains instructions about collecting rents, selling produce, planting hedges, and caring for horses and fences, illustrating his dedication to the comprehensive management of the farm.

In this correspondence the measured prose of Washington's military and governmental communications was displaced by denser, more impacted sentences. His mind raced ahead of his quill and he was often frustrated because distance and duty compelled him to depend on others to realize his vision. During the last year of his presidency, in a revealing 3,000-word "Memorandum" to his outgoing farm manager, William Pearce, he wrote: "There are so many things I wish to have done soon, and so many others that are essential to do, that I scarcely know what direction to give concerning them . . ."[14] One also perceives the imperious eye of the artist:

for the government of Mr. Anderson [the new manager] *repeat that no trees standing between the Visto's are to be cut down, or trimmed up. . . Where the trees stand very thick, leave circular clumps (of from 30 to 50 yards across) without trimming the Trees. But all single trees should be trimmed to one regular height, and as high as can be reached by a Chissel on a long staff; that the Corn may be less shaded in its growth. In leaving the clumps, if it can be done consistent with the thick growth of the Trees, pay attention to the look of them, in going to, or returning from the house.*

Turning to crops, Washington's orders are equally specific, and he carefully explained his reasoning to ensure that the managers had a full understanding of the situation:

All the ground within the inclosure . . . that was not in Wheat this year (and which was proposed to have been sown in Rye but not done so) I would also have put in Corn next Season; The part that was in Wheat, may be sowed with Oats and grass-seeds in the Spring; or, if judged better, might lye uncultivated; or be fallowed, so as to come into Rye in the Autumn with all the Corn ground in other parts at that place; or the Spring following may be wholly sown with Oats.[15]

Nothing was left to chance. In the same memorandum, when the subject changed to hedges, a previous explanation about preparing cedar berries for planting was repeated to ensure perfect understanding: "after being prepared in the way formerly mentioned you, that is by rubbing, or getting off in some way or other all the pulp, or glutinous matter which encompasses the Seed." The memorandum also discussed sand to be used in paint for the house. Washington noted where it was stored, and how it was to be prepared, and gave instructions for conducting an experiment using the paint with either sand or "pounded Stone" in order "to decide which will look best and most resemble stone." He also asked that the "Ice house be filled from the first Ice that forms," that "Such Sashes as are wanting in the Cupulo" be installed, and that "porkers (are) to be made fat."

That he was able to manage his estate and the construction of his house and farm buildings by letter during these extended absences testifies to Washington's exceptional organizational ability. His letters reveal his passionate preoccupation with every aspect of daily life at the five farms and his clear vision of the property as a 12-square-mile farm/garden. As much as any other of his achievements, Mount Vernon illuminates his character, ambition, and ability.

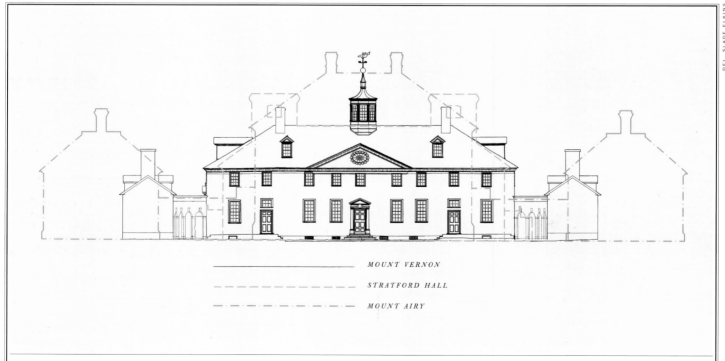

DEL. SLADE ELKINS

—————————————— MOUNT VERNON

– – – – – – – – – – STRATFORD HALL

— · — · — · — · — · — MOUNT AIRY

FIG. 7 *A drawing comparing the scale of Mount Vernon as it existed in the 1790s, after Washington completed the second phase of his building program, with the silhouettes of Stratford Hall (ca. 1738) and Mount Airy (1754–64), both in Virginia.*

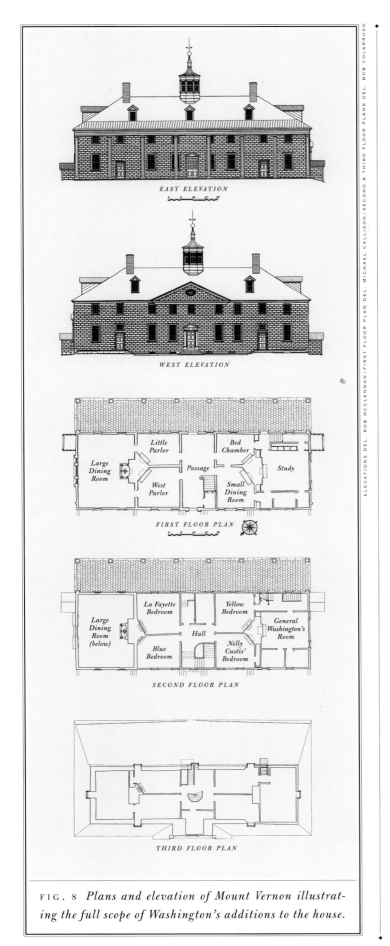

ELEVATIONS DEL. ROB MCCLENNAN/FIRST FLOOR PLAN DEL. MICHAEL CALLISON/SECOND & THIRD FLOOR PLANS DEL. BOB COLARRUSO

EAST ELEVATION

WEST ELEVATION

Large Dining Room / Little Parlor / West Parlor / Passage / Bed Chamber / Small Dining Room / Study

FIRST FLOOR PLAN

Large Dining Room (below) / La Fayette Bedroom / Blue Bedroom / Hall / Yellow Bedroom / Nelly Custis' Bedroom / General Washington's Room

SECOND FLOOR PLAN

THIRD FLOOR PLAN

FIG. 8 *Plans and elevation of Mount Vernon illustrating the full scope of Washington's additions to the house.*

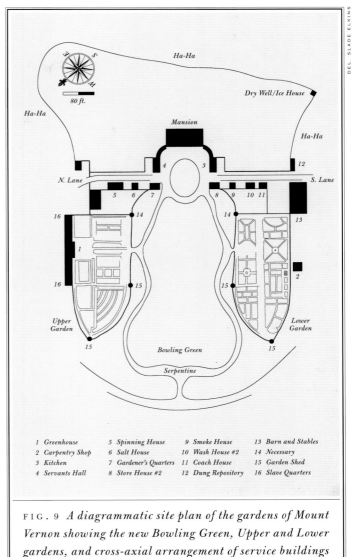

DEL. SLADE ELKINS

Ha-Ha / Ha-Ha / Ha-Ha / Dry Well/Ice House / Mansion / N. Lane / S. Lane / Upper Garden / Lower Garden / Bowling Green / Serpentine / 80 ft.

1 Greenhouse		5 Spinning House		9 Smoke House		13 Barn and Stables
2 Carpentry Shop		6 Salt House		10 Wash House #2		14 Necessary
3 Kitchen		7 Gardener's Quarters		11 Coach House		15 Garden Shed
4 Servants Hall		8 Store House #2		12 Dung Repository		16 Slave Quarters

FIG. 9 *A diagrammatic site plan of the gardens of Mount Vernon showing the new Bowling Green, Upper and Lower gardens, and cross-axial arrangement of service buildings on either side of the circle.*

THE APPROACH TO MOUNT VERNON IN ITS TIME

Descriptions of the estate in Washington's time evoke a place that is very different from the historic house and garden of today. In the eighteenth century, Mount Vernon could be approached either by ship or ferry boat across the Potomac from Maryland or by road from Alexandria and Colchester, Virginia. The ferry service, which Washington owned, brought travelers to a landing dock on Union Farm, on the south side of the estate. From the dock the traveler proceeded up a public access way across Union Farm to the road to Alexandria and Colchester, and then west to the estate's front gate. The road approach to the house was described in

FIG. 10 *From the entrance gate to the estate, Washington created a three-quarter-mile-long axial vista to the house. Seen across an undulating meadow and framed by trees and sky, this was the most dramatic entrance to any house in eighteenth-century America. Unlike most English and European estates, Washington chose not to locate the approach road on this axis.*

1796 by the newly arrived English architect Benjamin Henry Latrobe, who wrote that even before reaching the entrance to Mount Vernon, the traveler was aware of the "neatness" of the grounds, and the "Good fences, clear grounds and extensive cultivation, [which] strike the eye as something uncommon in this part of the World . . ."[16] When Sally Foster Otis, a relative of a friend of the Washingtons', visited in January 1801 shortly after Washington's death, she noted that "the estate is immensely large and enclosed by a high Virginia fence."[17] Samuel Vaughan, a merchant from London and an admirer of Washington who visited Mount Vernon in 1787, found "the farms neat, kept perfectly clean & in prime order." He speculated that Washington was "indisputably the best if not the only good farmer in the State."[18]

As the visitor approached the entrance gate to the estate (which is not used today), the house was framed by a vista across a meadow cut through the forest of trees on either side (fig. 10). In 1801, John Pintard, who had been appointed American Consul at Madeira in 1790, noted that these trees were "standing trimmed and cleared of underwood."[19] This view, which may be seen today, is approximately 1,200 yards long and is dramatized by the distance, the rise and fall of the rolling meadow, and the density of the groves of trees that line the vista.[20] From the entrance gate, the white-painted house

FIG. 11 *The driveway to the house moves off the visual axis, with its dramatic vista, and descends into a river valley 25–40 feet below the level of the surrounding meadow.*

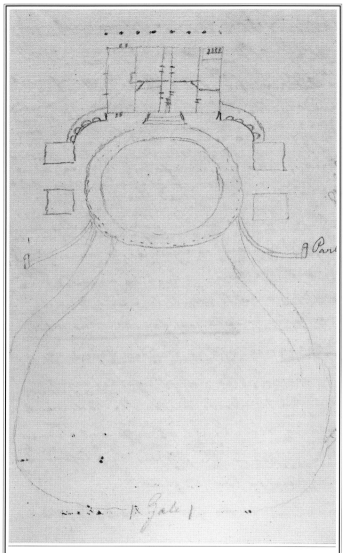

FIG. 12 *In 1787 Washington's friend from Philadelphia, Samuel Powel, visited Mount Vernon. He recorded this plan of the Bowling Green and the cross-axial forecourt in his diary.*

appears to be quite small. As Samuel Powel, Washington's friend from Philadelphia, described it in 1787:

The approach to this Seat is very pleasing. At the entrance from the Road you have a View of the House at the Distance of near a Mile. The Grounds on each Side of the Road are cleared of the underwood & the Saplings neatly trimmed so as to promise to form a handsome Wood in future. Passing thro' this young Wood the Road lies thro' a bottom till you approach the House . . .[21]

About 50 yards beyond the entrance gate, the driveway to the house moves off the main axis created by the alignment

of the entrance gates, the vista cut through the forest of trees, and the house. The road descends into a small valley formed by the bed of a rivulet, which Powel described as a "bottom" (fig. 11). The valley varies in depth from 25 feet to as much as 45 feet, twisting and turning for nearly three-quarters of a mile until, at last, the road rises again to the level of the house. Powel continues:

. . . after ascending the Eminence on which the Mansion is placed you enter a very large Court Yard, with a pavilion on each Side & proceed thro' a circular Road covered with rough Gravel till you come to the Offices, from which the Road is paved to the House. Within this road the ground is covered with Grass.

Powel's diary includes a plan he sketched, which shows that the lawn, or "Bowling Green," was entered through a gate (fig. 12). The plan also shows the house, the serpentine driveways and circle, the cross-axis formed by kitchen and farm buildings, and the low walls that connect the central buildings to the two octagonal pavilions, or outhouses, which mark the start of the walled gardens on either side of the Bowling Green. Vaughan, too, described the house as situated "upon an eminence." Confirming Powel's description, Edward Hooker, an 1808 visitor and one of many Americans who came to view the estate uninvited, wrote that " . . . you pass through a pleasant grove of neat, well trimmed oaks, follow the path in some parts strait, in others winding among hills, at length ascent a tolerably steep hill . . ."[22] Unfortunately, we have no record of the eighteenth-century location of the road from the "bottom" that brought visitors up the "tolerably steep hill" to the west garden gate of the Bowling Green (fig. 13). Nor do we know where these observers first experienced what Powel called the "Eminence on which the mansion is placed."

At the Bowling Green gate, the main axis is reestablished as the visitor sees the house once again, this time 200 yards away across a level lawn (fig. 14). In his diary, Count Julian Ursyn Niemcewicz, a Polish visitor and compatriot of

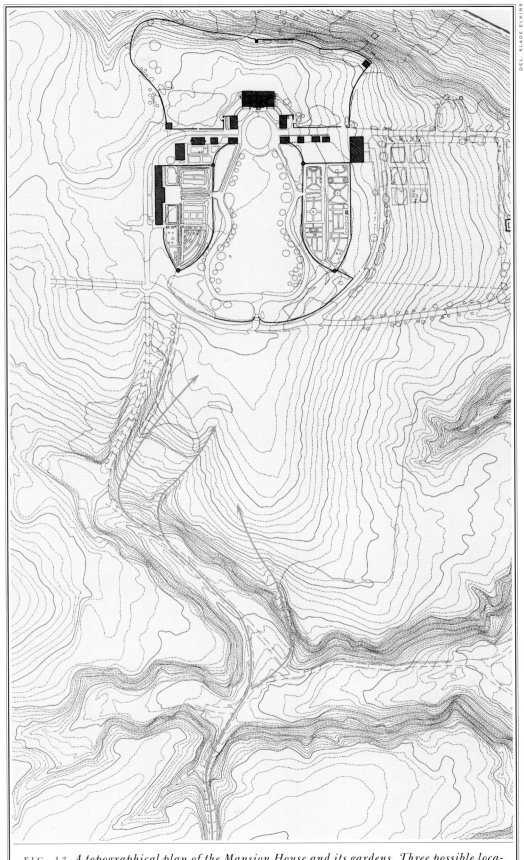

DEL. SLADE ELKINS

FIG. 13 *A topographical plan of the Mansion House and its gardens. Three possible locations for the lost road from the river valley to the west gate of the Bowling Green are indicated. Refer to fig. 64 to see the long vista through the trees and the approach road in the river valley.*

FIG. 14 *The first full view of the house, from the west garden gate of the Bowling Green, is framed by the trees and shrubs of the two "wildernesses." Open arcades signal the presence of the river on the other side of the garden. The authority of the strong massing is somewhat offset by the asymmetrical placement of windows.*

General Thaddeus Kosciusko, described the Mount Vernon of 1798 as

a rather spacious house, surmounted by a small cupola, with mezzanines [these may refer to the basement windows, which were wider than they were tall] *and with blinds painted in green. It is surrounded by a ditch in brick* [the retaining wall at the west end of the Bowling Green, also referred to as a ha-ha, or a hidden boundary wall to a garden] *with very pretty little turrets at the corners; these are nothing but outhouses.*[23]

Washington planted the groves of trees and shrubs, which he called "wildernesses," on either side of the lawn (fig. 15). These features frame the view of the house and shelter the two serpentine driveways on either side of the center lawn

that leads to the circle in front of the house (fig. 16).

Niemcewicz wrote that the Bowling Green was ornamented at its sides with "All kinds of trees, bushes, flowering plants."[24] He noted in detail: "a thousand kinds of trees, plants and bushes; crowning them are two immense Spanish chestnuts that Gl. Wash planted himself; they are very bushy and of the greatest beauty." He observed the tulip poplar, magnolia, "Sweet Sented Shroub . . . with a very deep purple, nearly black flower, (that) has a fragrance which from my point of view surpasses all the others, "catalpa, weeping willow, spruce, a tree "bearing thousands and thousands of pods like little pea pods." Also noted were a "thousand other bushes, for the most part species of laurel and thorn, all covered with flowers, of different colors, all planted in a manner

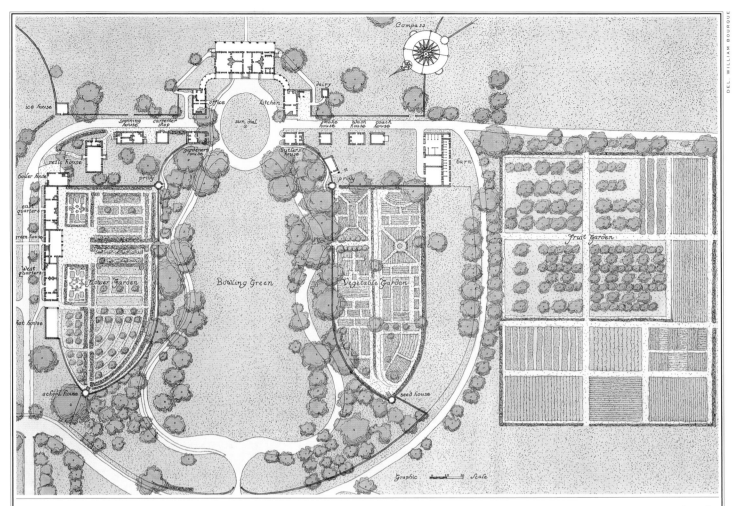

FIG. 15 *Washington designed a new garden on the western, entrance side of the house. The central driveway was removed and replaced by the Bowling Green. He created two walled gardens—the flower garden on the north side and the vegetable garden on the south side—and planted the two "wildernesses" on either side of the Bowling Green.*

to produce the most beautiful hues."[25] Sally Foster Otis described the Bowling Green as

an open lawn, —the walks are irregular & serpentine, cover'd by trees of various kinds but what pleased me most was a labyrinth of evergreens where the sun cannot even now penetrate. This must be a little Paradise in summer.[26]

These "wildernesses" appear to have been far more densely planted than is apparent at Mount Vernon today.

The 1787 plan drawn by Vaughan as a gift to Washington shows the ordered, orthogonally arranged world of the farmhouse, with its satellite buildings in place to house the cottage industries that were essential to the operation of a large farm. These included stables, dairy, smokehouse, wash

house, spinning house, blacksmith's forge and servant and slave quarters clustered around the "Mansion House" (fig. 17). On Vaughan's plan the buildings are laid out in a straight line on either side of the cross-axis formed by the circular driveway, the ends of the two dependencies, and the north and south lanes. Despite some errors, the layout is similar to what we see today.[27] The lanes, which Vaughan described as a "street," form a service road.[28] The walled cutting garden and its greenhouse are located on the north side of the Bowling Green (fig. 18). The vegetable garden is on the south side of the green, but at a lower level, for the ground slopes off (fig. 19). Both gardens are largely hidden by the trees and shrubs and are surrounded by brick walls that have an octagonal outhouse at each end nearest the

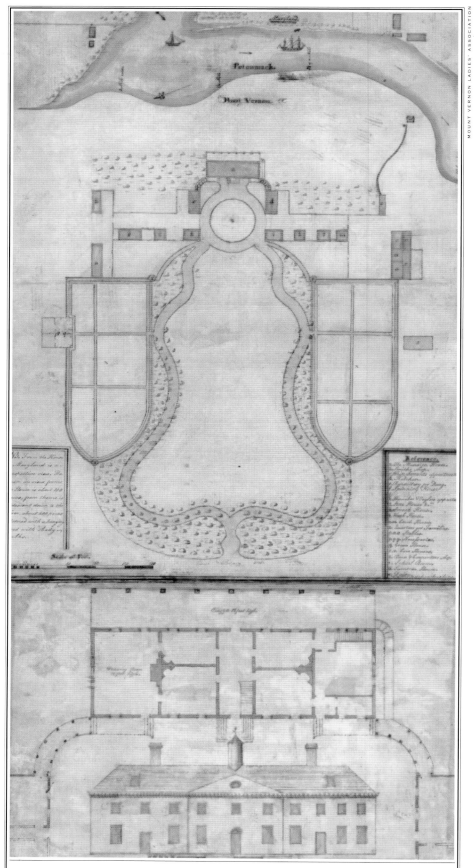

FIG. 17 *This plan of Mount Vernon's gardens was drawn in 1787 by Washington admirer Samuel Vaughan, who presented the drawing to the president.*

house, and gardeners' sheds at the ends farthest away (fig. 20). The views toward the house from these gardens and the serpentine walks are dramatic architectural compositions that, as one observer put it, form a *"tout ensemble* (a whole assemblage) of the green house, school house, offices and servants halls . . ."* The vista, this observer noted,

when seen from the land side, bears . . . a resemblance to a rural village, especially as the lands in that side are laid out somewhat in the form of English gardens, in meadow and grass grounds, ornamented with little copses, circular clumps and single trees.[29]

The arresting play of geometric masses testifies to Washington's skill as an architect and a planner (fig. 21).

Although Latrobe observed that the "approach is not very well managed," surely this was one of the most dramatic sequences of garden, house, and landscape in eighteenth-century American domestic architecture.[30] The long, arrow-straight view from gate to house and the sunny, ordered geometry of the farmhouse and its satellite buildings strike powerful contrasts with the meander through the "bottom,"

FIG. 18 *Washington completed construction of the Greenhouse in 1787. Slave quarters are in the low wings on either side of the taller conservatory.*

with its shady, romantic bower of trees and ferns. So does the picturesque beauty of the Bowling Green and its serpentine driveways through Washington's densely planted "wildernesses" as it gives way to the geometric order of the walled flower and vegetable gardens. The drive from the entrance gate to the forecourt of the house is not only an eloquent statement of the tension between the picturesque and the formal approaches to nature and to gardening, but a triumph of the artistic imagination as it harnesses difficult, almost impossible, terrain for its own ends.

THE MANSION

The Mansion is such a famous house and its owner is such a seminal figure in our history that one anticipates a more majestic building. What confronts us is a large house of surprising simplicity, one of intimate yet noble scale that is framed by the plantings on either side of the Bowling Green. The west elevation, which is the first view of the house that a visitor sees, is a subtle orchestration of powerful architectural elements within an asymmetrical façade. It is the carefully modulated asymmetry that creates the impression of a relatively modest house. This may be why Latrobe thought

FIG. 16 *A present-day view from one of the "wildernesses" to the house. Washington planted "a thousand kinds of trees, plants and bushes" to create "a labyrinth of evergreens where the sun cannot even now penetrate." The tall trees and openness we now see were not characteristic of this part of the Bowling Green. According to contemporary accounts, a visitor walking or driving through the "wildernesses" would have been more enclosed by shrubbery.*

FIG. 19 *Taking advantage of the dramatic topography, Washington planned the vegetable garden at a lower level than the Bowling Green. One of the octagonal garden sheds is visible in the distance at the end of the retaining wall.*

that "It has no very striking appearance," while he conceded that it was "superior to every other house I have seen here."[31]

The house is a two-story-high rectangular mass, built of wood designed to suggest stone, with an attic story; it is 96 feet long and 47 feet wide, including the 14-foot-wide portico facing the river (fig. 22). At either end are curved hyphens connecting 1½-story dependencies to the main house. These two buildings contained the kitchen and quarters for visitors' servants.[32] The hyphens are formed by a series of delicate segmental arches supported on small, square Tuscan columns (fig. 23). Arriving at the entrance court, the visitor is drawn to views through the bays of the arcade that frame the lawns and, beyond that, the river. Sailboats and other life on the Potomac shift in mood as the light, weather, and seasons change.

This arcade was an important architectural innovation, for at the time such hyphens were typically closed by walls on one side to hide service activities, as at Mount Airy (1754–1764) in Warsaw, Virginia (fig. 24).[33] In the rare case when arches were used, they were heavier and supported by substantial piers. The delicacy of Washington's thin, square columns and open arcades is further enhanced by the

"French," or scarlet, honeysuckle climbing up their supports and along the wall above the arches. This was an important feature of the design; in his diary of 1785, Washington noted that he planted honeysuckle "at each Column of my covered ways." Two years later, while he was attending the constitutional Convention, he instructed George Augustine Washington to replace any dead plants "near the Pillars of the Colonades, or covered ways" so that they may "run up, and Spread over the parts which are painted green."[34]

Washington was aware that the most impressive Virginia mansions of the time were built of masonry and had, as their most significant architectural feature, a symmetrical arrangement of windows around a centrally placed entrance door. In comparison with these houses, the west façade of Mount Vernon has three unusual qualities: asymmetry, wood rustication, and a coved cornice. Asymmetry is rarely a major fea-

FIG. 20 *A two-story octagonal building, used for an outhouse and garden-related storage, is part of the retaining wall of the kitchen garden. As seen from the Bowling Green, these buildings are one story high.*

FIG. 21 *The view from the flower garden to the Mansion House presents an arresting composition of geometric masses that testifies to Washington's skill as an architect.*

ture of the exterior elevations of an important residence (fig. 25). The large pediment and front door define the center line of the house's mass.[35] The lantern on the roof, which Washington called his "Cupulo," is noticeably about 14 inches off this center line.[36] Although an equal number of windows are placed on either side of the entrance door, the positions of those on the north are not symmetrical with their counterparts on the south. On the north, at the left of the entrance, the first windows are approximately five feet, ten inches from the center line of the house; on the south side this distance is about nine feet, ten inches. Washington appears to have wanted a similar relationship and proportion

of windows in the interior of the West Parlor and Small Dining Room, where the placement of the windows in relation to the side walls is almost the same within reflective symmetry—it is approximate because the West Parlor window is six inches farther from the passage wall than is its counterpart in the Small Dining Room (figs. 26 a & b). The exterior asymmetry of windows is the result of the Small Dining Room and West Parlor being, respectively, about nine feet and five feet on either side of the center line of the house. Washington may have considered that the house's interior design was more important than exterior symmetry. He may also have thought that the asymmetry was of little con-

FIG. 22 *Curved arcades connect the west façade of the house to the dependencies on either side. The asymmetry of the windows may have been designed to offset the monumentality of the house's mass.*

sequence and not worth altering, an attitude that would have been uncharacteristically accepting on his part.

A small line drawing by Washington of the west elevation, the only extant drawing of the exterior in his hand, provides insight into his thought process. The drawing was probably done in 1773, when he was planning the north- and south-side additions, before construction began in 1774. It shows a version of the house that is different from the one built (fig. 27). The most significant difference is the symmetrical, or almost symmetrical, elevation. Although the two windows north of the center doorway are about six inches farther away from the center line of the house than those

south of it, this disparity is little more than the thickness of a heavy pencil line and may be the result of the small size of the drawing or the fact that it was a study for which accuracy was not deemed essential; similar inconsistencies may be observed in other parts of the drawing. Because of the exterior symmetry, the windows in the West Parlor and Small Dining Room are in different locations (fig. 28). The latter has one window, and the first window on the south side of the center door is in the closet under the stair. Other differences include wider doors—probably double doors— with no transom lights; smaller first-floor windows with higher sills; and lower second-floor window sills. This draw-

FIG. 23 *The curved open arcades are set on delicate, square Tuscan columns and painted white and green. Washington pioneered, perhaps invented, the use of open arcades like this which draw the visitor's attention to the river and grounds on the other side.*

FIG. 24 *Mount Airy was built in Warsaw, Virginia, between 1754 and 1764. One of the largest and most magnificent houses in 18th century Virginia, it is noteworthy for the monumental polychrome masonry façade and rusticated entrance. The hyphens, which connect house and dependencies, were enclosed to prevent visitors from seeing service-related activities on the other side.*

ing shows that the exterior was not an afterthought and that Washington studied the aesthetic and practical consequences of alternative window locations and sizes, larger doors, and a symmetrical placement of windows. It is noteworthy to recall that an alteration to create a symmetrical exterior façade would have involved moving two windows on the first floor and two on the second, a very minor task in the overall scope of the construction. This lends credence to the idea that the asymmetrical window arrangement on the most public façade of the house, which remains one of its most characteristic features, was the result of Washington's considered choice.[37]

In this context, it is also significant that the other three façades of Mount Vernon are asymmetrical as well, and all exploit the aesthetic opportunities of asymmetry in different ways. The asymmetry of the north façade offers an intriguing juxtaposition of the high style and the practical. Here, Washington built a *serliana*, or Venetian window, the main feature of the Large Dining Room that was part of the 1774 expansion (figs. 29 and 30). This regal window shares the

elevation with the cellar door, which Washington could easily have hidden in a sunken areaway or moved to some other part of the building. To our twentieth-century eyes it appears that he wished to emphasize the contrast between the monumental window and the modest cellar door, between the high architectural statement and the candid, evocative expression of a functional farmhouse. It is more likely that for Washington there was no incompatibility between the ornamental and the practical and that he perceived the cellar door and *serliana* as perfectly comfortable side-by-side. The south side of the house is a more straightforward symmetrical composition of four modest windows and a dormer that shares the façade with another asymmetrically located cellar door. On the east side, each bay of the piazza, with the exception of the one in the center, frames an asymmetrical composition of windows and doors (fig. 31).

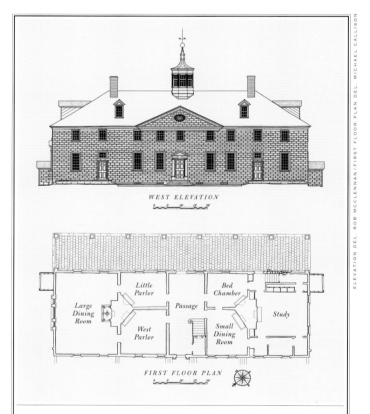

FIG. 25 *A measured drawing of the West Façade and First Floor Plan of Mount Vernon. These drawings are based on ones prepared in 1937 by Morley Jeffers Williams, Director of the Office of Research and Restoration at Mount Vernon.*

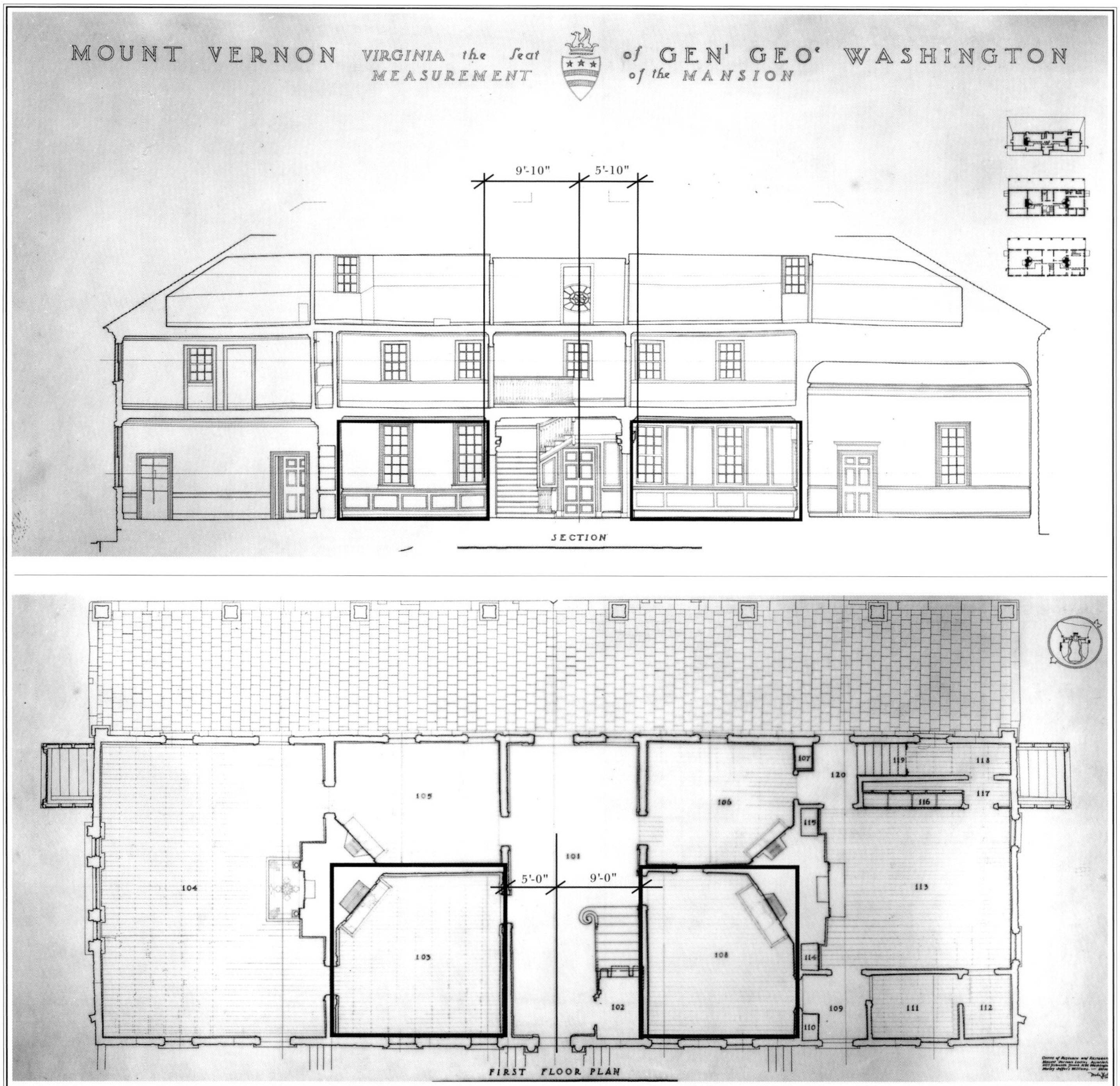

MOUNT VERNON LADIES' ASSOCIATION/DEL. SLADE ELKINS

FIGS. 26 A & B *The first-floor plan and a longitudinal section through Mount Vernon show the relationship between the center line of the house, the walls on either side of the passage, and the windows in the West Parlor and the Small Dining Room (respectively shown on the left and right sides of the Passage).*

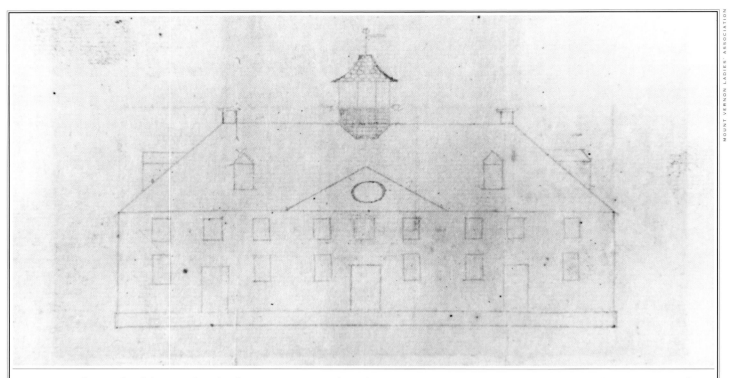

FIG. 27 *This study of the west façade of Mount Vernon is the only extant drawing by Washington of the building's exterior that has survived. He may have used it to assess the impact of placing smaller windows in different locations.*

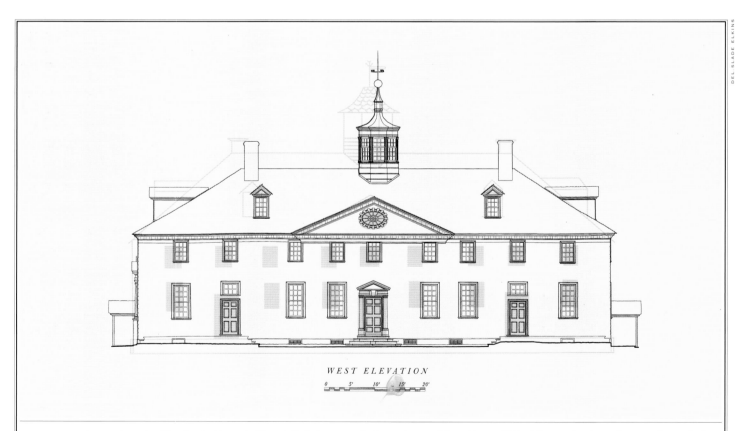

WEST ELEVATION

0   5'   10'   15'   20'

FIG. 28 *A montage to illustrate the relationship between window size and location of Washington's elevation study and the fenestration he eventually chose for Mount Vernon.*

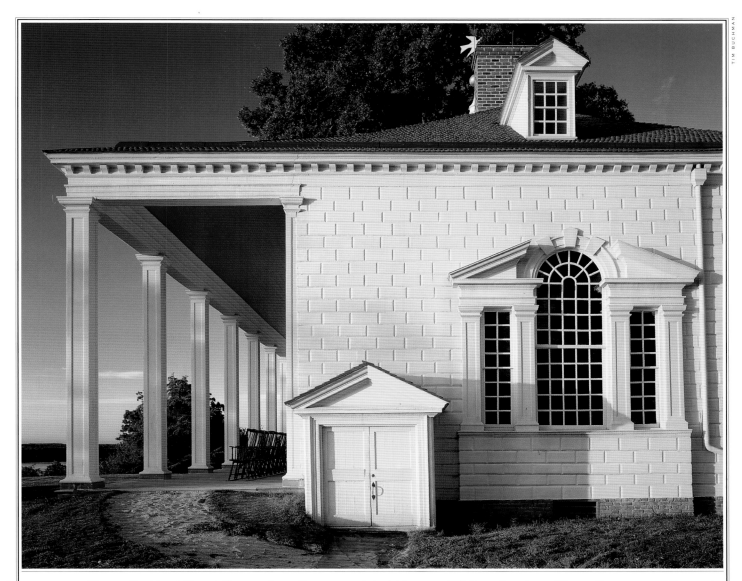

FIG. 29 *The north side of Mount Vernon shows the asymmetrical placement of the cellar door. The serliana, one of the most beautiful examples of this feature in the United States, is symmetrically located in the façade.*

Why did Washington use asymmetry? Samuel Powel, noting that Mount Vernon's west elevation was "not altogether regular as to the Windows under the Pediment . . ." but declaring the effect "handsome" nonetheless, posited that different parts of the house were "built at different Times."[38] The house was in fact built in phases over three decades, yet Washington easily could have achieved the "uniform Appearance" Powel found lacking by moving eight windows. Because asymmetry is used so consistently on each façade of Mount Vernon, Washington may have considered it to be a design theme that unifies the house. He may also have chosen to exploit the aesthetic opportunities offered by asymmetrical compositions of windows and doors to alter perception of the building's scale. The tension between the expectation of symmetry and the visual surprise of asymmetry diverts attention from the striking expanse of the façade. Perhaps he did not wish to create a grand manor house that dominated the surrounding gardens and farmland upon which his subsistence depended. It would seem that he wanted a farmhouse, in fact. He may have wished to retain a sense of the vernacular farmhouses in Virginia, which he saw on his extensive travels in the colony.

On December 30, 1798, Washington wrote to his friend Dr. William Thornton, whose design won the competition

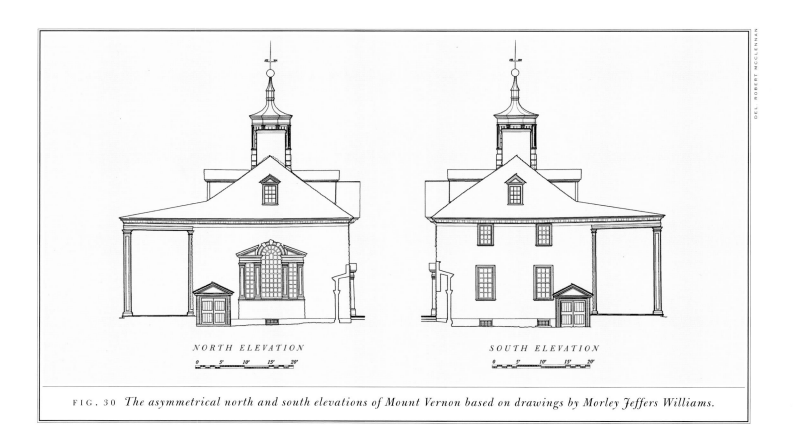

NORTH ELEVATION

SOUTH ELEVATION

FIG. 30 *The asymmetrical north and south elevations of Mount Vernon based on drawings by Morley Jeffers Williams.*

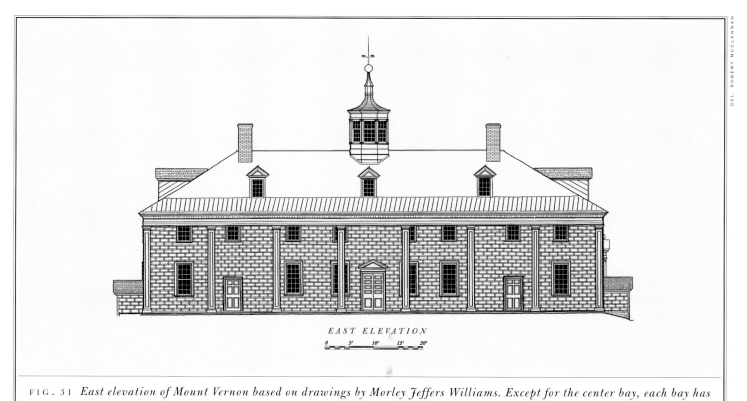

EAST ELEVATION

FIG. 31 *East elevation of Mount Vernon based on drawings by Morley Jeffers Williams. Except for the center bay, each bay has an asymmetrical placement of windows and doors between the square piazza columns.*

for the Capitol in the new Federal City, that his own ideas about architecture "proceed from a person who avows his ignorance of Architectural principles, and who has no other guide but his eye, to direct his choice."[39] Yet it is clear that his own eye was a precise guide (fig. 32). In his instructions to Lund Washington regarding the new Large Dining Room that was under construction in 1776, Washington was explicit:

The chimney in the new room should be exactly in the middle of it — the doors and every thing else to be exactly answerable and uniform — in short I would have the whole executed in a masterly manner.[40]

His sense of design was so keen that he would refer workmen to specific details in an existing building. Writing to his cousin on August 20, 1775, about the design of the "New Kitchen," he instructed, "I would have the Corners done so in the manner of our New Church [at Pohick]."[41] Although it was common practice to direct a builder to imitate a detail or part of another building, his choice of when to use, or to ignore, symmetry was based on a clear understanding of the effect he was striving to achieve (figs. 33 a & b).

The second unusual quality of the façade is the exterior finish, "painted to represent champhered [wood siding] rustic

FIG. 32 *Washington gave specific instructions that the fireplace in the Large Dining Room, with its beautiful marble mantle, "should be exactly in the middle" of the south wall of the room, "with the doors and everything else to be exactly answerable and uniform." The mantel was a gift from Samuel Vaughan.*

FIG. 33A *A detail of the rustication of the "New Church" at Pohick.*

and sanded,"[42] Latrobe noted. In Virginia, large houses are usually built of brick. Washington may have chosen wood because its suggestion of modesty helped to undermine the monumental scale implied by the massing. Its boards are much broader than typical siding, and their edges have been chamfered, or cut at an angle, so as to suggest dressed stone. To further imply the texture of smooth stone, sand was thrown onto the white boards when they were freshly painted (fig. 34). In a letter to Dr. Thornton, written in 1799, Washington observed that "sanding is designed to answer two purposes, durability, and presentation of stone."[43] Recent testing confirms Washington's assertion that sanding increases the durability of paint.[44] Of greater import is how the rustication affects the perceived scale and character of

the house. Because the boards are larger than those used for typical siding, and because they have pronounced joints that are emphasized by both the shadows cast on the upper surface and the highlight on the lower surface, the eye reads the wall as an incised surface. The visible texture of the sand-paint enhances the reflectivity of each rusticated board and the brilliance of the highlighted part of the joint. Thus the large expanse of the west façade is downplayed, making the house appear smaller than it actually is.

It is interesting to speculate about what precedents may have inspired Mount Vernon's rustication. Although there are no known examples in Virginia of a fully rusticated house, the use of brick walls with rusticated stone quoins was fairly common in both church and domestic architecture. The most conspicuous examples Washington visited or may have known about are the Aquia Church (ca. 1754–1757) in Stafford County; Gunston Hall (1755); the neighboring estate of his friend George Mason; the Thomas Nelson House (ca. 1710–1730) in Yorktown; Cleve (ca. 1750) in King George County; and the stucco-covered Carlyle House (1751–1753) in Alexandria (fig. 35).

FIG. 33B *Washington used the "New Church" as the starting point for the design of the corner rustication of the two dependency buildings at Mount Vernon.*

FIG. 34 *Photograph of the painted wood siding Washington used for the exterior of Mount Vernon when he expanded the house in the 1757–1760 building campaign. Latrobe described it as "painted to represent champhered rustic and sanded" wood siding.*

FIG. 35 *The Carlyle House in Alexandria, Virginia, was built between 1751 and 1753 by Washington's friend John Carlyle. The rusticated quoins that encase the front door and define the corners of the building make use of a "V" joint.*

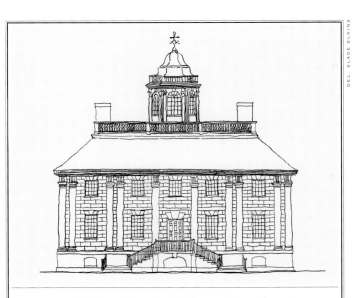

FIG. 36 *Shirley Place in Roxbury, Massachusetts, was built by the royal governor, William Shirley, ca. 1747. It is a rare example of a house with a completely rusticated façade. Washington may have seen the house when he visited Governor Shirley in February 1756.*

FIG. 37 *The Redwood library in Newport, Rhode Island, is completely sided with rusticated wood. It was designed by Peter Harrison and built between 1747 and 1748.*

A more likely source of inspiration for the use of rustication at Mount Vernon is Shirley Place (ca. 1747) in Roxbury, Massachusetts[45] (fig. 36). A rare example of a house with a completely rusticated façade, it was built by William Shirley, who served as royal governor from 1741 to 1756.[46] Washington met Governor Shirley in Alexandria in April 1755; in February 1756 he visited him in Massachusetts, though we do not know whether the Governor

FIG. 38 *The Lindens was built in 1754 in Danvers, Massachusetts. Rusticated wood siding with a "V" joint covers the front elevation. The house was dismantled and moved to Washington, D.C., in the 1930s.*

received Washington in Shirley Place or at the official residence, the Province House, in Boston.[47] It has been conjectured that Peter Harrison, architect of the Redwood Library (1747–1748) in Newport, Rhode Island, which was also completely sided with rusticated wood, may have influenced the design of Shirley Place, as Harrison was a relative of Julie Shirley, the Governor's wife (fig. 37).[48] We know that Washington might have seen the new Library when he traveled to Boston via Newport.[49] Rusticated wood siding also completely covered the front elevation of two residences in Massachusetts, the Benjamin Pickman House (1750) in Salem and the Lindens (1754) in Danvers (fig. 38).[50] Washington may have known about these buildings before 1757, when he began his first rebuilding at Mount Vernon. It was during this phase of construction that rusticated wood siding was applied to the exterior. Although Mount Airy was not completed before Washington began his project, he may have been aware that the design specified the entire central entrance section of the house as rusticated stone.

A more remote set of sources that possibly inspired the rustication of Mount Vernon's façade are Inigo Jones's Banqueting Hall in Whitehall, London (1619–1622), and Andrea Palladio's Palazzo Thiene in Vicenza, Italy, begun ca. 1542 (figs. 39 a & b).[51] Both buildings, as well as many of Jones's designs for gateways, had the unusual feature of a "V" for all vertical and horizontal joints (fig. 40).[52] This joint also occurs at Mount Vernon, Gunston Hall, the Nelson and Carlyle Houses, the Aquia Church in Virginia, and the Lindens and other New England houses. One precedent for façades that are completely rusticated is Palladio's recreation of the ancient Roman Pantheon, a design illustrated in his *Four Books of Architecture* (fig. 41).[53] The importance of the Pantheon as a possible source is that its upper and intermediate cornices have the same moldings and unusual form of block modillion, with cyma recta, or a reverse S-shaped, curved end that Washington used for the interior cornice of Mount Vernon's passage (fig. 42). A variation of this design,

FIG. 39A *Andrea Palladio began working on the Palazzo Thiene in Vicenza in ca. 1542. This drawing is from Book Two, Plate 9, of* The Four Books on Architecture. *It shows the first floor of the exterior of the Palazzo covered with rusticated stone using a "V" joint.*

FIG. 39B *Palladio's Palazzo Thiene may have influenced Inigo Jones's use of the same joint at the Banqueting Hall (1619–1622), in Whitehall.*

using a cyma recta, or S-shaped, block modillion, occurs at the exterior cornice of the house, arcades, and dependencies.[54] Washington may have been inspired by plate 75 in Batty and Thomas Langley's *Builder's Jewel*, which shows three cornices with block modillions, one of which has associated V-jointed rustication (fig. 43).[55]

The third unusual quality of the façade is the use of a cove in the base of the pediment that defines the center of the house. This pediment is supported by an entablature that has as its frieze an eight-inch-high cove, or quarter circle (fig. 44). Washington used the cove to set the pediment forward from the wall of the house to give it visual prominence. Typically, this would have been accomplished by a set of supporting columns or pilasters. The cove form is rarely found in the frieze of an entablature, and the appearance of a cove below a pediment is even more unusual. One of the earliest known uses is by Inigo Jones in his 1620s elevation

FIG. 40 *ca. 1618 drawing by Inigo Jones of the "Italian Gate" at Arundel House in London shows rustication with a "V" joint.*

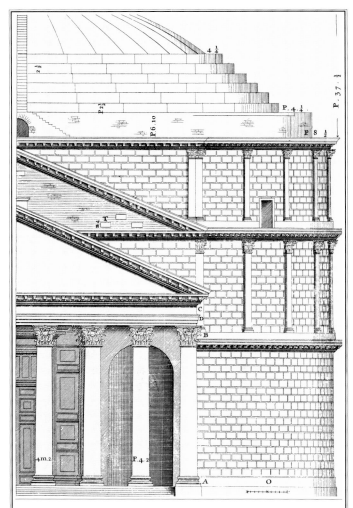

FIG. 41 *Andrea Palladio's recreation of the ancient Roman Pantheon is illustrated on Plate 53, Book 4, of his* Four Books of Architecture. *He shows the building completely covered with rusticated masonry. The upper and intermediate cornices of the Pantheon are also possible sources for cornices that Washington used for the exterior of Mount Vernon and for its interior Passage.*

(drawn by John Webb) for Sir Peter Killigrew's house, Blackfriars, London (fig. 45). It is also found on a few late-seventeenth-century and early-eighteenth-century houses in England.[56] In the colonies, examples of coved cornices survive at the Presbyterian Church (ca. 1735) and the Amstel House (ca. 1740) in New Castle, Delaware; at St. Anne's Church (ca. 1768) in Middletown, Delaware; and at the Town Hall (1707), the Friends' Almshouse (1729), and Bellaire (1720) in Greater Philadelphia, Pennsylvania (fig. 46).[57] Sabine Hall (1733–42) in Richmond County, Virginia, uses a cove as part of the cornice in the interior passage. The

cove also appears on small dairy buildings in Virginia, such as the one at the Archibald Blair House in Williamsburg (fig. 47). Washington may well have derived it from a number of plates in Batty Langley's *The City and Country Builder's and Workingman's Designs: Or the Art of Drawing and Working the Ornamental Parts of Architecture,* a handbook he probably consulted for other features of his house.[58] Nevertheless, we cannot pinpoint the actual source of the unusual coved form that supports the projecting pediment of Mount Vernon's west front. In such situations, the lack of documentation is frustrating. So much that was taken for granted at the time, that seemed too obvious to require specific explanation in diaries or letters, turns out to be vital data. Without this documentation we are reduced to speculation about sources of ideas and reasons for their employment.

THE PIAZZA

The most celebrated and imitated feature of Mount Vernon is the two-story-high piazza on the east side of the house. Supported on eight square Tuscan columns, it provided a setting for family activities and pleasing views across the Potomac River (fig. 48). Latrobe made a number of sketches of it, including a watercolor of George and Martha Washington

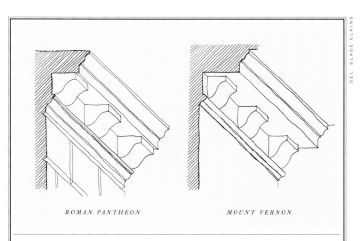

ROMAN PANTHEON MOUNT VERNON

FIG. 42 *A comparison drawing of the exterior cornice of the Roman Pantheon and the interior Passage cornice at Mount Vernon. Although they are delineated at the same size—in order to compare molding profiles—the ancient Roman cornice is significantly larger.*

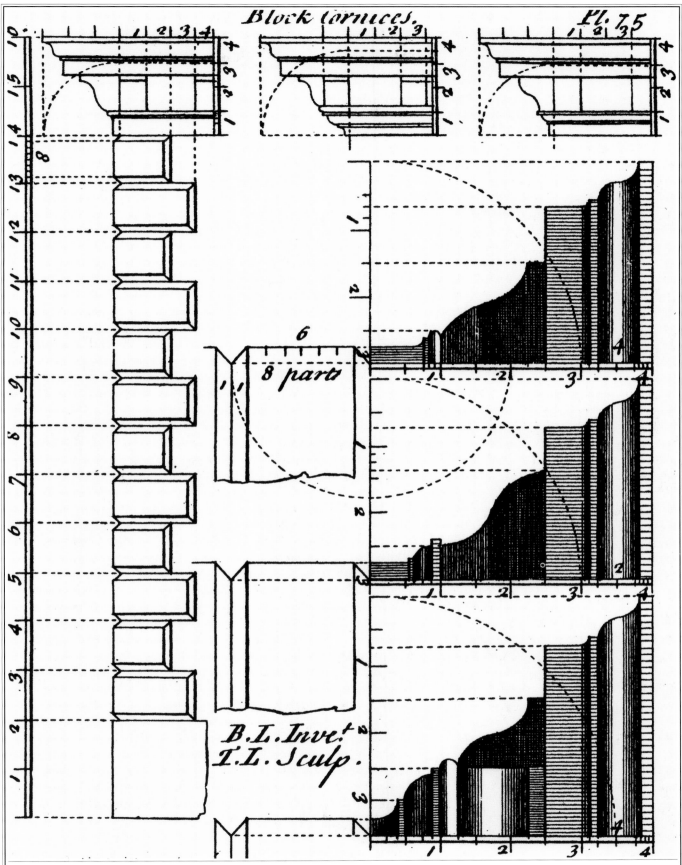

FIG. 43 *Washington's source for the designs of the exterior cornice at Mount Vernon and interior Passage cornice may have been Plate 75 of Batty and Thomas Langley's* Builder's Jewel. *Note that Langley's design shows "V" jointed rustication.*

FIG. 44 *Washington used a cove molding as part of the entablature below the pediment of the west façade at Mount Vernon.*

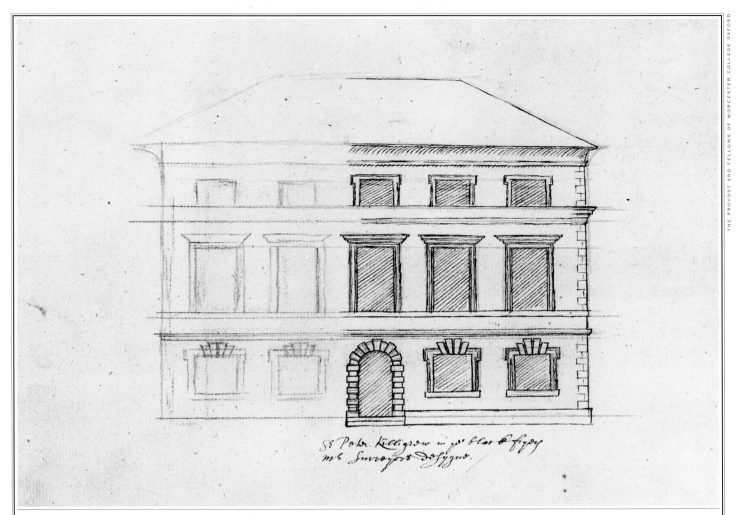

THE PROVOST AND FELLOWS OF WORCESTER COLLEGE OXFORD

FIG. 45 *Inigo Jones's design for Sir Peter Killigrew's house (ca. 1620s), Blackfriars, London, is unusual for the use of a coved cornice. This drawing is by Jones's disciple John Webb.*

TIM BUCHMAN

FIG. 46 *A rare form, the coved cornice survives at the Amstel House (ca. 1740) in New Castle, Delaware. The use of the cove here, below the pediment, is similar to Washington's design at Mount Vernon.*

COLONIAL WILLIAMSBURG FOUNDATION

FIG. 47 *The coved cornice was sometimes used for small dairy buildings in Virginia. This example is at the Archibald Blair House in Williamsburg, which was built between 1775 and 1800.*

having tea on the piazza with Martha's granddaughter Nelly Custis and a guest (fig. 49). The piazza serves as an exterior extension to the Passage and Large Dining Room, and to a lesser extent, the Study. The absence of pilasters on the inside wall, the absence of axes—such as would be present if there were a pediment to transform the piazza into a portico—and the relaxed and intimate scale contribute to the sense of ease and comfort that visitors today feel as they sit here and watch their children playing on the lawn, or follow the boats sailing by on the river. Latrobe's description of the piazza's architecture and setting is the longest single section of the journal pages he devoted to his Mount Vernon visit. He wrote:

Towards the East Nature has lavished magnificence, nor has Art interfered but to exhibit her to advantage. Before the portico a lawn extends on each hand from the front of the house . . . Down the steep slope trees and shrubs are thickly planted. They are kept so low as not to interrupt the view but merely to furnish an agreeable border to the extensive prospect beyond. The mighty Potowmac runs close under this bank the elevation which must be 250 perhaps feet. The river here is about 1 ½ miles across and runs parallel with the front of the house for about 3 miles to the left and 4 to the right.[59]

The portico was such a striking feature of the house that visitors to Mount Vernon lavished some of their most poetic descriptions on its architecture and the views obtained from it. Niemcewicz notes that from the

immense open portico supported by eight pillars. . . . one looks out on perhaps the most beautiful view in the world. One sees there the waters of the Potowmak rolling majestically over a distance of 4 to 5 miles. Boats which go to and fro make a picture of unceasing motion. A lawn of the most beautiful green leads to a steep slope, covered as far as the bank by a very thick wood where formerly there were deer and roebuck, but a short time ago they broke the enclosure and escaped. [There are] robins, blue titmice, Baltimore bird, the black, red and gold bird. It is there that in the afternoon and evening the Gl., his family and the gustes [guests] go to sit and enjoy the fine weather and the beautiful view. I

enjoyed it more than anyone. . . . The opposite bank, the course of the river, the dense woods all combined to enhance this sweet illusion. What a remembrance![60]

William Loughton Smith, an English visitor to Mount Vernon in 1790, was equally enthusiastic:

From the grand portico which fronts the river, the assemblage of objects is grand beyond description, embracing the magnificence of the river with the vessels sailing about; the verdant fields, woods, and parks."[61]

Abigail Adams, wife of John Adams, considered the piazza to be the house's "greatest ornament."[62] In his recent book *The Pleasure Gardens of Virginia*, Peter Martin observes that a common thread connected all these descriptions: "this portico, with its pillared and elevated elegance . . . was a stage, in effect, a framing artifact, from which the scene could be leisurely contemplated. . . . One is not really in the landscape but rather is an observer from an artificially arranged vantage point."[63]

Nestled into the sloping terrain between the house and river was a deer park built by Washington. There a visiting journalist noted "wild deer . . . seen through the thickets, alternately with the vessels as they are sailing along, adding a romantic and picturesque appearance to the whole scenery."[64] Vaughan called it a "hanging wood with shady walks."[65] "Hanging" may refer to Washington's having trimmed the trees and shrubs so that they would, in Latrobe's words, "furnish an agreeable border" to better frame the view.[66] In the eighteenth century, "hanging" also referred to land that is too steep to be cultivated, to a garden or walk situated on a steep slope, and to trees with branches hanging over sloping ground so that the brow of a hill was not visible.[67] Trimming the trees would ensure that the house could be seen from the river. Today, when most of the planting in the area of the deer park directly in front of the piazza has been lost, only the top half of the house is visible from the river's edge, 125 feet below the level of the piazza.

FIG. 48 *View of the Potomac and the Maryland shore from the piazza at Mount Vernon.*

FIG. 49 *Benjamin Henry Latrobe made a number of sketches of the piazza during his visit to Mount Vernon in 1796. This watercolor shows George and Martha Washington having tea on the piazza with Martha's granddaughter Nelly Custis and a guest.*

Even from the middle of the Potomac, or from the distant Maryland shore, the dense growth of trees and shrubs on either side of the hanging garden, described by Niemcewicz, would hide most of the house (fig. 50). During Lawrence Washington's tenure, and before Washington trimmed the trees and shrubs, it is likely that the house would not have been visible from the river except during the winter months, when the deciduous trees lost their leaves.[68]

Washington planned a serpentine ha-ha wall to separate the deer park from the grounds on the north and south sides of the piazza and from the hanging garden to the east, on the sloping lawn. His sketch and instructions, presumably prepared for a mason, survive. In these notes, thought to date from October 1798, he explained how the wall should relate to the contours of the land. It was his wish that the wall be not "very serpentine nor would I have it quite strait if I could—a little curving and meand[e]ring would be my choice" (fig 51).[69] At the deer park gate, which is 70 feet above the river, only the cupola may be seen; as visitors approach the house, first the roof and then the piazza columns gradually come into view. Seen frontally from below the piazza floor level, the columns take on a monumental scale. The transformation to intimate and inviting gathering space becomes complete as one then enters under the shelter of the piazza's roof. Although erosion has made the slope steeper today than it was in the late eighteenth-century, this experience today is very similar.

Certainly, some of Washington's guests must have arrived at Mount Vernon by river and landed at the small, private dock at the foot of the slope southeast of the house.

FIG. 50 *A visitor arriving by boat at Washington's small wharf would have been able to see only the upper portion of the house beyond the deer park.*

Winthrop Sargent, who visited in 1793, noted that

The Front [of the property facing] *towards the Waters of the Potowmack is of greater Declivity—a small Deer Park in that Quarter and a good road to the River with a small Wuay or Landing Place . . .*[70]

The "small Wuay or Landing Place" may refer to a dock that has since disappeared. One is indicated on the 1770 map of the properties of Mount Vernon. The map also shows a pathway to the river's edge (fig. 52). The location of this pathway from the dock to the house is not known.[71] From the shoreline, only the top half of the piazza is visible.

Latrobe's sketches convey the intimacy and sociability of the space under the open piazza. "This is a delightful place to walk in & admirably adapted to the Climate," Samuel Powel confirmed. The use of rusticated wood siding on the rear wall, the delicate scale of the wood columns, and the inviting proportion of the piazza create a sense of comfort, ease, and gracious hospitality. This extraordinary transformation of scale, from abstract to monumental to intimate, may help explain why the piazza is the most imitated feature of the house. Greek Revival houses throughout the south, with their two-story-high porches, as well as houses by

McKim, Mead & White, John Russell Pope, Donn Barbor, Neil Reid, and more recently Robert Venturi and Denise Scott-Brown, have been modeled after Washington's two-story piazza (fig. 53). It is his most significant architectural innovation and has strongly influenced the design of embassies and of public, exposition, and commercial buildings.[72] Variations of it, at a much reduced scale, may be seen in suburbs throughout the nation (fig. 54).

This unusual and influential element of the house appears to be Washington's own invention. There is no documentary evidence in Washington's papers, or in records of conversations with him by others, of the sources he may have

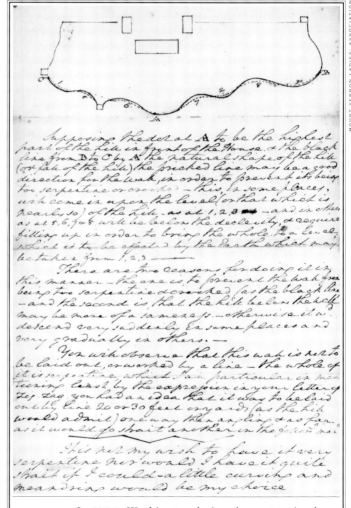

FIG. 51 *In 1798, Washington designed a serpentine haha wall to separate the deer park from the hanging garden overlooking the Potomac River. His sketch shows how the convex and the concave shapes of the wall weave around the contour line that is its median.*

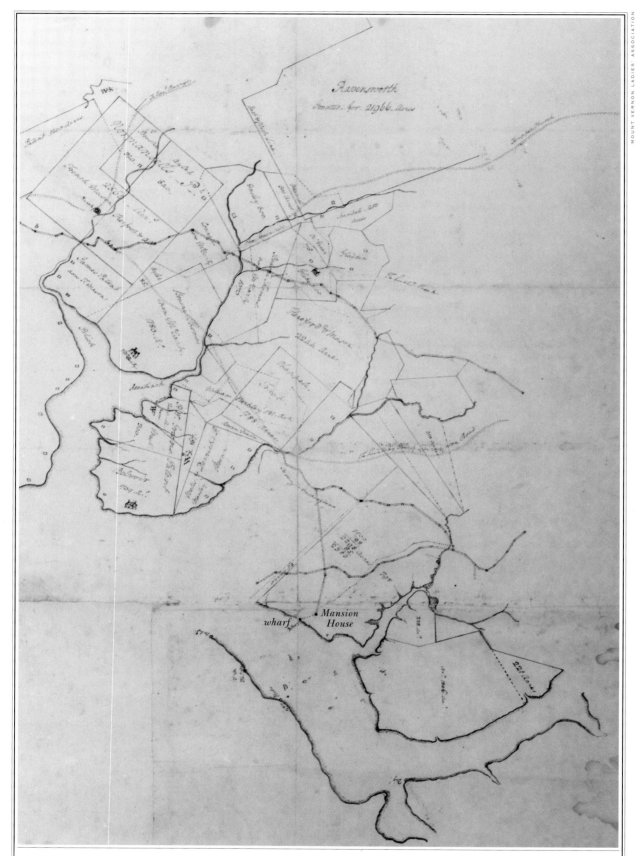

FIG. 52 *This detail of Washington's 1770 survey map of the properties of Mount Vernon indicates a wharf southeast of the house. It also shows a pathway from the house to the wharf. The precise locations of the wharf and pathway are not known.*

FIG. 53 *The influence of Mount Vernon may be seen in the piazza of a house in Connecticut designed by Allan Greenberg in 1988. The five-bay portico has round Doric columns.*

used.[73] Therefore it is possible only to speculate on its origins. Although Washington visited Barbados in 1751 with his ailing half brother Lawrence, there is no direct connection between the island's architecture and Mount Vernon's piazza. One reasonable and hitherto unnoticed source may be Greenway Court (ca. 1752), near White Post, Virginia (fig. 55). This unpretentious house was the home of Thomas, Lord Fairfax. Although only one-and-a-half stories high, its piazza extended all the way across one façade, was integrated into the mass of the house, and had thin columns that were widely spaced. Washington visited the house during the course of his duties as one of the surveyors employed by Lord Fairfax to chart his vast estate but left no recorded comment about its architecture.[74] Perhaps the piazza is a transformation of a plate in Palladio's *Four Books of Architecture,* such as the pedimented portico or the one-

story-high colonnade of the Villa Trissini or the two-story columns of the Villa Sarego (fig. 56). Of the latter, Palladio commented that it is

placed in a very beautiful situation, that is upon a hill . . . which discovers a part of the city and between two small vales. All the hills about it are very agreeable, and abound with most excellent water, therefore this fabrick is adorned with gardens . . . The part of this house which serves for the use of the master, and of the family, has a court round which are portico's. The columns are . . . made of unpolished stones; as it should seem a villa requires, to which plain and simple things are more suitable than those which are delicate. These columns support the outward cornice, that forms a gutter; into which the water falls from the roof.[75]

Although there is no evidence that Washington owned this book, he may have borrowed a copy or been told about this description of a house that was also sited on a hill with a wonderful view and had a two-story portico, albeit one with two levels.

Another unusual feature of the piazza is the design and the proportioning of its 18-foot-high, 17-inch-square columns. Each side of each column is articulated by a recessed panel. This feature is likely derived from plate 51 in Batty Langley's handbook or from plate 79 in William Pain's *Practical Builder* (figs. 57 a & b). Both plates show square columns with recessed paneling. Although cruciform in plan,

FIG. 54 *Suburban houses from the Atlantic to the Pacific show two-story features developed from the piazza at Mount Vernon.*

FIG. 55 *Greenway Court, the unpretentious western home of Thomas, Lord Fairfax, had a piazza that was integrated into the mass of the house and supported on thin, widely spaced columns. One-and-a-half stories high, it extended all the way across one façade. As a young man, Washington often visited Lord Fairfax here. This piazza may have influenced the design of the piazza at Mount Vernon.*

the thin shafts of Pain's Greenhouse design are similar in their proportions to both the piazza and the arcade columns.[76] According to Langley, the height of a Tuscan column is typically seven times its diameter.[77] Following this formula, an 18-foot-high column would measure 31 inches in diameter if round. Washington's square columns depart from this for-

mula with intriguing results. Typically, the side of a square column is equal to the diameter of its round counterpart. When viewed obliquely, a square column appears to be more massive than a round column because the eye measures it by the diagonal. A square with 31-inch sides has a 44-inch diagonal (fig. 58a). If a square column is proportioned so that it fits inside its round counterpart, however, its diagonal equals the diameter of the round column that circumscribes it. With this proportion, a 22-inch square column appears to have the same mass as a 31-inch round column (fig. 58b). Since Washington's column is only 17 inches square, its diagonal measures 24 inches (fig. 58c). Twenty-four inches is one-ninth of the 18-foot height, which is the classic proportion of an Ionic, not a Tuscan, column.

If indeed Washington based the proportion of his square Tuscan columns on that of the Ionic order, he had developed an intelligent formula for the well-established colonial precedent of making the wooden columns of wooden buildings slenderer than stone columns. The 13-foot, six-inch-wide inter-columniation does not accord with conventions in handbooks, or with European precedent derived from stone buildings. Rather, it reflects American wood building

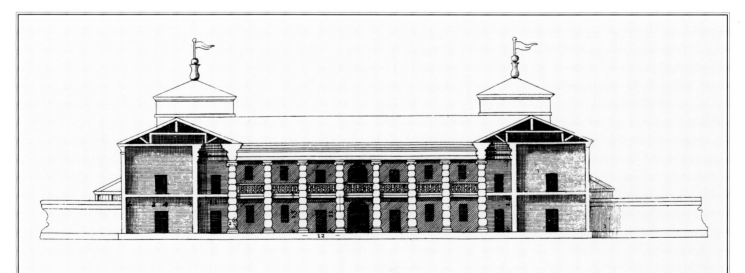

FIG. 56 *The Villa Serego at Santa Sofia, built between 1565 and 1569, is one of Palladio's most magnificent houses. Its U-shaped plan forms an open courtyard that is defined by unusual two-story-high columns. The drawing of this house, illustrated on Plate 49, Book 2, of the* Four Books of Architecture, *may have suggested to Washington that tall columns might be appropriate at Mount Vernon's piazza.*

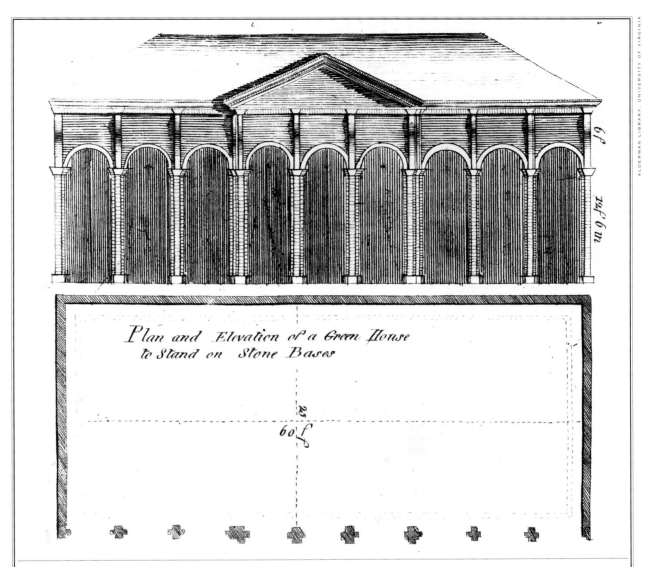

Plan and Elevation of a Green House
to Stand on Stone Bases

FIG. 57A *The drawing on plate 79 of William Pain's handbook,* The Practical Builder, *illustrates a greenhouse design with slender cruciform-shaped columns.*

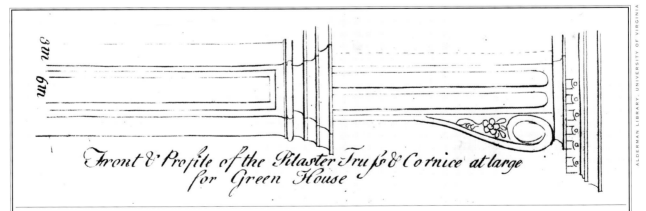

Front & Profile of the Pilaster Truss & Cornice at large
for Green House

FIG. 57B *The detail drawing, shown here horizontally, illustrates that these columns have recessed panels and the same slender proportions as the square columns Washington used for the piazza and arcades at Mount Vernon. Another possible source of Washington's inspiration may have been plate 51 in Batty Langley's* Builder's Treasury of Designs *(see fig. 96).*

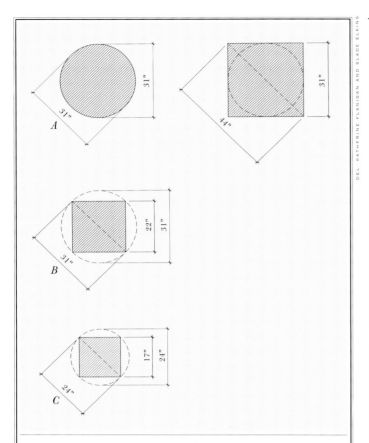

FIGS. 58 A–C *Drawing a) shows that a square column with a side dimension equal to the diameter of a round column appears to be more massive because the eye measures its mass by the diagonal. Drawing b) illustrates a square column that is proportioned so that its diagonal is equal to the diameter of the round column that circumscribes it. These columns are perceived as having the same mass. At drawing c) Washington's 17-inch-square column has a diagonal that measures 24 inches, or one-ninth of the 18-foot-high column. This is the conventional proportion of an Ionic column.*

practices, which allow for longer spans. Sadly, the information that has come down to us about Washington's knowledge of architecture is so minimal that we do not know whether he resolved such problems by combining his intuition and his eye for proportion; by studying handbooks and sketching alternative solutions; or by seeking the advice of friends and artisans.

Washington's modulation of the terrain in front of the piazza is masterful. To dramatize the view across the river as well as the relationship of the house to the grounds, he created two important features. First, he elevated the piazza

floor three feet above the surrounding lawn by creating a berm that slopes down from the edge of the piazza to the lawn. This feature is precisely captured by Samuel Seymour's 1804 engraving, after a sketch by William Birch (fig. 59). Because the floor of the piazza rises gently above the land in front of it, the spectator's awareness of the view to the river is enhanced. Washington must have sensed that the introduction of masonry steps from the piazza down to the grass would have separated the house from the landscape and imposed architectural features of an identifiable scale that may have made the piazza appear larger and more monumental. Instead, when the berm around the piazza is seen from the surrounding lawn, or from a boat on the river, it functions as a grass ramp that establishes an almost seamless shift from the house to the landscape. It binds the house to the site and allows the scale of the piazza to remain ambiguous.

Second, Washington formed a concave depression on the river side of the hill on which the house stands. This remarkable feature begins about 55 feet in front of the piazza and extends another 100 feet to the low wall at the edge of

FIG. 60 *Washington sculpted a concave depression out of the hill on which the house stands. Facing the river, this remarkable feature is on the main axis of the house. It begins in front of the piazza and extends 100 feet to the low wall at the edge of the lawn. This gentle hollow emphasizes the continuity of the axis through the house to the river and serves to anchor Mount Vernon to the site.*

FIG. 59 *Samuel Seymour's 1804 engraving of the east side of Mount Vernon, made after a sketch by William Birch, illustrates how Washington elevated the piazza floor three feet above the surrounding lawn. He created an angled berm that slopes down from the edge of the piazza to the lawn.*

the lawn (fig. 60). Because it is situated on the main axis of the house, which starts at the entrance gate, this slight hollow emphasizes the continuity of the axis through the house to the river and serves to anchor the house to the site. To accent the beauty of the land form he created, and to frame the view over the hanging garden, Washington raised gentle mounds on either side of the hollow.[78] On July 3, 1799, the Reverend John E. Latta watched Washington sculpt the garden's contours: "Between the home and the descent of the bank is a very beautiful and extensive green, and to enhance its beauty still more, the General, whilst I was there, was engaged in . . . modeling its form, that to the beauties of nature he might add the embellishments of art; but in such a

manner that the improvements would still appear natural."[79]

In 1776 Washington planted two substantial groves of trees—one on each side of the piazza. Seen from the river, they frame the house and piazza and screen the lawns on the river side from the service buildings to the west (fig. 61). He outlined this plan to his farm manager, Lund Washington, in a letter written from New York on August 19, 1776, in which he described the location of the two groves. This letter also provided instruction on how the

groves of Trees at each end of the dwelling House . . . these Trees to be Planted without any order or regularity (but pretty thick, as they can at any time be thin'd) and to consist that at the North end, of locusts altogether & that at the South, of all the clever

FIG. 61 *The view to Mount Vernon from the Potomac River was a particularly important aspect of Washington's design. At a time when road travel was very limited, the river provided the most public view of the house. In 1776 Washington planted substantial groves of trees on each side of the piazza. Seen from the river, they continue to frame the house's most memorable façade.*

kind of Trees (especially flowering ones) that can be got, such as Crab apple, Poplar, Dogwood, Sasafras, Lawrel, Willow (especially yellow & Weeping Willow, twigs of which may be got from Philadelphia) . . . these to be interspersed here and there with ever greens such as Holly, Pine, and Cedar, also Ivy—to these may be added the Wild flowering Shrubs of the larger kind, such as the fringe Tree & several other kinds that might be mentioned.[80]

Niemcewicz notes that the locust is "a charming tree, with a smooth trunk and without branches leaving a clear and open space for the movement of its small and trembling leaves. The ground where they are planted is a green carpet of the most beautiful velvet. This tree keeps off all kinds of insects."[81]

For Washington, the view to the house from the Potomac River was a particularly important aspect of Mount Vernon's design. A major traffic route at a time when road travel was

very limited and difficult, the river provided the most public view of the house. Seen from the river, the piazza is framed by trees and presents a memorable façade. The simple, almost diagrammatic, design—eight columns and a roof—is strengthened by the deep shadow the roof casts on the piazza's rear wall, by the slenderness of the columns, and by the dramatic counterpoint of the asymmetrically placed windows and doors in the column bays (fig. 62). The result is architectural eloquence that becomes more powerful when seen from afar. From the river, the ambiguity of scale and the schematic, attenuated quality of the east front also create an unsettling, even haunting, verticality that is apparent from some of the early views of the house. Although the trees in the 1790s may have been smaller than they are today, one cannot gauge the height of the piazza. From the river, the

MOUNT VERNON LADIES' ASSOCIATION

FIG. 62 *The east elevation is a simple design formed by eight slender columns and a roof. It is strengthened by the deep shadow the roof casts on the piazza's rear wall and by the dramatic counterpoint of the asymmetrically placed windows and doors in the column bays. This concise quality of Washington's design is illustrated by this painting, ca. 1792, by an unknown artist.*

simplicity of the piazza's design and the absence of features with an easily identifiable scale contribute to the sense that the house occupies its prominent site with the ease of a natural feature.

GARDENS AND FARMS

The mansion is the centerpiece of the garden and farms. The main axis from the house to the entrance gate is the reference line around which the estate is organized; it is manifest by the view from the west entrance door of the house that takes the eye across the Bowling Green to the west gate and, in the distance, to the entrance gate at the end of the vista cut through the woodland (fig. 63). Throughout this designed landscape most circulation moves off the main east-west axis so that the latter is used as a visual and con-

ceptual organizing device. Circulation intersects with the main axis at critical junctures, like those of the west garden gate and the front door. Here, the visitor is reminded of the main axis and the larger estate (fig. 64). The route of movement off the main axis is picturesque and intimate, descending into the rivulet valley and the shaded serpentine walks. On the two cross-axes, movement usually coincides with an axis, but at the actual cross point the axis is not defined. For example, at the Bowling Green the pathways to the flower and vegetable gardens begin at the serpentine walks and do not extend across the lawn; this helps to fully define the cross-axis. Similarly, no path crosses the circle in front of the house although the north and south lanes extend out from it on either side to form a powerful cross-axis. In order to maintain the primacy of the Bowling Green lawn and the circle and avoid cluttering them with pathways, Washington decided to merely imply the presence of the cross axes. He also created long views to the surrounding fields and meadows that, like the numerous cross-axes, are used as organizing devices to unify the five farms.

The subtlety and variety of Washington's landscape plan make Mount Vernon the most dramatic, and one of the most beautiful, eighteenth-century landscapes in the United States. The cutting and vegetable gardens, on the north and south sides of the Bowling Green, are largely hidden from view by brick walls so they become elements of discovery as the visitor explores the estate. At each end of these lozenge-shaped walled gardens, as previously noted, are small octagonal pavilions. Opposite the gate to the cutting garden is a

FIG. 63 *The view from the west entrance door of the house, looking across the Bowling Green, focuses a visitor's eye on the west garden gate and beyond, to the entrance gate of the Mansion House Farm. The roof of the barn at Dogue Run Farm would have been visible in the distance, framed by the vista through the woods and behind the entrance gate.*

Greenhouse, which is approached on a pathway between the constricting walls of hedges. Planted parterres open out on either side of the pathway, becoming visible only when the visitor reaches the Greenhouse and turns around (fig. 65). On the other side of the bowling green, the vegetable garden is symmetrical with the cutting garden except that it is some ten feet lower, as the site slopes down to the valley on the south side. The stables, "dung repository," and barns at the south side of the line of service buildings also occupy lower grades and sloping ground. By these subtle arrangements, Washington integrated the vegetable garden into the sloping site and related the house and its immediate gardens to the surrounding landscape, blending them all into a richly textured composition (fig. 66).

The house and surrounding landscape afforded carefully planned views to the cultivated fields and meadows of the other four Mount Vernon farms. In his journal entry, Latrobe described the view north from the piazza to River Farm:

An extent of 1500 acres perfectly clear of wood, which borders the river on the left bank on the Virginia side boldly contrasts the remainder of the Woody landscape. It is a farm belonging to the President. The general surface is level, but elevated above all inundations. Beyond this Sheet of verdure the country rises into bold woody hills . . . . The Maryland shore has the same character. Opposite to the house, where its detail becomes more distinct it is variegated by lawns and copses.[82]

A 1791 account of a visit to Mount Vernon published in *Osborne's New-Hampshire Spy* describes one of the views:

over a small creek to the northward, an extensive plain exhibits cornfields and cattle grazing, affords in summer a luxuriant landscape to the eye; while the blended verdure of woodlands and cultivated declivities, on the Maryland shore, variegates the prospect in a charming manner.[83]

The same author noted that a view to the south from the vegetable garden "slopes more steeply, in shorter distance and terminates with the . . stables, vineyard and nurseries."

From Washington's diaries and letters to his estate managers, we learn of his ongoing preoccupation with opening vistas from one part of his estate to another in order to unify the farms. Washington's diary indicated that on March 15, 1785, he "Began to open Vistos throw the Pine grove on the Banks of H. Hole."[84] On October 14, 1792, he wrote from Philadelphia to Anthony Whiting, his farm manager, about the "second Visto which I mentioned to you . . . (as) I am anxious to know over what ground it will pass; but this may be done by a line of stakes in an avenue not more than Six feet wide."[85] Two months later, he informed Whiting that

I would have you open the second Visto 20 feet wide, as far as Muddy hole branch, and let me know whether the hill on the other side of it is high or low . . . for as to opening it beyond the hill I conceive it to be as unnecessary, as it was in the first Visto . . . [86]

Later, on January 13, 1793, he explained to Whiting,

My object in clearing the grounds out side of the pasture, along the Road from Gum Spring, was that you might see the Mansion house as soon as you should enter the little old field beyond it. [87]

On December 2, he had reminded Whiting "to mark out another Visto on the West front of the Mansion house," and referred to a second one where he might wish "to make a pond . . . along the Visto that was opened in a line between the two doors."[88] In March 1793, he asked again, "Have you got the second Visto so much opened as to be able to form any opinion of the view, and how it will appear from the House?"[89]

The four other farms were tied to the center farm by views from the main house, gardens, and approach roads. The farms afforded their own views to the main house on its hill—part of the "Mansion House farm" designated by Washington on his 1793 plan. In a letter to William Triplett in 1786, Washington described this careful process of integration and how, by acquiring the "French Manley" property, he hoped "to blend them & my other plantations together, & to form entire new ones out of the whole."[90]

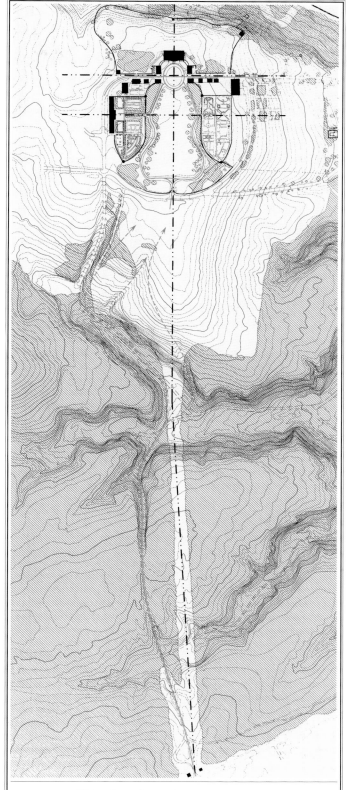

FIG. 64 *This plan shows the main east-west axis from the entrance gate to the Mansion house and how circulation moves on and off this axis. Circulation and axis intersect at critical junctures — the gate into the estate, the west garden gate, and the front door. The circulation route meanders into the rivulet valley in contrast with the direct formal axis.*

FIG. 65 *The walkway into the cutting garden is framed by tall hedges. The Greenhouse is at the end. Planted parterres that open out on either side of the pathway become visible only when the visitor reaches the Greenhouse and turns around.*

A significant element in the composition of these views is the use of hedgerows, which Washington referred to as "live fences." On November 22, 1795, he wrote to William Pearce that "there is nothing which has relation to my farms — not even the Crops of grain that I am so solicitous about as getting my fields enclosed with live fences." He continued: "At least 15 years have I been urging my managers to substitute live fences in lieu of dead ones — which, if continued upon the extensive scale my farms require, must exhaust all my timber." Washington then proposed English thorn for "inner" fences, honey locust along Mill Road and Union Farm, "Cedar hedge from the Barn . . . to the Mill road," and cross fences of Lombardy poplar wattled to form hedges.[91] In his letter to Whiting on October 14, 1792, he issued instructions to plant "cuttings of the Weeping Willow, yellow willow,

or Lombardy Poplar . . . at the distance of a foot, or 18 Inches apart . . ." around certain fields "because it is indispensably necessary to save timber and labour; and . . . because it is ornamental to the Farm, and reputable to the Farmer."[92]

The meadow enclosures were for cattle to graze in. This was part of Washington's plan for crop rotation and the revitalization of his fields, which is not only good farming practice, but was an important element in picturesque garden composition. The hedges have the practical purpose of defining and enclosing different parts of the farms, as well as the aesthetic function of composing views from the house and gardens to the farms.

Washington was constantly aware of the importance of trees in these garden and farm compositions. In his Memorandum of 1796 to William Pearce, he wrote (as we have noted earlier) that "Trees . . . except where they stand in clumps, be trimmed in one even height from the ground" to reduce shade on crops and improve "the appearance of the trees when they get to be of larger growth."[93] Clearly he understood that he was planning for future "beauty." After losing thousands of trees by transplanting them, he discovered that

FIG. 66 *On the south side of the Bowling Green, set some 10 feet lower, the vegetable garden is symmetrical with the cutting garden on the north side. The site continues to slope down to the valley. The orchard, stables, and service buildings define the far edges of the vegetable garden.*

MOUNT VERNON LADIES' ASSOCIATION

FIG. 67 *Four etchings after Claude Lorrain decorated the Passage in Mount Vernon. One such reproduction in the manner of Lorrain was painted by John Browne after an original by Herman van Swanvelt (ca. 1600–1655). Washington may have used these paintings and etchings for inspiration in his garden planning as well as to bring the artful landscape to the inside of the house. His interest in creating views from one part of his estate to another may also have been inspired by Lorrain's work.*

"with respect to the transplanting of Cedar (or any other evergreen) I am persuaded there is no other sure way of getting them to live, than by taking them up in the winter with a block of frozen earth around the Roots (and as large as it can conveniently be obtained, proportioned to the size of the plant)." [94]

The house was the heart of the composition. Together with the surrounding village of support and farm buildings and the gardens, it forms an exceptional expression of the integration of architecture and picturesque gardening. Perhaps the most unusual aspect of Washington's achievement was how gracefully he was able to meld the farms into the overall composition of landscape and architecture. He may have found his inspiration for these composed views in paintings or etchings, such as the four etchings in the style of Claude Lorrain that decorated the Passage in Mount Vernon. But it's just as likely that Washington selected these works of art to bring his artful landscape into the house (fig. 67).[95]

Washington's 1793 plan of the estate also includes a grist mill, described by Niemcewicz as "very large" and "built in stone," barns, fisheries, and numerous service buildings.[96] Niemcewicz also visited a distillery there. Like most Virginia

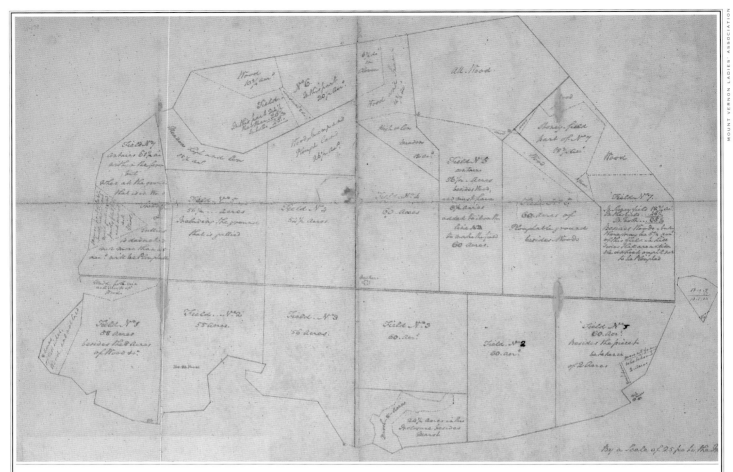

FIG. 68 *George Washington's 1747 survey map of the properties that he eventually acquired and consolidated into Union Farm shows field subdivisions for a three-crop rotation.*

farmers, Washington began by using a three-crop rotation, planting tobacco followed by maize, and then leaving the field fallow for a year. This mode of farming required subdivision of the land into smaller fields with overseers' dwellings, slave quarters, and tobacco houses scattered about the farms (fig. 68). In the mid-1760s he decided to drastically reduce reliance on tobacco because the soil on his farms was poorly suited to the cultivation of a high-quality tobacco leaf. He first switched some fields to corn production for which there was not a profitable market other than whiskey, and built his own still. Like many of his neighbors in the Alexandria and Colchester regions who were turning to the flour trade, Washington gladly substituted wheat for tobacco as his main cash crop.

As we have observed, Washington was one of a number of Tidewater farmers who sought ways of improving farming methods. Not only was diversification a means to limit imports and to protest reprehensive imperial measures such as the Stamp Act, but it reduced reliance on one crop and averted the economic privations that came when they had a poor harvest or a surplus.[97] Despite Washington's careful attention to farm management and field production, the proceeds of the sale of his tobacco in England seldom met his expectations. In order to better the quality of his soil and its output, Washington strove to become a more innovative farmer. This is evident in his diaries in 1760. That year also marked the beginning of a new approach to agriculture in England. Washington was particularly attracted to the revolutionary ideas of agronomist Jethro Tull, who advocated using forage crops, root vegetables, and non-native grasses together with deep plowing. Tull proposed that crops be drilled in rows, spaced so that the cultivating implements could pass between them.[98] Washington also investigated the market potential of grain, flour, hemp, and flax and enlarged the fishery at Mount Vernon.[99] To avoid having to import cloth, he purchased weaving equipment. By the end of the decade 1,200 yards of homespun were being produced at Mount Vernon.

It was in 1783, after he returned from the war, that Washington determined to totally replace the three-crop rotation with the more productive and scientific seven-crop rotation system. This mandated reconsidering his entire mode of farming. A period began of intensive experimentation with new scientific methods of farming that lasted until Washington's death in 1799. At this time he and the English agronomist Arthur Young (1741–1820) began a correspondence about improving farming that lasted many years. Washington experimented with dozens of crops, different methods of sowing seeds, alternative spacing for seeds, and varying the rates of seeding. He bred animals to improve his stock, assessed the efficacy of various plows and different manures, including dung, marl, plowing-under green crops,

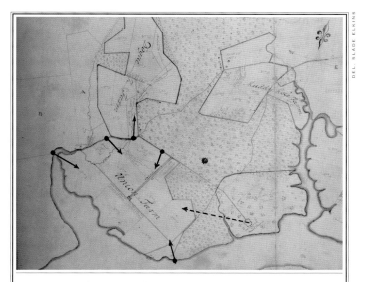

FIG. 69 *This map of Union Farm is an enlargement of Washington's 1793 survey of Mount Vernon. It shows the new sub-division into larger fields to accommodate a seven-crop rotation and the tree-lined road to the New Brick Barn. The arrows indicate views to the New Brick Barn from the Alexandria to Colchester Road, the approach road to the house, the Mansion House, and the ferry wharf.*

and even Potomac mud.[100] His seriousness of purpose and careful documentation yielded methods comparable to those of contemporary agronomists.[101]

To implement the seven-crop rotation, he reorganized his land into five larger, contiguous farms: Mansion House Farm, Dogue Run Farm, Union Farm, Muddy Hole Farm, and River Farm (refer to fig. 3). These were in place by 1786, when his land holdings totaled 7,400 acres. He subdivided each farm into larger, discrete working fields and created a system of numbering to identify each field; planned new, larger barns to process and store the crops; created a program to repair, move, and expand existing buildings or build new ones; and improved roads, fences, and ditches (fig. 69). He also sought better ways to improve the soil. "When I speak of a knowing farmer," he wrote to his friend George William Fairfax on June 30, 1785,

I mean one who understands the best course of Crops; how to plough—to sow—to mow—to hedge—to Ditch & above all, Midas like, one who can convert every thing he touches into manure, as the first transmutation towards Gold: in a word one who can bring worn out & gullied Lands into good tilth in the shortest time.[102]

Each farm was transformed into a well-ordered unit with its own barns, sheds, overseers' houses, slave quarters, and network of roads. Washington strengthened the farm management system to improve communication with his manager and overseers, to monitor his experiments, and to record the labor and production of each field. He altered his labor management to suit his new crop system.[103] Specific crop schedules were developed for the seven years of the rotation. This required planting two fields of wheat—the principal cash crop—three of clover or grasses for cattle-grazing and soil revitalization, one of corn and potatoes for domestic use, and one of buckwheat. Legumes were also used to rejuvenate the soil. Washington never stopped searching for optimal results in the quality of livestock and

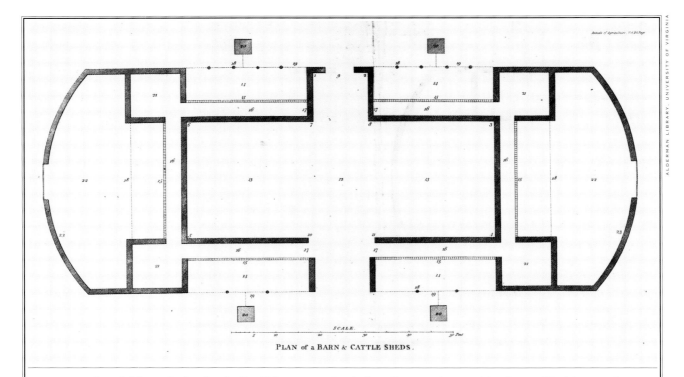

PLAN of a BARN & CATTLE SHEDS.

FIG. 70 *A model barn design by the English agronomist Arthur Young, who sent his plan to Washington. Later, this design was published, in 1791, in Young's journal* The Annals of Architecture and Other Useful Arts. *It served as model for Washington's design for the New Brick Barn.*

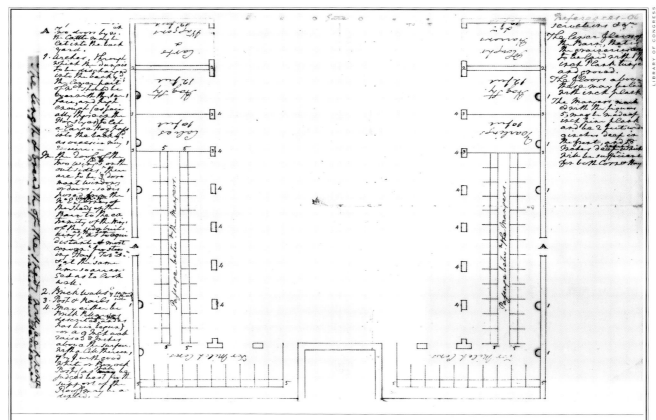

FIG. 71 *Washington's drawing of the stable building, erected on the south side of the New Brick Barn at Union Farm in 1791. The recess in the center of the stables probably accommodated the projecting center of the barn.*

soil. As a result, Mount Vernon became a stronger economic and architectural unit. The words used by the poet Jean Garrigue to describe Emily Dickinson's poetry apply equally to Washington's love of farming: "No substances were common for her. She saw them all as rare."[104]

Among the most noteworthy improvements were three major barns he designed and built. The two most important were the brick barn, reputed to be one of the largest in the new nation, that he built at the center of Union Farm, and the innovative 16-sided treading barn that he designed for Dogue Run Farm. In front of both barns are carefully composed groups of satellite support buildings that he planned as distinct architectural compositions. Each group was very different in character as he sought to dramatize the architectural setting and take advantage of the picturesque views to the barn from the surrounding roads and farms.

In 1788, Jean-Pierre Brissot de Warville, a visitor from France noted that the

celebrated General . . . has lately built a barn . . . one hundred feet in length, and considerable more in breadth, destined to receive the productions of his farm, and shelter his cattle, horses, asses, and mules. It is built on a plan sent him by that famous English farmer Arthur Young (fig. 70). But the General has much improved the plan.[105]

Brissot de Warville was referring to the great brick edifice at Union Farm. And though the design's origins are correct, Washington also gathered information from journals and books, and corresponded with friends and other progressive farmers. From this data, including Young's plan, he developed "a hybrid design specific to his particular needs and ambitions."[106] Construction of the brick barn began in 1787; by late 1790 it was in use. An adjoining brick stable complex for hogs, cows, calves, and farm equipment was completed in 1791 (fig. 71).[107] In 1793 Washington wrote Young that the complex at Union Farm was "equal perhaps to any in America, and for conveniences of all sorts . . . scarcely to be exceeded anywhere."[108]

The 1793 plan of the estate shows that the barn was sited at the junction of the main cross-axial road serving Union Farm and a newly constructed access lane from the main approach road to the Mansion House. The access lane was lined with an allée of trees and mown lawn; post and rail fences defined the cultivated fields on either side. A visitor approaching the house could look down the lane and see the new brick barn at the end of its formal tree-lined axis, a preview of the nearly mile-long tree-lined vista that awaited at the entrance gates to Mansion House Farm. Washington further embellished the barn's approach lane with a line of farm buildings sited on the east side of the access lane, midway between the barn and the main approach road. These were the farm and residential buildings distributed among the small farms that became Union Farm; Washington dismantled and reassembled them, repairing, modifying, or building a new one as necessary, to better serve the seven-crop rotation plan.[109] The barn and service buildings also were visible to travelers on the Colchester to Alexandria road, part of a pleasing

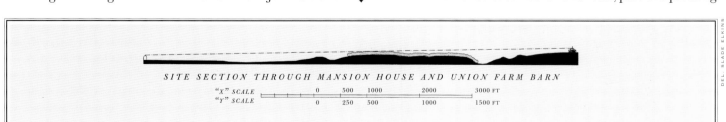

SITE SECTION THROUGH MANSION HOUSE AND UNION FARM BARN

"X" SCALE   0   500   1000   2000   3000 FT
"Y" SCALE   0   250   500   1000   1500 FT

FIG. 72 *A section through Union Farm and Mansion House Farm, to illustrate the contours of the land between the house and the New Brick Barn. It shows that the brick barn may have been visible from the upper floors of the house, especially in winter when the trees had lost their leaves.*

composition of fields, ditches, hedges, farm buildings, and trees, with the new brick barn and adjacent stables marking the center of Union Farm. The top of the new barn roof may have been visible from the Mansion House, particularly in winter when the trees lost their leaves, as well as from the adjacent Woodlawn Plantation and Belvoir (fig. 72).

Later, Washington built an innovative two-level, 16-sided treading barn that is also a functional structure of rare eloquence and ingenuity. Orlando Redout and John Riley describe it as "a unique landmark in the history of pre-industrial agricultural building."[110] Constructed at Dogue Run Farm, this barn was designed specifically for threshing grain. At the time, grain was usually threshed with a hand flail on a sturdy wood floor in the center bay of a barn, a time-consuming and labor-intensive process. Poorer farmers used well-packed dirt floors prepared in the open air. On some large farms, horses, mules, or oxen tread over the crop so that their hoofs beat out the grain: the crop was spread out in a large circle, in an eight-foot-wide swath, and the horses would be ridden around and around the circle. Workmen were required to continuously turn and stir the wheat piles, immediately remove manure, and see that the horses were driven in an orderly manner.[111]

Washington wanted a more efficient system that would protect the crop from the carelessness of his staff.[112] To this end, he designed and built the 16-sided, nearly circular

FIG. 73 *In 1793–94, Washington designed and built an unusual 16-sided, two-story treading barn on Dogue Run Farm. Designed to thresh crops more efficiently, the barn included a center building and wings forming a courtyard. The wings contained pens for livestock and corn cribs. This is a landmark in design of pre-industrial agricultural building.*

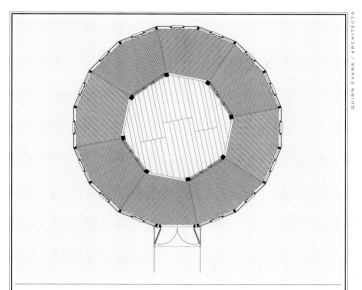

FIG. 74 *The upper floor plan of the treading barn shows a 28-foot-diameter storage area in the center for the unthreshed harvest. This is surrounded by a twelve-foot-wide wood threshing floor that is broad enough to accommodate teams of horses trotting around it.*

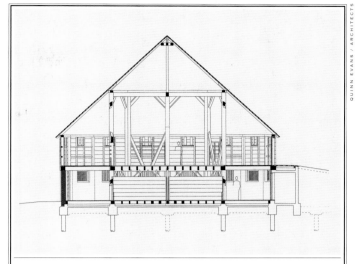

FIG. 75A *The section through the treading barn shows a two-level structure. Washington provided spaces between the floor boards of the treading floor so that the heads of grain, once separated from the straw and some of the chaff, would fall through to a granary below. The center of the lower level was used for piling the unwinnowed grain.*

building of 52 feet in diameter (fig. 73). In its center was a 28-foot-diameter storage area for the unthreshed harvest, enclosed by a low wall. Between this wall and the exterior was a 12-foot-wide wood threshing floor, broad enough to accommodate teams of horses trotting around it (fig. 74). To improve the efficiency of the basic treading process, and to reduce opportunities for theft, Washington ingeniously planned to leave spaces between the floor boards of the treading floor so that the heads of grain, once separated from the straw and some of the chaff, would fall through the spaces to a granary one level below. The optimal width of the opening between the boards was the subject of a series of experiments conducted by William Pearce, the farm manager, under the anxious guidance of Washington in Philadelphia. The President advised that

If the section . . . which you have left an inch apart, is not apt to choke or pass too much straw through try another section at an inch and a half and so on . . . until you hit the mark exactly; and then regulate all the sections accordingly.[113]

Eventually they determined that one-and-a-half inches was

the most efficient opening. The two-level structure used the center of the lower level for piling the unwinnowed grain (figs. 75 a & b). The result was a building that was really a machine. Niemcewicz observed the treading barn in use and noted that "all around the building there are windows for a draft."[114] The horses' hoofs stirred up dense clouds of dust and the windows facilitated circulation of fresh air. Wash-

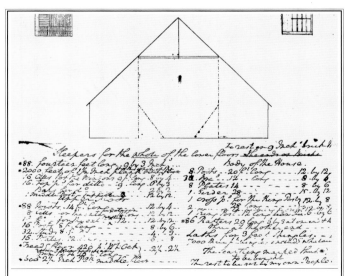

FIG. 75B *Washington's own drawing of the upper part of the barn includes calculations that established the size of every piece of wood used to build the barn.*

ington started construction of this handsome structure in 1793 and work was completed in 1795.

The treading barn was framed by a symmetrical forecourt with a row of buildings on each side for stables, corn cribs, and storage (fig. 76). It was beautifully sited at the head of an access lane from the Alexandria-Colchester Road. This lane had a forest on its east side and fields to the west. For the traveler going north, the treading barn was prominently visible from the road (fig. 77). It was set in the middle of fields of grain, and its unusual cylindrical form probably aroused considerable curiosity. Across the road from Dogue Run Farm were the fields of Union Farm and the new brick barn. The two farms were contiguous, separated only by the Alexandria-Colchester Road, but related by the stream—the Dogue Run—that ran south from the northern end of Dogue Run Farm through Union Farm to the Potomac, and by the same neat hedges and fences that

visitors admired at Mount Vernon. This barn was located on the main axis of the house and approach road (fig. 78). Its roof may have been a beacon of reference to travelers to and from Mount Vernon.

Washington built a third barn at River Farm, a threshing barn that improved upon the brick barn at Union Farm. In front of it were two rows of service structures, composed at right angles to each other. This picturesque group of buildings was ingeniously sited to form an interesting composition in front of the large barn. The group was visible from the Mansion House and the gardens to the north of the Bowling Green (figs. 79 & 80). That it was composed with less formality than the other barns tells much about Washington's pragmatic approach to design and his brilliant eye for taking advantage of the landscape to create arresting visual effects.

Constructed of stone, Washington's Grist Mill (1771, rebuilt 1932–33) is subtly sited on a hillside adjacent to

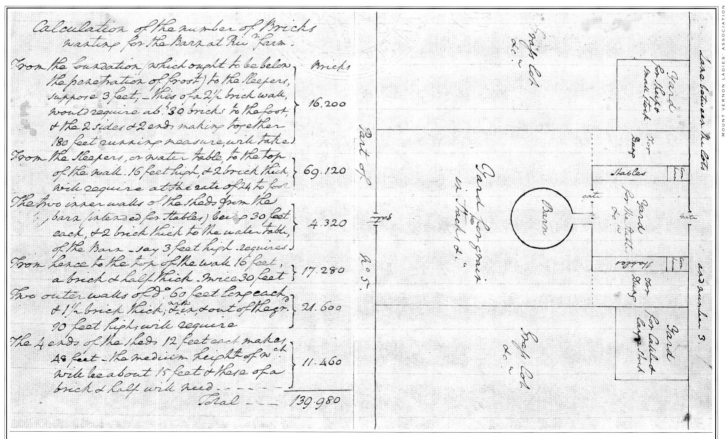

FIG. 76 *Washington's site plan shows the barn and wings for "stables" and "cornhouses." The symmetrically composed group of buildings is surrounded by a "yard for grain in stacks."*

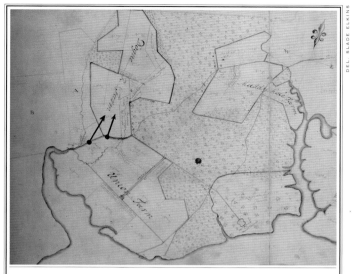

DEL. SLADE ELKINS

FIG. 77 *The treading barn was visible from the road. Its unusual cylindrical form set in the middle of fields of grain probably aroused considerable curiosity.*

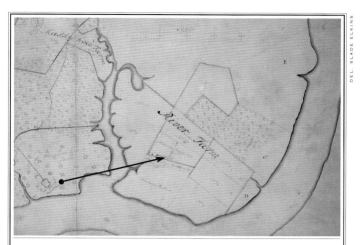

DEL. SLADE ELKINS

FIG. 79 *At River Farm, Washington ingeniously sited rows of service structures at right angles to each other, in front of the large barn. The picturesque composition differs from the more symmetrical site plan of the two other new barns.*

Dogue Run Farm. It was the first building a traveler from Colchester would have seen (refer to fig. 77). The three barn complexes form the centers of the largest farms. Visible from the surrounding roads or the river, they were satellites of the Mansion House in the middle of the estate. As such, they formed key elements in the system of "Vistos" that bound farms, house, and gardens together in pleasing, often dramatic compositions. It is probable that the roofs of the barns at Union Farm and Dogue Run were visible from the cupola and

possibly the second floor of the main house, particularly in winter when the deciduous trees were bare of leaves. Each barn also served as a focal point from various parts of the estate; two were visible from the river. Is it possible that Washington was trying to unify his estate with views to and from distant structures in the same way that Peter Charles L'Enfant's 1791 plan for the new Federal City offered distant views down streets and diagonal avenues to parks, buildings, and the Mall.

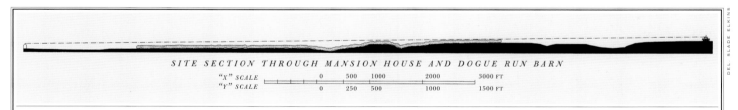

DEL. SLADE ELKINS

SITE SECTION THROUGH MANSION HOUSE AND DOGUE RUN BARN

"X" SCALE   0   500   1000   2000   3000 FT
"Y" SCALE   0   250   500   1000   1500 FT

FIG. 78 *The Treading Barn was located on the main axis of the Mansion House. This cross section shows that the cylindrical roof of the barn may have served as a beacon of reference for travelers going to and leaving Mount Vernon.*

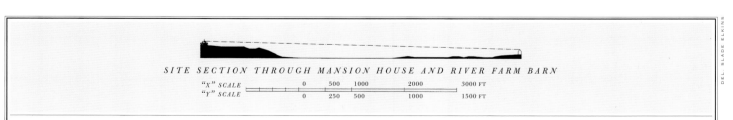

DEL. SLADE ELKINS

SITE SECTION THROUGH MANSION HOUSE AND RIVER FARM BARN

"X" SCALE   0   500   1000   2000   3000 FT
"Y" SCALE   0   250   500   1000   1500 FT

FIG. 80 *A section cut between Mansion House Farm and River Farm shows that the barn at River Farm was easily visible from the Mansion House.*

The 1754 inventory Washington prepared of his late brother's estate indicates the layout of the first Mount Vernon and the starting point for Washington's own additions and alterations (refer to fig. 4). Lawrence Washington's farmhouse had a 13-foot-3-inch-wide central hall, or "Passage." At either end of this passage were two sets of rooms: on the west side a hall and a bed chamber, called the Red Room, faced the entrance court, and on the east, two bed chambers overlooked the Potomac.[115] There was a storeroom under the stair and an attic that contained four bed chambers. The very conjectural floor plan and the west elevation of the house shows that the hall had two windows, while the Red Room and storeroom under the stair each had one window. The result was a nearly symmetrical elevation.

Washington began rebuilding Mount Vernon in 1757 by raising the roof and creating a full second floor and a new attic (refer to fig. 6). It was during this 1757–1760 rebuilding that he covered most of the outside of the house with rusticated wood siding, a change whose significance was discussed in the chapter entitled The Mansion. The rustication was not incorporated into the gables at either end of the house; for these he selected a beaded siding. All the exterior walls were painted with a sand finish.[116] As noted earlier, he also added two buildings, possibly outhouses, that were connected to the east side of the house by angled fences, which he called "running Walls for Pallisades."[117] Finally, he created new gardens by enclosing two matching rectangular parterres on either side of the driveway (refer to fig. 5). Washington also modified the interior of the house in significant ways. The majority of these changes were to create a more elaborate interior decoration. The passage was the most public room in Virginia houses of the eighteenth century, and it is understandable that he wanted to improve this room. No longer restricted by the space limitations of an attic, the staircase was rebuilt in walnut and on a more comfortable scale. Lawrence Washington's house may have had an arch, or sim-

ilar form, separating the stair section of the Passage from the rest of the room.[118] This was removed by George Washington, who then added new paneling and cornice moldings above the chair rail and painted it a yellow ochre color (fig. 81). As noted earlier, the new cornice is unusual because it is similar in form, with the same unusual block modillion on the cornice that Washington used on the exterior of the house (refer to fig. 42).[119] The only difference is that the end of the interior modillion has a cyma recta while the exterior cornice has a cyma reversa. The simple, bold character of the moldings distinguishes this cornice from the more elaborate and less monumental ones in the other rooms. This design decision is appropriate because the Passage was more than just an entry hall and stair to the second floor: Farm and other business would have been conducted here, servants interviewed, and visitors received. Thus, as architectural historian Mark R. Winger notes, the passage was "instrumental in restricting access" to the "most important, most symbolic," and more private rooms in the house.[120] By the mid-eighteenth century the Passage or summer hall was the only room to cut through the width of the house and to trap summer breezes.[121] Because it was the most comfortable room in hot weather, it was also used for dining.[122]

Lawrence Washington's Red Room became the Small Dining Room. It was enhanced by the addition of paneled wainscoting and a second window overlooking the entrance court. This window may have been removed from the storeroom under the stair.[123] Washington also relocated the existing window in the room so that the new window locations were in the same relative position in the room, when viewed from the inside, as the windows in what probably was the former Hall, now called the West Parlor. As we have noted, this alteration had a significant consequence on the exterior: It created the asymmetry that is such a key characteristic of the Mansion House's west façade.

The most challenging of the projects of this 1757–1760 phase of rebuilding was the West Parlor. The room was pan-

FIG. 81 *The Passage at Mount Vernon was for receiving visitors. It was also used for dining in summer and conducting the owner's public affairs and farm business. George Washington added the paneling and cornice moldings above the chair rail. This was first painted a yellow ochre color. Later in 1797, he applied the wood-grain finish to the panels.*

FIG. 82 *During his 1757–1760 building campaign, Washington paneled the West Parlor. He also added an elaborate pedimented door frame using the Ionic order to articulate the doorway to the Passage.*

eled and two elaborately pedimented door frames using the Ionic order were installed (fig. 82). The entablature may have been inspired by the "Ionick Entablature" illustrated on plate VI in Batty Langley's *Builder's Treasury of Designs* (fig. 83). The capital is based on Palladio's rendition of the Ionic order, as illustrated on plate 20, Book One, of his *Four Books of Architecture*, and plate 23 of the Langleys' *Builder's Jewel*, which is the more likely source. Palladio's capital is not used in Langley's *Builder's Treasury*, which follows Inigo Jones's precedent at the Banqueting House and combines Vincenzo Scamozzi's capital with Palladio's entablature.[124] The mantel and overmantel were inspired by plates 50 and 51 in Abraham Swan's handbook, *The British Architect* (figs. 84 & 85 a & b). A red mahogany graining was used to paint the chimneypiece, doors, and door frames. The wall paneling was covered with a stone-colored paint that contained ochre and umber pigments mixed with white lead.[125]

Both rooms on the east side, facing the river, were decorated as bed chambers. The one on the north side of the Passage is a very simple room, dating from Lawrence Washington's time, with a modest decorative scheme of chair rail and cornice with plastered walls (fig. 86). It continued to serve as a bed chamber until Washington stepped down from the Presidency, at which time it became the "Little Parlor" and music room, housing the harpsichord he purchased in 1793 for Martha's granddaughter Nelly Custis, who lived at Mount Vernon. Washington paneled the downstairs bed chamber on the south side of the passage in 1758. (This room is thought to have served as the master bed chamber until the extension of the south side of the house was finished in 1775. Thereafter, the downstairs bed chamber was probably used for guests.) The modest mantel in this room was probably similar to the mantels in the West Parlor and Dining Room prior to Washington's improvements (fig. 87). On the second floor were now five bed chambers. They were comparatively simple in design, featuring a small cornice molding and chair rail with plaster walls (fig. 88).

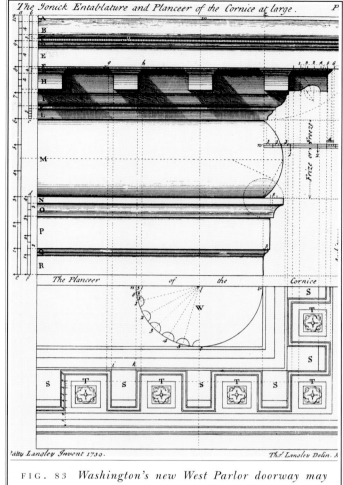

FIG. 83 *Washington's new West Parlor doorway may have been inspired by the "Ionick Entablature" on Plate 9 in Batty Langley's* Builder's Treasury of Designs.

By 1770 Washington had retired over half of his debts to English merchants. The profits from his cottage industries, crops, fishery, and livestock had reduced his dependency on imports to a minimum. He had completely changed his way of life. As a result, in 1773, Washington began to consider the second phase of the house's expansion. This would be a statement of his new-found economic independence and the successful transformation of Mount Vernon from a tobacco plantation to a diversified farm.

Construction started in the summer of 1774. Along with interior improvements, he planned substantial additions on both ends of the house, erected the new two-story piazza facing the river; and added the arcades connecting the new dependencies to the house on the west. This phase also included a complete redesign of the west garden. Washington

FIG. 84 *For a corner fireplace, the elaborate mantel and overmantel in the West Parlor are unusually elaborate in their design.*

removed the central drive and symmetrical parterres and created the Bowling Green and the serpentine walks, the north and south service lanes, and the flower and vegetable gardens. He also undertook an extensive program of tree planting.

Construction began on the south end with Washington's new study and some storage rooms on the first floor, and the master bed chamber and two dressing rooms on the second (fig. 89). The plaster walls of this wing were covered with

FIGS. 85 A & B *The mantel and overmantel in the West Parlor were inspired by Plates 50 and 51 in Abraham Swan's handbook,* The British Architect.

whitewash; burnt umber paint was used for the doors and blue-gray paint for other woodwork. The Washingtons' bed chamber decor and mantel are modest, similar to those of the upstairs bed chambers in the older parts of the house (fig. 90). The Study and Master Bed Chamber suite was completed in 1775 (fig. 91). Sheltered as a zone that was insulated from the daily routines of the house and the many visitors to Mount Vernon, it had its own stair. In planning this suite, Washington used two small vestibules, the Small Dining Room, and the downstairs bed chamber as additional barriers between the Passage and the Washingtons' bedroom and study. This innovative plan provided a sphere of privacy for the couple. Martha's grandson, George Washington Parke Custis, who was raised at Mount Vernon, relates that the Study was "a place that none entered without orders."[126] After the Revolution, the arrangement allowed the Washingtons to welcome guests, some of whom were total strangers, into their home in a fashion that might have been impossible given another design. Samuel Powel observes

FIG. 86 *This modest room on the north side of the Passage may date from Lawrence Washington's time. It served as a bed chamber until 1796 when it became the "Little Parlor" and music room. The perimeter ceiling molding with small rosettes was added in 1787.*

FIG. 87 *Washington added paneling to the downstairs bed chamber in 1758. This room may have been the master bed chamber until 1775. Thereafter it was used for guests. The modest mantel in this room may date from Lawrence Washington's time.*

FIG. 88 *The second-floor bed chambers were eloquently austere in design. The cornice molding, chair rail, and mantel are simple profiles that are delicate in scale.*

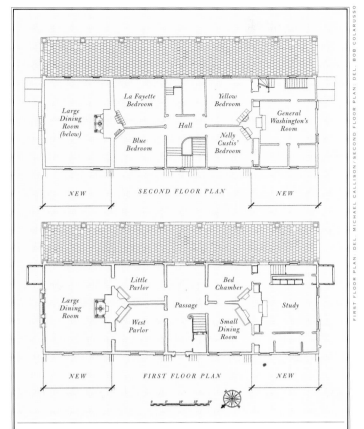

FIRST FLOOR PLAN DEL MICHAEL CALLISON / SECOND FLOOR PLAN DEL BOB COLARUSSO

SECOND FLOOR PLAN

FIRST FLOOR PLAN

FIG. 89 *Washington's extension at the south end of the house shows a new study and storage rooms on the first floor and a master bed chamber and two dressing rooms on the second. With privacy a priority, this wing had its own stair and the study was screened from the rest of the house by two small vestibules, the Small Dining Room, and the downstairs bed chamber.*

that privacy was "absolutely requisite" because of the "perpetual & elegant Hospitality exercised" at Mount Vernon.[127] It seems that even complete strangers felt a form of kinship with Washington and were comfortable arriving at his doorstep without invitation. Washington himself likened the house "to a well resorted tavern," because "scarcely any strangers who are going from north to south, or from south to north do not spend a day or two at it."[128]

In 1775, Washington added an ornate mantel and overmantel in the Small Dining Room (fig. 92). This flamboyant rococo creation was made by Bernard Sears after plate 50 in Abraham Swan's handbook, *The British Architect*. At the same time an elaborate decorative plaster ceiling was executed by a French artisan whose name has not survived (fig. 93).

The design was probably developed from plate 62 in William Pain's *Practical Builder*.[129] Lund Washington reported to Washington in November 1775:

it is I think very Pretty[.] the Stucco man agrees the Cielg [ceiling] is a Handsomeer one than any of Colo[nel] Lewises [Washington's brother-in-law and owner of Kenmore] altho[ugh] not half the worck in it [.][130]

The walls in this room were covered with whitewash.

Washington began work on the Large Dining Room on the north side of the house in 1776 (fig. 94). Used for both grand and intimate entertaining, this room is the most architecturally ambitious part of the mansion, with measurements "32 by 24 feet, and 16 feet in pitch."[131] Washington probably intended it to be in the family of English cube and double cube rooms, although its 2:3:4 proportions suggest

TIM BUCHMAN

FIG. 90 *The Washingtons' new Bed Chamber is modest. Plaster walls are covered with whitewash. Burnt umber paint was used for the doors and blue-gray for other woodwork.*

FIG. 91 *Washington's private study has a built-in wall of book cabinets that was added in 1786, and all the woodwork in the room has an applied wood-grain finish. Initially, the room was painted with whitewash. In order to reduce stains from chimney smoke, it was repainted a stone color.*

an association with ancient Greek musical harmony.[132] In his *Lectures on Architecture*, Robert Morris wrote that "Architecture has its Rules dependant on those [musical] Proportions which are Arithmetical Harmony."[133] The new dining room's fireplace and serliana, or Venetian window, are among the most beautiful such features of any era (fig. 95). The serliana was derived from Batty Langley's handbook *The City and Country Builder's and Workingman's Treasury of Designs* (fig. 96). In the text explaining the plate, Langley states that Venetian windows "are most proper for a grand Staircase, Saloon, Library . . .or for a Dining Room, Etc. whence fine

Views may be seen."[134] Washington used it to take advantage of the dramatic views from his new dining room to the river and to River Farm.

The marble mantel, made in England, was a gift from Samuel Vaughan. The symmetry, the scale of the room, and the complexity of the decoration all suggest an owner / architect who was highly attuned to the taste and refinements of his age. It was in 1776, with the Continental Army retreating from New York, that Washington, in a statement of sublime confidence, instructed Lund Washington to proceed with the construction of this room in a "masterly manner."[135] The room would take nearly twenty years to complete; General Washington was away from Mount Vernon from 1775 to 1783, and several years passed thereafter before he could find craftsmen skilled enough to realize his vision.

The large center medallion in the plaster ceiling of the Large Dining Room is framed by four panels, each with a center design that incorporates farming implements (figs. 97 a, b, c, & d). Their theme relates to the carved frieze of agricultural scenes decorating the English mantel. The delicacy of the plasterwork adds to the room's architectural splendor, in the service of which the chairs were arranged to line the walls, and removable trestle tables were used for dining and entertaining. The room's architectural wallpaper border, printed in France, may have been the first to appear in the United States; it was still a new product in Europe at the time.

As part of the 1774 building campaign, Lawrence Washington's outbuildings in the entrance court were realigned.

FIG. 93 *The elaborate decorative plaster ceiling in the Small Dining Room was executed by a French artisan whose name has not survived.*

FIG. 92 *Washington added an ornate mantel and over-mantel in the Small Dining Room in 1775. Initially, the walls in this room were also covered with whitewash.*

The two curved, arcaded hyphens, which Washington called "covered ways," were added to connect the newly enlarged house to the two new dependencies—a kitchen on the south, and quarters for visitors' servants on the north. In 1777, the piazza facing the Potomac was constructed, although the paving was not set in place until 1786. As we have noted, in 1778 a lantern, which Washington called the "Cupolo," was built on the roof of the house. This added drama to the building's silhouette and also facilitated ventilation by allowing hot air to escape and drawing fresh air into the house by convection (fig. 98).

In 1785, Washington began the Greenhouse: It was completed two years later. He also repainted the Small Dining Room a brilliant verdigris green, replacing the whitewash. In 1786, he added a wall of built-in bookshelves to his study—an unusual feature in an American home at the time. He also applied a wood-grain finish that resembled light English walnut to all the woodwork in the room. Earlier, he had repainted the room a stone color because the smoke from the chimney stained the whitewashed walls. In 1787, he introduced the Prussian blue color in the West Parlor, together with the new ceiling decoration that followed the style made fashionable by Robert Adam (1728–1792), who was the most influential British architect and decorator of the late eighteenth century.

At this time a weather vane in the form of a dove of peace was added to the top of the "Cupulo." In July 1787, Washington wrote to Joseph Rakestraw, a carpenter in Philadelphia:

I should like to have a bird (rather than a weather vane). . . with an olive branch in its Mouth. The bird need not be large (for I do

not expect that it will traverse with the wind and therefore may receive the real shape of a bird, with spread wings), the point of the spire not to appear above the bird.[136]

His instructions to George Augustine Washington for proper installation of the weather vane illustrates his knowledge of construction:

The sooner it is put up the better; but before it is done, the wood part (of what is sent) must receive a Coat of white paint. The Spire . . . must have that of black; the bill of the bird is to be black. and the Olive branch in the mouth of it must be green . . . Great pains (and Mr. Lear understands the Compass) must be taken to

FIG. 94 *The fine proportions, intimate scale, and complexity of decoration make Washington's Large Dining Room one of the glories of American architecture. Begun in 1776, the work that Washington wanted to be executed in a "masterly manner" would take nearly twenty years to finally complete.*

FIG. 95 *The serliana or Venetian window in the Large Dining Room is one of the most splendid exemplars of this feature of any era.*

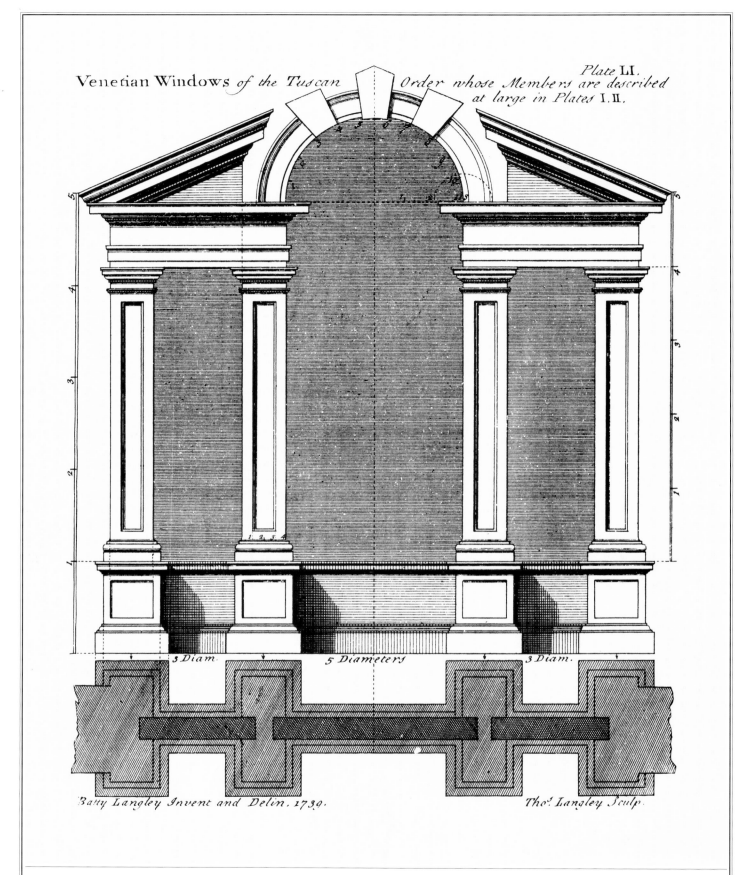

Venetian Windows *of the Tuscan* Order *whose Members are described at large in Plates* I. II.

Plate **LI**.

Batty Langley Invent and Delin. 1739.

Thos. Langley Sculp.

FIG. 96 *The Venetian window on Plate 51 in Batty Langley's handbooks* The City and Country Builder's and Workingman's Treasury of Designs *inspired Washington's design for the Large Dining Room.*

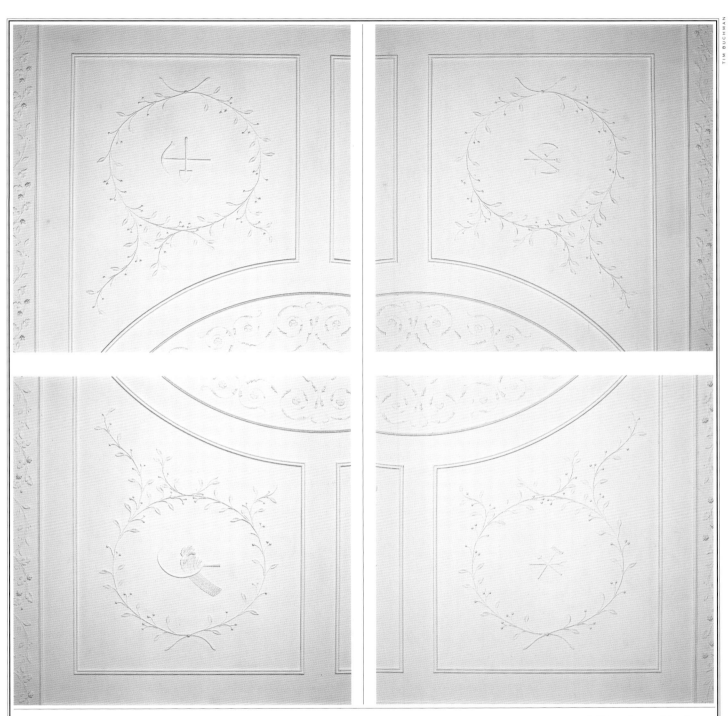

FIGS. 97 A, B, C, & D *The plaster ceiling decoration in the Large Dining Room has a large center medallion framed by four panels, each with a center design that incorporates farming implements. The delicate plasterwork is an important component of the room's architectural splendor.*

FIG. 98 *In 1778 Washington added the "Cupolo" to the roof of the house. It contributed drama to the building's silhouette and facilitated ventilation by convection.*

FIG. 99 *Prior to 1796, the roof shingles of the two dependencies were painted in a bold, deep blue color that contrasted dramatically with the red painted roof of the house. Washington then decided to reduce this element of unexpected drama by also painting the dependency roofs the same red color.*

fix the points truly; . . . What the paper means by cutting of[f] the top of the present Cupulo, is no more than a small octagon at the very top so that the work of the old & the New may fit together; and this, if the sizes of the two do not exactly accord, must be so ordered as to do it. Let particular care be used to putty, or put copper on all the joints to prevent the leaking, & rotting of wood as it will be difficult, & and expensive to repair it hereafter.[137]

In 1792, Washington erected the slave quarters adjacent to the Greenhouse. Four years later, in 1796, he installed Venetian shutters, with horizontal slats to filter the light, on the first—and second-floor windows on the west front. The panel shutters, which were removed from the first floor of the house's west side, were retained on the first floor of the east and south sides.[138] At this time the roof shingles of the two dependencies were painted the same red as the roof of the house; previously they had displayed a bold, deep con- trasting blue color, which added an element of unexpected drama to the entrance court (fig. 99). Finally, in 1797, Washington applied a wood-grain finish to the doors in the Large Dining Room and to the Passage, similar to the woodwork and paneling in the Study. This may have been an attempt to enhance the Passage in relation to the adjacent Small Dining Room and West Parlor. Mark Wenger notes that since the 1760s, passages had overtaken dining rooms in importance and their decorative schemes were more elaborate. The rich embellishment of the Small Dining Room and West Parlor at Mount Vernon reflected the "old scheme of order."[139]

THE ARCHITECTURAL CHARACTER OF THE INTERIOR

If the architectural character of a house and the internal arrangement of its rooms reflect something about the way of life of its builder and residents, what can we learn from Mount Vernon? In the 1780s and 1790s, visitors often remarked on the uniqueness of this estate and, typically, their assessments revealed contradictory experiences. For example, Brissot de Warville described "a country house, of an elegant and majestic simplicity."[140] Another visitor, Roger Griswold, called it "large, convenient and venerable, with a mixture of grandeur about it . . ."[141] Did these two men employ paradoxical terms like "majestic" and "simplicity," or "convenient" and "grandeur," to encapsulate a contradictory quality of Mount Vernon that is difficult to define? Abigail Adams, expecting a grander house, was disappointed, noting that the "house has an ancient appearance and. . . the rooms are low and small." Describing the Washingtons' personal accommodations, Sally Foster Otis thought it significant that there was "nothing to distinguish them from chambers in any other house."[143]

Most visitors commented on Mount Vernon's surprising modesty. Expectations were confounded by the exterior asymmetry of Mount Vernon's four façades, which undermined the large scale of its exterior mass; and by the subversion of the powerful axial vista from the entrance gate to the house by the curved, depressed road in the rivulet basin and gentle meander of the pathways in the wilderness areas. Contradiction is an integral part of the mansion's interior arrangement as well. Anticipating a grand suite of rooms, the visitor experiences relatively small-scaled interiors with corner fireplaces; finely scaled cornice moldings; and non-axial and informal circulation through these rooms. All are qualities typical of more modest houses. One may well be surprised by the warmth of the interior.

In the Passage, which was used for entertaining, Washington chose not to employ pilasters and a full entablature. Its decoration is modest in comparison with the more monumental designs of the center halls in such earlier Virginia mansions as Carter's Grove (1745–1755) or Gunston Hall (1755). The West Parlor, Small Dining Room,

Little Parlor, and downstairs bed chamber are modest in size and have corner fireplaces, vestiges of Lawrence Washington's house. Corner fireplaces are economical to build because two fireplaces, in adjacent rooms, require only one chimney; they are efficient at conserving heat; and they reduce the appearance of formality in a room. Even the most elaborate mantle looks more casual when it is located in a corner rather than symmetrically placed along the middle of the long wall of a room. This is because a corner makes the fireplace, with its associations of warmth and domestic harmony, the focus of the room; it precludes the use of symmetry and axes, which give a room formality. Both the West Parlor, which is paneled, and the Small Dining Room, which has a wainscot, have an elaborate mantel with an overmantel, but their corner fireplaces, modest areas and ceiling heights, and fine proportions mitigate the grandness of the mantels' design and execution.

In this context, it is important to note that the plan of the house is arranged so that no powerful internal axial organization governs the interior architecture or circulation through rooms. This characteristic is particularly evident in the relationship between the Passage and the Large Dining Room, on one side, and the Study on the other. Movement through the West Parlor is at an angle, and the doors to the Passage on one side and the Large Dining Room on the other do not align. This is also true of the circulation through the Little Parlor, the first-floor bed chamber, and the Small Dining Room. Washington's Study is symmetrical, but it is approached from the side through small, modest vestibules. These qualities suggest comfort, privacy, and informality, and are very different from the axial arrangements of the major rooms and the formal circulation and fireplace locations in many of Virginia's great mansions (fig. 100).

As the Large Dining Room was used for entertainment, its placement at one side of the house, with its own entrance, rather than in a location with a strong axial relationship to the Passage, is unusual. Situated in the house's coolest area, it permitted entertainment of a relatively public nature without requiring that guests enter the main part of the house. As with the Study and Master Bed Chamber, the Large Dining Room's location suggests that creating separate zones of privacy within the house was an important planning priority. The Large Dining Room is approached obliquely, by diagonal movements through the West Parlor and Little Parlor, an arrangement that precluded a more dramatic and formal alignment of doors from the Passage to the Large Dining Room. Washington further muted the visitor's perception of the Large Dining Room by separating circulation from the room's main axes. He simply located all the doors leading into the dining room from the rest of the interior, or directly from the outside, in corners.

Washington evidently did not favor either an architecturally unified set of rooms based on a restricted number of decorative elements, or an interior where rooms were characterized by separate design themes, such as those at Gunston Hall. He preferred a more subtle order that provided continuity from one room to another and also preserved a sense of the history of the house and its associations with his revered half-brother Lawrence, and with his father. The sense of continuity he sought was achieved by the careful use of common decorative elements; by subtle suggestions that encourage the eye to notice certain similarities of moldings; and by related organizational principles in the designs for the plaster ceilings. Washington also delighted in commissioning artisans like Bernard Sears and the French artisan, whose identity has been lost, to display their technical virtuosity in the redecoration of the Small Dining Room.

Mount Vernon's interior design made nuanced use of thematic variations in the decoration. For example, the carving in the West Parlor incorporates five or six designs that are based on the lotus, a symbol of fertility and renewal

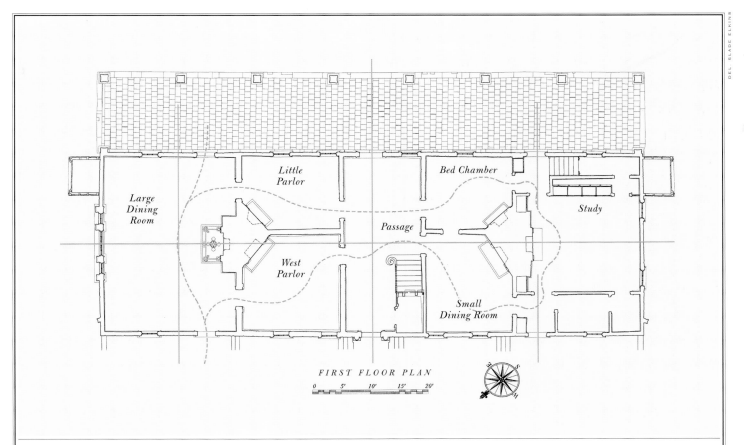

FIG. 100 *Plan of the first floor of Mount Vernon illustrating the relationship between formal axes, in orange, and circulation routes from room to room, in green.*

FIGS. 101 A & B *The lotus form recurs in decorative carving at Mount Vernon. In the West Parlor, the surround to the fire box has a lotus separated by shells. This theme is repeated twice in the mantel's cornice. It is also used in the overmantel and door architrave.*

(figs. 101 a & b). The marble surround to the fire box has a lotus separated by shells, and on a much smaller scale, the lotus appears in the cornices of the mantel and overmantel. A lotus alternating with an egg shape appears at the door architrave and the frame of the overmantel; it turns up again, in a variety of sizes, and alternates with rosettes in other parts of the overmantel. Rosettes are also used in the four corners of the overmantel, in the face of the scrolls of the pediment, at the vortices of the whorls on either side of the overmantel, and in the door head cornice between modillions (figs. 102 a & b).

Decorative themes also suggest continuity from exterior to interior, and from one room to another. In the Passage the most striking decorative feature is the cornice, which, except for the different form of cyma modillion, has the same moldings as the exterior cornice of the house, arcades, and dependencies. A cyma reversa is used inside and a cyma recta outside (refer to figs. 42 & 43). Continuity from room to room begins with the cornice over the door from the Passage to the piazza, which incorporates a dentil course based on a meander. This form is also found in the West Parlor, on the chair rail, and in the Large Dining Room, in the cornice of the *serliana* and four door heads (figs. 103 a, b, &c). A pulvinated (convex) frieze is used in the mantel of the downstairs bed chamber, the Little Parlor, and, in a slightly modified form, in the Nelly Custis bed chamber upstairs. Croisettes, or little ears, are part of the four corners of the overmantel in the downstairs bed chamber and the Small Dining Room. The overmantel in the West Parlor has two croisettes at the top. All three mantels have dentil courses.

The ceiling medallions in the West Parlor, the Small Dining Room, and the Large Dining Room share the graceful geometry of a circular pattern of lines radiating outward from a small center medallion to a perimeter of connecting concave and convex arcs of circles. In the Little Parlor a perimeter molding is set parallel to the walls; it is broken in the middle of each wall by a small rosette. A similar edge molding with rosettes appears in the West Parlor. It is prob-

FIGS. 102 A & B *Rosettes are another decorative motif. They are used in the corners of the overmantel and in the door-head cornice between modillions.*

able that this feature was added in the Little Parlor in 1787, when the West Parlor ceiling was created. The same small rosette is used in the decoration of the coved ceiling in the Large Dining Room (figs. 104 a, b, & c).

Washington used pediments to distinguish between the entrances to major and secondary rooms. The primary doors—from the west garden court and the piazza into the house and from the West Parlor to the Large Dining Room—all have pediments, while the secondary doors on each of the sidewalls of the Passage have split pediments.[144] Doors with a horizontal cornice represent a third tier in the hierarchy and occur in the Large Dining Room and above the door from the Passage to the piazza.

THE MEANING OF WASHINGTON'S MOUNT VERNON

T. S. Eliot has asserted that "it is a function of all art to give us some perception of an order in life, by imposing an order upon it."[145] At Mount Vernon, Washington created a very subtle idea of order. His perceptions developed from a carefully composed balance between symmetry and asymmetry; between farms and gardens; between the man-made and the natural; between geometric clarity and picturesque variety; between stillness and motion; between art and life. It is a balance that is profoundly humanistic, arresting but never intrusive or overwhelming. The eloquent, classical symmetry projected by the exterior façade of Gunston Hall or Mount Airy may not have satisfied Washington. Or perhaps it could have been attained only by demolishing his house and starting again, a quest that engaged neither his pragmatic nature nor his sense of continuity and tradition. In any case, the remarkable qualities of his mind were drawn to a more subtle and elusive definition of architectural order and to a richer, more interactive relationship between architecture and its landscape setting.

Today, because we approach the house from different roads and directions, the drama of the two-thirds-of-a-mile-long vista across the rolling landscape through the woods and the descent into the valley is not available to most visitors, and the sense of the house set on an "eminence" has been lost. The Mount Vernon we see today is a shadow of the 8,000-acre plantation Washington owned. Only 500 acres are still intact, five percent of its size in the 1790s, and the visitor has access to only 40 or 50 acres. The density of the trees and shrubs has been lost as well, and the farms, barns, and extensive forest tracts we see on Washington's 1793 plan of the estate have been redeveloped as suburban housing. As a result, the most innovative aspect of Washington's genius as a designer—his vision of a unified composition of house, landscape, barns and other farm buildings, woods, and cultivated lands framed by hedgerows, fences, and ditches—is now barely discernible or completely gone.

Before Washington redesigned his rectangular and axial garden in 1774, Mount Vernon was an example of a seventeenth-century formal garden with a center-passage type of house. Sadly, we know little about Washington's familiarity with English or American picturesque gardens, or with the historical association between picturesque garden planning and the ideals of liberty, mixed government, republicanism, and pastoralism in this country.[146] We do not even know whether he visited any of the well-known picturesque gardens of Virginia and Pennsylvania. His library contained one book on garden design, Batty Langley's *New Principles of Gardening*, of 1729, which he acquired in 1759. Because his diary, letters, and surviving library contain little on architecture or garden design, it is difficult to find direct precedents for his most accomplished innovations: the piazza; the brilliant integration of the farms, landscape, and garden; and the dynamic relationship between the architecture of house and surrounding grounds. This point may be strikingly demonstrated by comparing Vaughan's plan of the house and grounds, which depicts a pleasure seat in the English manner, with Washington's own 1793 plan, showing river, farms, barns and service buildings, roads, ferry dock, and house. Washington's plan is a functional document for a man who is concerned with every detail of his estate.

Washington wrote little about garden design, yet, as Peter Martin notes, the very precise instructions that he gave his managers for planting trees, shrubs, and flowers "leave no doubt that he considered carefully and deeply the styles and arrangements he desired."[147] That we have no records of his design and planting plans, or of his thoughts on gardening, in no way suggests that they never existed; he may have laid out the gardens from ideas he formulated in his head so clearly that there was no need to explore them in letters, journal entries, or alternative plan studies. The planting arrangements may have been developed empirically, from day to day as he watched his gardens grow and develop.

Such a process is described in his diary entry for January 12, 1785. He recorded how he searched for "the sort of

FIGS. 103 A, B, & C *A carved meander pattern suggests visual continuity from room to room. It occurs in the cornice over the door from the Passage to the piazza, on the chair rail in the West Parlor, in the cornice of the serliana, and in the four door heads in the Large Dining Room.*

Trees I shall want for my walks, groves, & Wildernesses" at the bowling green. On January 19, he noted being "Employed until dinner in laying out my Serpentine road & Shrubberies adjoining."[148] The activity was repeated on March 18, 1785:

I went to my Dogue run Plantation to make choice of the size, & to direct taking up of Pine trees, for my two wildernesses. Brought 3 waggon load of them home, and planted every other hole round the Walks in them. . . Also planted 20 Pine trees in the lines of Trees by the sides of the Serpentine roads to the House."[149]

On March 22, he wrote:

Mrs. Grayson sent me 8 Yew & 4 Aspan trees & Colo. Mason some Cherry Grafts. Planted the intermediate holes round the Walk in the Wilderness on the right and filled the spaces between with young Pines.

On March 23 and 24, he "Finished Planting the Pine trees in the wilderness on the left and planted 4 of the live Oak Trees in the Shrubberies. . ." and "Finding the Trees round the Walks in my wildernesses rather too thin I doubled them by putting (other Pine) trees between each."[150]

In a letter to Edward Newenham of April 20, 1787, Washington wrote of the cultivation of "fruit, forest, trees, and Shrubs" as

certainly among the most rational avocations of life; for what can be more pleasing, than to see the work of ones own hands, fostered by care and attention, rising to maturity in a beautiful display of those advantages and ornaments which by the Combination of Nature and taste of the projector in the disposal of them is always regaling to the eye at the sametime in their seasons they are grateful to the palate.[151]

Here is how George Washington Parke Custis, Martha Washington's grandson, who grew up at Mount Vernon, characterized his step-grandfather's work: Washington was his own architect and builder, laying off everything himself. The buildings, gardens, and grounds all rose to ornament and usefulness under his fostering hand."[152] Custis's description was echoed by Robert Hunter, Jr., who visited Mount Vernon in 1785, and wrote that Washington

often works with his men himself; strips off his coat and labors like a common man . . . The General has a great turn for mechanics. It's astonishing with what niceness he directs everything in the building way, condescending even to measure the things himself, that all may be perfectly uniform.[153]

Washington's friend Samuel Powel records a similar thought in his journal, describing Mount Vernon as "altogether the most charming Seat I have seen in America. It is kept with

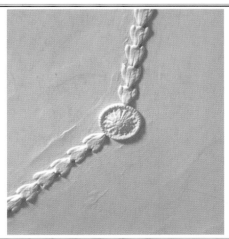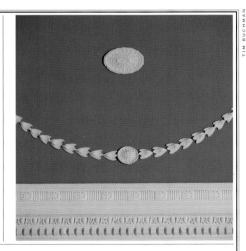

FIGS. 104 A, B, & C *A small rosette is used in the perimeter molding of the Little Parlor ceiling, in the edge molding of the West Parlor, and in the decoration of the coved ceiling in the Large Dining Room. Repeated use of the same form in three rooms provides an element of continuity to enhance the visitor's experience of the house.*

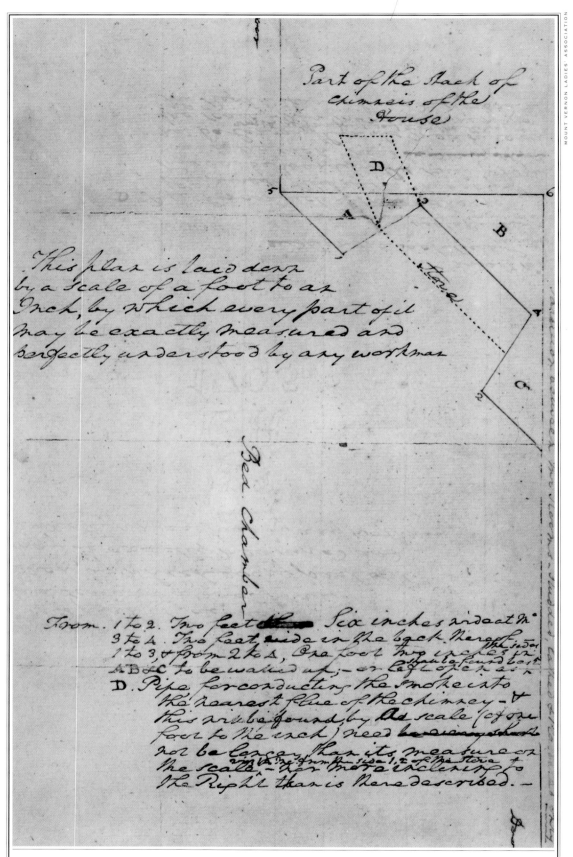

FIG. 105 *This page of a letter from Washington contains very detailed notes for the building of a chimney stack. The precise drawings and the intricate instructions illustrate a mind that understood the construction process.*

great Neatness & the good Order of its Master Mind appears extended to every Thing around it."[154]

Perhaps the best evidence we have of the precision of Washington's creative vision is his comment to Samuel Vaughan about the latter's plan of Mount Vernon, which

describes with accuracy the houses, walks, and shrubberies etc. except in the front of the Lawn, west of the Ct. yard. There the plan differs from the original; in the former you have closed the prospect with trees along the walk to the gate; whereas in the latter the trees terminate with two mounds of earth on each side of which grow Weeping Willows leaving an open and full view of the distant woods. The mounds are at sixty yards apart.[155]

Indeed, Vaughan had closed off the view to the west, beyond the Bowling Green, through the swathe cut through the woods to the entrance gates and approach road from the Alexandria-Colchester Road. For Washington it was important to correct this fundamental error.[156]

So tight is the weave between the architecture and the landscape that it is not possible to determine whether the house was the genesis of the landscape design around which the surrounding gardens and farms were organized, or whether the landscape was an independent creation that enhanced the architecture. The integration of the house and surrounding landscape and the importance of the gardens and "vistos" to river, house, and farms also served to divert attention away from the singularity of the house. Its west façade both received and generated the axis that extended to the entrance gates and was framed by large trees of the two "wildernesses" on either side of the Bowling Green. Its east façade was framed by two clumps of flowering trees on either side, and the piazza extended out, its berm gently binding the architecture to the surrounding lawn. The house was tied to the river by the concave depression Washington sculpted into the hillside in front of the piazza. Both Count Niemcewicz and Henry Latrobe testified to the way in which the visitor's attention was lured away from the comforting framework of the piazza to the Potomac and the surrounding

landscape and from the west façade by the forest-like groves of trees, shrubs, and flowers on either side of the Bowling Green. Within this composition the house was a subtle fulcrum that animated the entire scene. It is in the deft integration of house and landscape that the full authority of Washington's design ability is apparent, and the very subtlety of his hand makes it difficult to isolate the architecture of the house and to appreciate its unique qualities.

Although he was a surprisingly inventive and sophisticated designer, Washington was self-taught. We know very little about the process of his education; we have observed that his library had very few books on design and his diary and correspondence contain only tantalizingly spare comments on architecture.[157] Neither do we know much about his interaction with the craftsmen who realized the house's moldings, carvings, and plaster decorations, or the extent to which he may have relied on friends like George Mason and the Fairfax family for guidance. Because almost none of the correspondence between husband and wife survives, we cannot assess the role Martha Washington may have played in the design or the furnishing of Mount Vernon. Our basic resource is the evidence of the work itself, and even here archaeological data is often limited, for some of the house's original fabric was removed to strengthen the floor structure. A few of Washington's architectural drawings survive (fig. 105). From these and his written instructions it is clear that he understood construction and that he had a more comprehensive knowledge of architecture than may be apparent from his correspondence or library. This lack of data may be one reason why so little has been written about Mount Vernon as architecture and about Washington as an architect.[158]

In his important study of the complex process by which churches were designed in colonial Virginia, Dell Upton observed:

If we cannot conceive of traditional craftsmen reeducated by cultivated gentlemen, we cannot locate design entirely in the builder to the exclusion of his client either. Who designed the churches?

They all did. The fracture of high style and vernacular, of design and execution, along clear class or craft lines is impossible.[159]

Likewise, in the eighteenth century a house's design was based on close collaboration by owner and artisans. The nature of such collaborations and the allocation of responsibility for various tasks depended on the personalities and knowledge of the owner and builder.[160] The type of detailed architectural drawings and studies for Monticello that Jefferson produced are a rarity in eighteenth-century America. Houses were typically built from simple sketches, almost diagrams, such as Washington's elevation study for Mount Vernon's west façade. Typically, in a vernacular tradition, no plans were necessary because new houses were simply variations of previous ones. Colonial builders worked in a similar way, using pattern books or drawings of other houses for floor plans and elevations.[161] Given the close personal attention that Washington lavished on every detail relating to life at Mount Vernon and to the planning of its farms and buildings, it is likely that he played a pivotal role in the design of the house and its interiors. At the same time, he was a good listener and, no doubt, approached design matters with the same open-minded pragmatism that is evident in his other fields of endeavor.

We can still speculate, however, about some of the sources of his inspiration. While seventeenth-century colonial houses developed out of sixteenth-century, or older, English models, many eighteenth-century property owners and builders of Virginia were informed by the newer English designs presented in architectural handbooks. Upton notes that the eighteenth-century vernacular house is actually closer in spirit to the architectural ideals of a seventeenth-century house. This is because both the exterior cornice and the other decorative moldings are less important in their own right than as secondary elements designed to reinforce a house's cubic mass. Thus, the Mansion House suggests seventeenth-century aesthetic models because its mass is a singular, primary form. Its plan is typical of vernacular buildings because all four of its first-floor rooms, on either side of the Passage in the house Washington acquired from his brother Lawrence, have dissimilar dimensions. The form of houses illustrated in many eighteenth-century architectural treatises is very different. Like Mount Airy or Brandon (ca. 1765), in Prince George's County, Virginia, they are usually composed as an assemblage of discrete parts that are grouped together to form a whole (fig. 106 and refer to fig. 24).

As an architect Washington was more ambitious than a vernacular builder, but he employed the vernacular method of pragmatic adaptation to his design decisions. This is evident in his strategy for expanding the house and planning for privacy in his study and the master bedroom. In most eighteenth-century houses, expansion was usually accomplished by adding rooms to the back of the house. Again, his approach was unconventional. He expanded to the side. The great houses of the seventeenth and eighteenth centuries had to fulfill both public and residential functions. The hall, or parlor, and the dining room were used for public entertainment; so was the passage. Bed chambers were adjacent to public rooms, and privacy—a much less important matter in the seventeenth and eighteenth centuries than it is today—was obtained by closing a door. After construction of the new study and bed chamber suite at the south side of Mount Vernon, the Small Dining Room and downstairs bed chamber served as an additional barrier between the Passage and the Washingtons' suite. There may not be an earlier house with a similar cubic mass and two layers of rooms on either side of the central passage. In planning this lateral expansion, Washington may have been influenced by Mount Airy, where one dependency was used for auxiliary bedrooms. An alternative source may have been houses like Battersea, which had two rooms on either side of a taller center mass, and were based a very different aesthetic model such as plate 3 in Robert Morris's handbook, *Select Architecture* (fig. 107).[162]

FIG. 106 *Brandon (1765) in Prince George County, Virginia, is formed of an assemblage of discrete parts that are grouped together to create a whole. Houses like this are illustrated in many eighteenth-century architectural treatises.*

The historian Rhys Isaac writes that the plan of the seventeenth-and early eighteenth-century house provided

little segregation of persons and particular rooms were not set aside for such activities as cooking, eating, and bedding down. The communal area, usually called 'the hall,' lay immediately open to anyone who crossed the threshold.

The basic house was restructured by the introduction of "a 'passage' between the outside door and the now specialized rooms for sleeping, taking meals, and sitting at ease."[163] Washington's unusual plan of a sequestered master suite on the south side, and the equally isolated large dining room on the north side, allowed his family to maintain their privacy while welcoming strangers into their home.

One of the few statements Washington made about architecture occurs in a letter of December 30, 1798, to his friend Dr. Thornton. He wrote:

Rules of Architecture are calculated, I presume, to give Symmetry, and just proportion to all the Orders, and parts of (the) building in order to please the eye. Small departures from strict rules are discoverable only by the skillful Architects, or by the eye of criticism; while ninety nine of a hundred, deficient of their knowledge, might be pleased with things not quite orthodox.[164]

Washington does not define by example or explanation what "small departures" from the rules denotes, or why people might derive pleasure from "not quite orthodox" solutions. We have noted that asymmetry is an important feature of Mount Vernon, but symmetry is an equally significant component, and he carefully cultivated a relaxed formality by balancing and juxtaposing symmetry and asymmetry. While asymmetry is a feature of all four façades of the house,

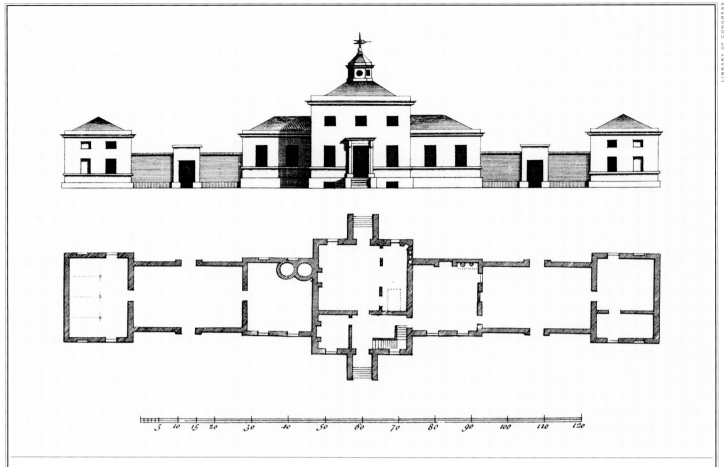

FIG. 107 *Plate 3 from* Select Architecture *by Robert Morris (London, 1755) may have been a design source for houses like this one in Brandon, Virginia.*

Washington would not consider even "small departures from *strict* rules" in, say, the north or south elevations of the Large Dining Room, the serliana, or the east façade's colonnade. And his selection of Thornton's design for the New Capitol building, which was both symmetrical and monumental, suggests that Washington appreciated the role of symmetry, "grandeur and beauty" in civic architecture, and that, despite his disclaimers to the contrary, he was a shrewd judge of architecture.[165]

Sometimes Washington drew on designs illustrated in the new handbooks as a source for ideas, but he typically consulted them for only general guidance. Thus, he used a coved cornice as part of the entablature of the base of the exterior pediment without feeling impelled to extend it into the house cornice on either side of it. While the integration of house cornice and pediment would seem to be an obvious

design choice, he apparently wanted to avoid defining the top of the house by a coved cornice because its exaggerated scale would distract the viewer's attention from the house's compact, unified mass. Here and elsewhere, his method of pragmatic adaption allowed the inconsistency to be incorporated into the design.

Washington was remarkably adept at making the most of the opportunities that were available to him. Judge Thomas Jones, a loyalist, observed that "no other person could have kept such a heterogeneous army together as he did."[166] As a second son with no expectation of a significant inheritance, Washington knew that he would have to make his own way in the world. He learned to survey and practiced it with great success. He constantly experimented with crop rotations and different ways to restore the depleted soil on his estate— until he became one of the best farmers in the new nation.

He strove to overcome obstacles and to succeed in the Virginia militia. And he quickly learned from setbacks and developed battle tactics appropriate for the Continental Army. At Mount Vernon, he added to the existing house rather than demolishing it and beginning anew. He made the most of the existing topography, and rather than separating the two, incorporated the farms into the landscape.

Mount Vernon's aura of domesticity and comfort is as gratifying to the visitor today as it was in Washington's own time. In his letter of February 5, 1785, to Samuel Vaughan, thanking him for the gift of the marble mantel for the Large Dining Room, Washington wrote that the "Chimney piece is . . . too elegant & costly for my room & Republican stile of living."[167] This is a rare example of an architect in the new nation relating design to contemporary politics. Brissot de Warville exemplified the feelings of other contemporary visitors by observing that "Everything has an air of simplicity in his house."[168] In this context it is appropriate to recall that Washington lit his own fire every morning. His personal modesty and his concern for modesty in the expression of the way in which he lived were paramount.

When he visited Mount Vernon in the year before Washington's death, Count Niemcewicz wrote:

In a word the garden, the plantations, the house, the whole upkeep, proves that a man born with natural taste can divine the beautiful without ever having seen the model. The Gl. has never left America. After seeing his house and his gardens one would say that he had seen the most beautiful examples in England of this style."[169]

Although Niemcewicz compared Mount Vernon to English models, Washington was not emulating a Georgian mansion or its grounds. On the contrary, the enlarged house, gardens, and reorganized farms at Mount Vernon were a statement of Washington's economic, political, and cultural independence and his new "Republican stile of living." The forms of this architecture, and the landscape he created around it, embodied the ideals he articulated in his 1783 "Farewell to the Army":

The foundation of our empire was not laid in the gloomy age of ignorance and superstition, but at an epoch when the rights of mankind were better understood and better defined than at any former period; . . . the free cultivation of letters, the unbounded extension of commerce, the progressive refinement of manners, the growing liberality of sentiment, and above all, the pure and benign light of revelation, have had a meliorating influence on mankind and increased the blessings of society. At this auspicious period, the United States came into existence as a nation.[170]

These circumstances, he noted, created, for Americans, "a fairer opportunity for political happiness than any other nation has been favored with . . ." Such thoughts and ideals were incorporated in the architecture of the farm house at Mount Vernon, with its asymmetries, informal circulation, corner fireplaces, modest scale, and innovative piazza and open arcades; into the new garden with its tension between formal axes and informal circulation routes; and into the farms which, planned as a vast garden of field, meadows, and forest, became a paradigm for this new Eden.

The noted author and historian Wendell Garrett has observed that Washington was especially sensitive to his political role as the living symbol of the Revolutionary cause and notes that

Mount Vernon was vastly more than a country gentleman's residence. With no permanent national capital and no president's house, Mount Vernon was one of the most prominent buildings in America and the scene of impressive entertaining for renowned visitors.[171]

The rare and felicitous balance of the house's public and private realms is of particular importance in a nation in which public buildings all have a domestic suffix: court*house*, congress *house* (the first name for the U.S. Capitol), state*house*, school*house*, and town*house* (city hall in the seventeenth century).[172] Between the Declaration of Independence and the completion of the White House in 1800, Mount Vernon, and the unfailing hospitality of its owner, may have served as an inspiration for a new American architecture that proposes a revolutionary definition of the public realm. In the new republic, citizens form the government. Elected representatives and appointed officials are temporary occupants of office and their responsibility is to serve the citizenry. This new order was most eloquently represented in the architecture of the new U.S. Capitol, where the primary symbolic space was the rotunda under the dome, designated by Latrobe and President Thomas Jefferson as the "Hall of the People."[173] The chambers for senate and representatives were located to the sides, on the building's cross-axis.

In this way, architecture serves as an instrument for embodying a system around which a family or institution may organize its daily routines and present itself to the world. Thus, great architecture may serve as a force that binds a family, state, or nation together by providing continuity, by reminding people of who they are and where they came from, and by encouraging rational conversation about the nature and purpose of the institution it houses. Such systems of architectural organization are not inevitable. They are created. Washington's accomplishments as general, President, agronomist, civic leader, explorer, city planner, and regionalist are extraordinary. What is common to his achievements in each endeavor is a passion for creating the appropriate form, whether to find the right "form" for the new Continental army; for his farms and fields; for the most productive plan of crop rotation; for a new constitution to create an enduring republican government; for the model new capital city and public architecture that would embody the ideals of the Constitution; or for the architecture of his own house and its surrounding landscape and farms, which he created as both a public and private place, as a pleasure garden and a working farm.

Authentically creating enduring forms, whether for policy or architecture, requires the ability to analyze complex questions, to define and balance variables, and to synthesize this information in comprehensive and innovative solutions to contemporary problems. Great leaders are citizens who understand the necessity of creating form, or of searching for the right form, by which to solve their nation's problems. At its best, this quality becomes realized in a vision of a noble future for the nation, based on justice for all. It is also realized in the design of buildings in the landscape. Great American Presidents, men like Washington, Jefferson, Madison, Lincoln, Theodore Roosevelt, and Franklin Delano Roosevelt, all understood the purpose of form. And all were concerned about architecture. Jefferson was one of the most profound architects of the early nineteenth century. Lincoln, although not a designer of buildings, understood the value of architectural symbolism: Despite an order to cease all work because of the Civil War, the building contractor Janes, Fowler, Kirtland and Company continued to construct the new dome of the Capitol in Washington. Lincoln turned the contractor's unusual action into a symbol of national resolve and, as the new dome burgeoned above the horizon of Washington, D. C., transformed it into a symbol of the enduring Union.[174] Franklin Delano Roosevelt created the therapeutic center at Warm Springs, Georgia, for children stricken with polio.[175] He also designed the most moving memorial to a twentieth-century president, the simple marble block inscribed "In memory of Franklin Delano Roosevelt 1882–1945," and he placed it in front of the National Archive Building he admired.

At Mount Vernon, George Washington's vision embodied an Arcadian ideal of human beings living and working together. In the unity of farms, gardens, and landscape it integrated the prerogatives of work and pleasure; in the design and planning of the farm house it stabilized the tensions of family life and public office; and in the dynamic interdependence of architectural form and the surrounding environment it presented a prospect of human aspiration in harmonious alignment with nature (fig. 108). Washington remains the nation's exemplary form giver. This is true not only because he was the first President, but because his comprehensive dream of the future resounds with us still.

FIG. 108 *The simple and eloquent design of Mount Vernon's front door serves to focus the visitor's attention on the center of the house. The lack of ostentatious decoration and the modest scale tell us about Washington's strength of character and humane ideals.*

PART TWO

"SHOULD HIS SERVICES BE LOST, I KNOW NOT HOW TO REPLACE THEM"

THE COLLABORATION OF

GEORGE WASHINGTON AND PETER

CHARLES L'ENFANT ON THE PLAN

OF WASHINGTON, D.C.

URING THE LATE EIGHTEENTH AND EARLY NINETEENTH CENTURIES THE CLASSICAL ARCHITECTURAL HERITAGE OF EUROPE WAS TRANSFORMED TO SERVE THE NEW AND VERY DIFFERENT NEEDS OF THE YOUNG UNITED STATES. THE CITIZENS AND FOUNDERS of the new nation were acutely aware that their revolution had established only the second democracy in history. Whether it was in writing the Constitution, creating a citizen's army, developing battle strategy and tactics for this army during the revolution, designing the nation's Great Seal, or planning its public buildings, Americans took great pains to recognize the special prerogatives of their unique form of republican government and especially the revolutionary principle of government by the people. Nowhere was this mandate executed as boldly and ambitiously as in the city plan for Washington, D.C., designed in 1791 by Peter Charles L'Enfant by commission from President George Washington (fig.1).

The collaboration of the American President and the young French-born engineer and city planner could have evolved only in a world in which architecture and city planning were regarded as vehicles to express political ideals as well as formal beauty. This point of view was summarized by Sir Christopher Wren, writing in England a century before the American Revolution: "Architecture has its political Use; public building being the Ornament of a Country; it establishes a Nation, draws People and Commerce; makes the People love their native Country, which Passion is the Original of all great Actions in a Commonwealth."[1] Because such a perspective assumes the existence of a nation, it could be properly applied to America only after the Revolution. And even Wren did not imagine forging a new country from scratch. Yet architecture turned out to be a potent tool with which the new republic could create and solidify its identity. L'Enfant would affirm this view in the explanatory text he wrote directly on his drawing of the final plan of the federal city, which he submitted to President Washington in August 1791: "This mode of taking possession of and improving the whole district at first must leave to posterity a grand idea of the patriotic interest which prompted it."[2]

Although the debate relating to the decision to build a new capital is well documented, only a hazy outline of the genesis of the plan may be gleaned from a few letters, reports, and sketches. It is difficult to trace the unusual collaboration between these two men and the process by which a city plan came to embody the ideals of democracy articulated by the young nation's founders. However, insights can be derived from restudying the plan itself; relating its creation to other fields of artistic endeavor; and developing a fuller understanding of its relationship to contemporary towns and cities. Such a strategy may help foster a better

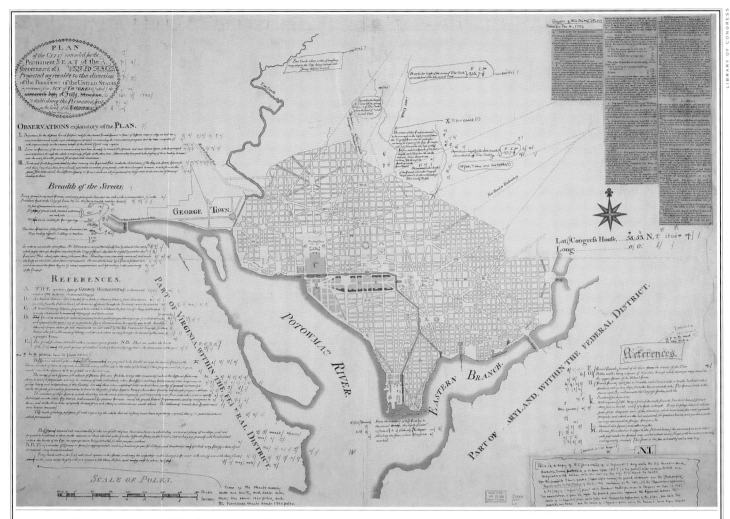

FIG. 1 *One of the most original examples of how new democratic ideals became incorporated in architecture is the city plan for Washington, D.C., designed in 1791 by Peter Charles L'Enfant by commission from President George Washington. The "Congress House" and the "President's House" are two major focal points of the plan. The park-like Mall represents the Constitution. The many small foci where major streets intersect are possible locations for important public buildings. Fifteen small parks are dedicated to the states that first accepted the Constitution.*

understanding of the symbolism in L'Enfant's plan and of the full scope of Washington's vision of the new city. Inevitably some elements of conjecture will remain. Scrutinized in the light of our growing knowledge of the period, they may serve to elucidate this masterpiece of the art of city planning.

The plan of the new federal city was created between March 1791, when L'Enfant arrived in Georgetown, and August of the same year, when Washington approved the design. From the outset of their collaboration the young military engineer and the new President established a close rapport. Although they met on only four or five occasions for

a few hours each time, they quickly came to an understanding on how best to proceed; the site was surveyed and design work completed in the astonishingly short time of five months. Washington concurred with almost every one of L'Enfant's design decisions and proposed only minor adjustments to the plan. The next six months were devoted to completing the survey work, refining details of the plan, and preparing to have it engraved for general distribution.

At the end of March 1792, L'Enfant's contract was abruptly terminated. The calamity arose from his failure to understand the mechanism of decision making in the new nation and the need to tactfully accommodate vested interests—or at least to give the appearance of doing so. L'Enfant's behavior was often perceived as impetuous and his detractors used this to precipitate a series of crises that eroded confidence in his ability to implement his plan. This eventually developed into outright opposition from some. Even many of Washington's closest associates, including Secretary of State Thomas Jefferson, opposed L'Enfant's further involvement, and their antagonism eventually succeeded in toppling Washington's support of him. To the end of his days L'Enfant, who never ceased to believe that he had implemented Washington's wishes, failed to grasp the reasons for his failure. Years later, he even petitioned the man who masterminded his ouster, now President Jefferson, for assistance in obtaining some remuneration for his services.

Among the great political thinkers who forged the nation and drafted its most important documents—the Declaration of Independence, the Constitution, and the Bill of Rights—were some who were deeply interested in architecture. The list is impressive, beginning with Washington himself. As the first part of this book describes, Washington designed the gardens and the extensive enlargements of his home, Mount Vernon. It was he who conceived the great two-story piazza and the Adamesque ornament there, both elements leaving their mark on American architecture to this day. And it was his vision of a great domed structure, the first one in the United States, that inspired the competition for the new Capitol building and the selection of Dr. William Thornton's winning design.[3]

FIG. 2 *Thomas Jefferson designed the new Virginia State Capitol in Richmond between 1785 and 1788, while he was in Paris. Benjamin Henry Latrobe's watercolor shows the eloquent and simple cubical form, noble scale, and lofty columns that "gave the building a novel dignity expressive of the majesty of the sovereign state." Historian Fiske Kimball noted that the "portico was a frontispiece to all Virginia."*

FIG. 3 *Jefferson's masterpiece, the* Academical Village *at the University of Virginia, may have been inspired by L'Enfant's great plan for the federal city. Both have a major building at one end of an open park that is lined on either side by smaller, freestanding buildings.*

Building ranked as a key vocation of Thomas Jefferson as well. In addition to his homes, Monticello and Poplar Forest, he designed the Virginia State Capitol at Richmond, the first monument of the classic revival in the United States, which preceded the Madeleine in Paris, the first European temple building, by more than twenty years. The Virginia Capitol is a landmark in architectural history. As described by Fiske Kimball, its "vast portico was united with the mass by an unbroken cornice. The simple and crystalline cubical form, the colossal scale of the columns, gave the building a novel dignity expressive of the majesty of the sovereign state. The portico was a frontispiece to all Virginia"[4] (fig. 2). With Benjamin Henry Latrobe, the architect of the national Capitol from 1803 to 1817, Jefferson created the first and most eloquent version of this important building after Thornton's design. By 1823 he completed the design of his masterpiece, the "academical village" at the University of Virginia. Although he did not help L'Enfant to retain his commission and oversee the construction of the new Capitol, Jefferson nonetheless based this complex on L'Enfant's great plan. Both have a major building at one end of an open park that is lined on either side with free-standing buildings (fig. 3).

James Madison evinced no less affinity for architecture. In 1797 and 1809 he altered and expanded Montpelier, his house in Virginia, adding a great white portico and wings. And throughout his presidency he supported Latrobe's work at the Capitol and the White House, patronage that became particularly important after the buildings were destroyed by the British in 1814. The next president, James Monroe, built Oak Hill (1822–23) in Virginia and continued to support Latrobe, as well as his successor, as Architect of the Capitol, Charles Bulfinch. The unusually high profile of Bulfinch's design for the dome of the first capitol was based on a suggestion made by Monroe.[5] Founding Father Alexander Hamilton commissioned John McComb, Jr., the architect of the New York City Hall, to design his own house, The Grange, in northern Manhattan, overlooking the Hudson River. As Secretary of the Treasury, Hamilton had invited L'Enfant to design new coins and later would help him to obtain the commission to plan the city of Paterson, New Jersey.[6] George Mason, an author of the Virginia Bill of Rights, was not involved in public architecture but became the first patron of William Buckland, who did much work on Mason's Gunston Hall (1755).

<hr />

WASHINGTON'S IDEAS FOR THE NEW CAPITAL CITY

In spite of the enormous burden of being the nation's first president, Washington lavished an extraordinary amount of time on planning the new capital. He typically relied on members of his cabinet and staff in managing affairs of state, yet, as one biographer notes, "he scarcely could have found the future seat of government more time-consuming"[7] had it been his only concern.

As late as 1790, Washington did not have a clear vision of what he wanted the new city to look like. Whereas Jefferson collected plans of European cities and studied them as potential models, Washington, though he traveled extensively in the United States, had no interest in visiting Europe, much less in seeing the design of its cities on paper. Like most Americans at the time, he thought the new republic had little of use to learn from European monarchies. There, governments served the King, who ruled by divine right. This authoritarian structure was reflected in most

European architecture and city planning as exemplified by Louis XIV's vast palace and garden at Versailles and by the plan of Carlshrue. Located at a powerful cross-axis, the palace at Versailles completely dominated the adjacent town, parks, and forests, embodying John Milton's words from *Paradise Lost*, "Thrones and imperial power, off-spring of heav'n." The palace at Carlshrue was the focal point of thirty-two avenues that radiated out into the surrounding region. (figs. 4 a & b).

Like Wren, who was also writing about architecture at a time of radical political change—the aftermath of England's Glorious Revolution of 1688—Washington believed that part of the architect's responsibility was to incorporate political symbolism into the design of public buildings. New architecture and city plans, he proposed, should respond to the needs of democratic forms of government so that citizens could feel that it was they who constituted the government and that elected officials and civil servants were there to serve them. For Washington, the planning and design of a new capital city was of paramount importance, for it would set an example for the states and cities to follow. While he clearly believed that Europe had little it could teach the new nation about such matters, he was well aware that democracy and republicanism were classical ideals and knew that he was working within a larger tradition of classical architecture and city planning.

Washington left no clear statement of his goals for the new capital. While this suggests that he lacked a preconceived image of the city's final form, we know he wished to see certain ideas incorporated into its plan and architecture. As a professional surveyor, he knew how important it was to have a sound plan, and he had a strong intuitive conviction that the plan needed to embody, in its structure and symbolism, the new relationship between the nation's citizens and their government. The President was also concerned about the political process by which the new city was to be created. At no point in planning the capital did Washington ask

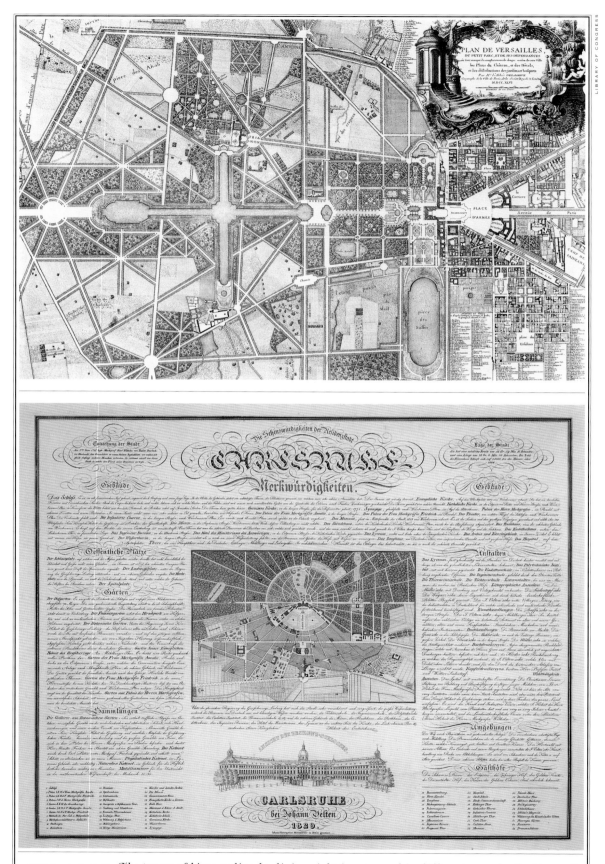

FIGS. 4 A & B *The power of kings ruling by divine right is expressed in different ways by the plans of Versailles (a) and Carlshrue (b). Both royal palaces are the focal points of their regions. The axes of Louis XIV's palace extend to the horizons; at Carlshrue the palace is the focal point of thirty-two radial avenues.*

Congress for the funds or the power of eminent domain to expropriate land. The process of patient negotiation that led to this acquisition was itself a paradigm of what an elected government in a republic could achieve.

Washington's aspirations for the capital were grounded in three important ideas. First, he believed it should help unify the new nation by offering a common realm of interest to all the states. The city therefore had to be newly created. An important existing city would have ancient and powerful associations with the colonial era, and both its plan and public buildings would lack republican symbolism. Second, he wanted the capital to be large and bold in scale. For Washington, size would mark the city's importance to the new nation and optimistically assert its future significance to the world. Third, he believed the city's plan should express the noble ideals upon which the United States was founded. Here was an opportunity to forge a design with a unique iconography. For many people, the American republic, with its respect for personal liberty based on inalienable and natural rights, symbolized a rebirth of civilization.

THE NEW CAPITAL AS A UNIFYING FORCE. It was hoped that a city centrally located without belonging to any state could help consolidate the new nation. When the Continental Congress met at Philadelphia in 1776, it represented thirteen sovereign entities united primarily in their resolve to fight for independence from outside domination. Not until five years later, in 1781, did they enter into an alliance under the Articles of Confederation, which declared "a perpetual union between the states." Dissatisfied with this Union's lack of cohesion, the states' representatives met once again in Philadelphia, in 1787, to form a "more perfect union," one that had a greater likelihood of succeeding. The underlying purpose was to discourage the states from engaging in war with one another and, in Washington's words, disintegrating "into insignificant and wretched Fragments of Empire." Since signing the Treaty of Paris in 1783, many states had refused to contribute to common national expenses;

passed laws that made it difficult for foreign creditors to collect debts; imposed tariffs on goods in transit to other states; argued over unresolved land claims; issued inflationary amounts of paper money; and undercut retaliatory commercial legislation aimed at Great Britain.[9] By August 1, 1786, a frustrated Washington was writing to patriot and diplomat John Jay that leading citizens had "begun to speak of a monarchical form of Government without horror."[10]

Events from 1783 to 1787 testify to animosity among the states that could have erupted into warfare. The first nine *Federalist Papers*, written by Alexander Hamilton, James Madison, and John Jay, attempted to persuade the citizens of New York to adopt the federal Constitution by contrasting their own situation with the incessant warfare among the unfederated sovereign states of Europe, and earlier, among the city states of ancient Greece. A decade before, the French economist and statesman Baron de l'Aulne Turgot had warned that the new nation would cease to be "the hope of the world" if it degenerated into an "image of our Europe, a mass of divided powers contending for territory and commerce."[11]

The Constitution transformed the loose alliance of thirteen independent states into a single nation and the first democratic federal republic in history. The "more perfect union" embraced a concept distinctly different from that of all previous constitutions: the plurality of sovereignty by which the federal government ruled in concert with state government.[12] Clearly, Washington believed that the unity of the thirteen separate states as "one people" could be further enhanced by the new capital city. Because the national government under the Articles of Confederation had almost ceased to function by 1784, Washington needed to establish common spheres of national interest for the states and their citizens, or in his words, "to apply the cement of interest, to bind all parts of the Union together by indissoluble bonds."[13] Adopting a constitution to create a single nation and establishing a new capital provided crucial elements of that unity.

The site represented another opportunity for cohesion.

Washington insisted that the new capital city be centrally located so as to be equally important both to the eastern seaboard states and the new territory of the West. No doubt it would have been far easier to designate either New York, where the capital was situated when Washington took office, or Philadelphia, the nation's most important commercial center, as the permanent capital. Philadelphia had been described by a contemporary observer, the Duc de Liancourt, as "not only the finest city in the United States, but . . . one of the most beautiful cities in the world."[14] In his "Notes on the Permanent Seat of Congress" of April 13, 1784, Jefferson made an impressive case in favor of Philadelphia as capital. Perhaps this was to foil efforts to confer that privilege on New York. On June 17, 1785, he explained his larger purpose to Monroe, writing that "It is evident that when a sufficient number of Western states come in they will remove it [the capital] to George town. In the mean time it is our interest that it should remain where it is . . ."[15] His arguments must have appeared overwhelming, for the proposed site of the future city of Washington was mostly undeveloped land.

On July 1, 1790, Congress passed the Residence Act, a bill establishing the "permanent seat of the government of the United States." The bill set the location of the new capital at the geographical center of the nation, identified as a 105-mile-long stretch along the Potomac River between the mouths of two of its tributaries: the Eastern Branch—also called the Anacostia River—and the Connogocheque, twenty miles south of the Pennsylvania state line (fig. 5). This choice, devised by Washington, Jefferson, Madison, and Hamilton was a compromise balancing the demands of various groups. The site's centrality ensured uninhibited and open intercourse with all the states and their cities, towns, and rural areas. Like London, historian Elbert Peets observed, "It was at the head of a tidal estuary, giving it accessibility to the sea yet relative safety from sea attack, the river above the site gave access to the hinterland, it was at the first bridge or ford, and

it was on the principal north-south national highway. The site was thus by no means an arbitrary one."[16]

The central location and river site were related to another crucial consideration in Washington's mind: access to the West. Virtually alone among the Founding Fathers, Washington believed that the frontier territory beyond the Allegheny and Appalachian mountains should be part of the United States. In this he was opposed to Jefferson who, for at least a decade after writing the Declaration of Independence, envisioned "our Western friends . . . formed into separate states [nations]."[17] It is not clear whether this idea grew out of Jefferson's desire to see the new republic remain a nation of farmers, or out of a belief that democracy could flourish only in a small state, a viewpoint he shared with Baron Charles-Louis de Secondat de Montesquieu. In either case, Washington disagreed. Like Madison, he was convinced that democracy would thrive if the nation grew. And he was certain that one key to realizing this goal was to establish a trade route, by water if possible, to connect the Ohio River valley and the eastern seaboard.[18] In 1788 Washington described this commerce "as the best, if not the only cement that can bind those people to us . . ."[19] Such a trade route would integrate and expand the economies of both regions, he asserted, making the future of the West, together with that of the new capital, another common cause among all the states.

Washington was also concerned about defense. He noted that "the flanks and rear of the United States are possessed by other powers and formidable ones too," which should be preempted from controlling the West.[20] So important did this issue loom in his mind that within months of resigning his commission as Commander of the Continental Army he set out on a journey to find a satisfactory water route to the West. He spent much of 1784 traveling on his own, exploring the western parts of Virginia and Pennsylvania, and concluded that a route using the Potomac and the Monongahela rivers was optimal; the 300-mile journey from the Ohio

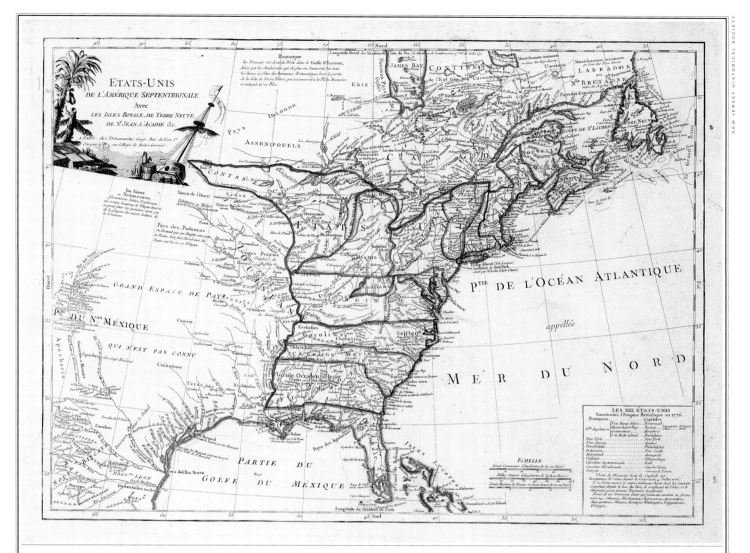

FIG. 5 *The enabling legislation created a new capital city located at the geographical center of the nation. This was identified as a 105-mile-long stretch along the Potomac River between the mouths of two of its tributaries: the Eastern Branch — also called the Anacostia River — and the Connogocheque, twenty miles south of the Pennsylvania state line. Abel Buell's* A New and correct Map of the United States of North America Layd down from the latest Observations and best Authority agreeable to the Peace of 1783 *was engraved in 1784 and is the first map of the new nation. It sites the new capital midway between the northern border with Canada and the southern border with Spanish/French Florida.*

River required only twenty miles of portage (figs. 6 a & b). On Washington's return to Mount Vernon, he helped to form the Potomac Navigation Company which opened the route. There is no record that anyone before Washington had explored this area so thoroughly or realized that it offered an opportunity to build a short east-west canal that crosses ranges of mountains running north and south.

The task of improving the water connection between the Ohio and Potomac became increasingly urgent as the next 20 years saw a "spectacular trans-Allegheny migration of people and goods."[21] Its magnitude was large enough for one observer to predict that in the next decade the population of the West would exceed that of the eastern seaboard states.[22] By 1800 some trade had begun moving up and down this route.[23]

Washington never lost his faith in the goal of westward expansion. On April 8, 1792, he wrote to his close friend and stepson-in-law David Stuart:

There is such an intimate connection in political and pecuniary consideration between the federal district and the inland navigation of the Potowmac, that no exertions, in my opinion, shou'd

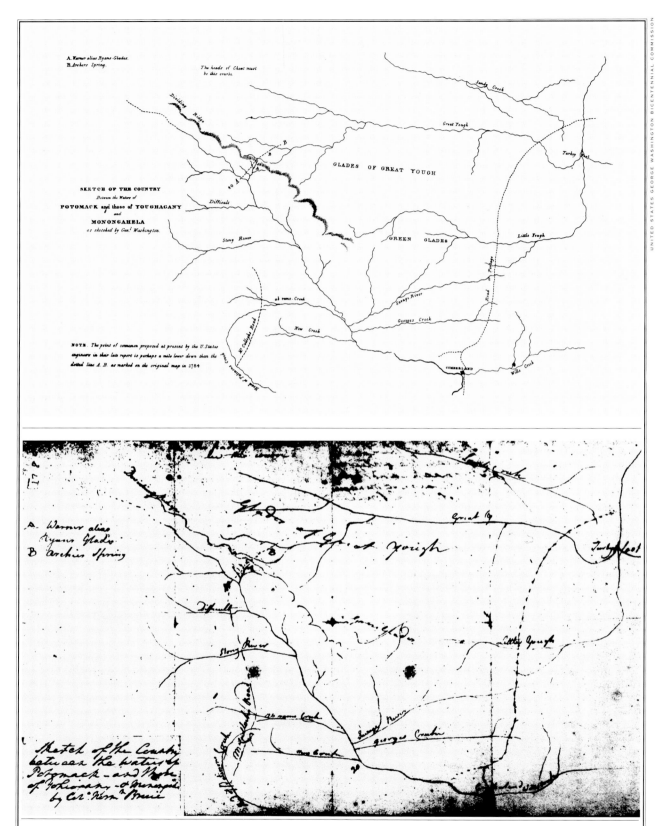

FIGS. 6 A & B *George Washington discovered a water route between the Ohio River system and the Potomac River via the Monongahela and its tributaries. Fig. 6A shows a map of the border between Virginia, now West Virginia, and Pennsylvania marked with the site of a proposed canal connecting the Great Yough, a tributary of the Monongahela, to the tributary system of the Potomac. Fig. 6B shows the survey map of the site of this canal commissioned and annotated by Washington. It was prepared by Normand Bruce in 1784.*

be dispensed with to accomplish the latter. For, in proportion as this advances, the City will be benefited. Public and private motives therefore combine to hasten this work.[24]

In 1784, when he returned from his expedition, he had thought Alexandria would become a major port of trade between the West, the Atlantic seaboard states, and Europe. Now he wanted the new federal city to fulfill this role. In a letter to Arthur Young, the English agronomist, Washington described the new city's future as the eventual "emporium of the United States" because of "advantages given to it by nature, and its proximity to a rich interior country, and the western territory. . ."[25] This general perception explains why Jefferson, in the first plan he drew for the federal city, made provisions for extensive docks, and why L'Enfant's plan provided for both harbor and commerce.

In a far-sighted and comprehensive approach to coordinated urban, transportation, and economic planning, officers of the Potomac Navigation Company planned to use federal, state, and local government monies in combination with the private capital to promote regional development and construct locks and canals necessary to make the river more easily navigable. Transportation by water between the East Coast and the Ohio River was essential for stimulating economic development in all the territories. The scope of Washington's proposed regional plan was significantly more ambitious than the contemporary city planning practice of subdividing land by imposing small grid plans. Washington's advisors advocated this as the expedient way to realize the new capital.

THE SCALE OF THE NEW CAPITAL. The second component of the President's vision for the capital city was its magnitude. Washington did not have in mind a precise definition of area so much as an intuitive sense that one of the city's special characteristics should be substantial scale. Size is a quality associated with importance, and the federal city was to be a statement the new nation was making to its citizens as well as to the world. Washington also sensed that a larger and more ambitious capital would be of greater use in helping to unify the nation than a smaller town.

Between March 28 and 30, 1791, Washington was in Georgetown meeting with local landowners to discuss the selection of the actual site of the federal city and its major buildings. The events of these three days served to clarify and focus his concern about the size of the city and establish the dominant role of L'Enfant as planner.

Preparation for these meetings had begun the previous summer. Once the Residence Act was passed, Washington and Jefferson turned to defining the precise location of the ten-square-mile area of federal territory it called for. Washington had decided upon the general area between the Eastern Branch and Georgetown as the optimal site, and they were contemplating a variety of different locations within this 100-square-mile area. Two places were under serious consideration: Carrollsburg, laid out in 1770, where the Eastern Branch flowed into the Potomac, and Hamburgh, south of Georgetown, which had been platted in 1768 (fig. 7). Both were small, sparsely developed settlements. Nonetheless, they were ambitious projects that were approximately 170 and 110 acres, respectively, and could accommodate a combined population at least double that of Georgetown, which was at the time about 135 acres.

Jefferson first turned his thoughts to possible configurations of the city's plan in the summer of 1790. He prepared for the President a "Draft of Agenda for the Seat of Government," dated 29 August, which proposed a grid plan with 200-square-yard blocks, streets 100 feet and 120 feet wide, and 15-foot-wide foot-ways.[26] Two weeks later, on 14 September, he presented a report to Washington on a meeting with local landowners held at Georgetown, and recommended that 1,500 acres of land be required for the federal city, of which 300 acres would be set aside for "public buildings, walks &c" with 1,200 acres "to be divided into quarter acre lots."[27]

The Secretary of State did not discuss why he believed 1,500 acres to be an appropriate area, but the number may have been derived from William Penn's 1682 plan for Philadelphia, the largest city in the new nation. The report also included a sketch of a plan for the city showing it facing the "river" on one side, presumably the Potomac, at right angles to a "creek." This most likely was St. James Creek, about which Jefferson queried, "Will it not be best to lay out the long streets parallel with the creek, and the other crossing them at right angles, so as to leave no oblique angled lots but the single row which shall be on the river?" (fig.8) Jefferson's drawing indicates that this sensible if undistinguished grid plan was probably located on the west side of St. James Creek, opposite Carrollsburg, but his text suggests

the location as Carrollsburg itself; it is similar in configuration to the plat for that city, though considerably larger. The plan's total area may be calculated by using Jefferson's recommended square-block size and street and sidewalk widths and multiplying this area by the number of blocks in the plan. The resultant area is approximately 470 acres.[28] Of the 1,500 acres Jefferson recommended for the capital, this left 1,000 available for future expansion. The site maximized potential harbor facilities, anticipating the role Washington envisioned for the future capital as the "emporium of the United States."

By the late fall of 1790, both Washington and Jefferson

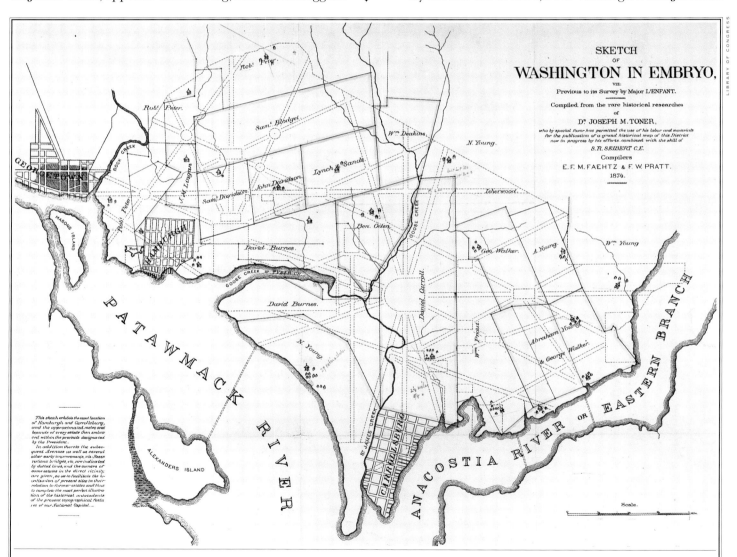

FIG. 7 *Two possible sites were under serious consideration for the federal city. Carrollsburg was platted in 1770 at the junction of the Eastern Branch and the Potomac. Hamburgh, south of Georgetown, was platted in 1768. This map shows both sites as well as the property lines prior to 1790. L'Enfant's plan is indicated by the broken lines.*

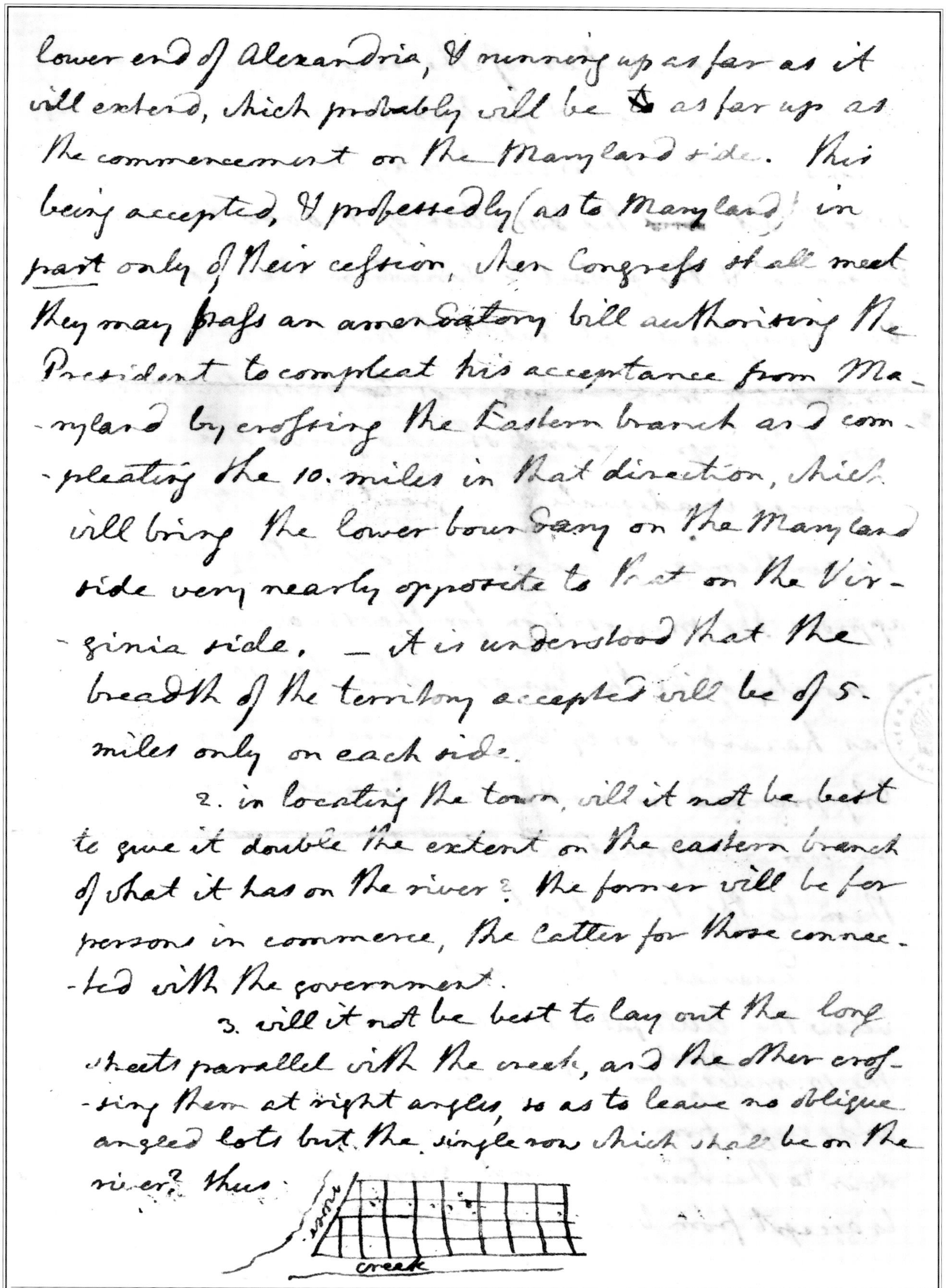

lower end of Alexandria, & running up as far as it will extend, which probably will be as far up as the commencement on the Maryland side. This being accepted, & professedly (as to Maryland) in part only of their cession, then Congress shall meet they may pass an amendatory bill authorising the President to compleat his acceptance from Maryland by crossing the Eastern branch and compleating the 10. miles in that direction, which will bring the lower boundary on the Maryland side very nearly opposite to that on the Virginia side. _ It is understood that the breadth of the territory accepted will be of 5. miles only on each side.

2. in locating the town, will it not be best to give it double the extent on the eastern branch of what it has on the river? the former will be for persons in commerce, the latter for those connected with the government.

3. will it not be best to lay out the long streets parallel with the creek, and the other crossing them at right angles, so as to leave no oblique angled lots but the single row which shall be on the river? thus.

FIG. 8 *Secretary of State Thomas Jefferson prepared a crude sketch of a new capital on the site of Carrollsburg. He proposed a town planned with major streets laid out at right angles to St. James Creek.*

had decided that the Carrollsburg area might not be the best site. Washington's choice of location shifted to the area around Hamburgh. In a confidential letter written on February 3 to William Deakins, Jr., and Benjamin Stoddert, his agents in the field, he explained the reasons for the change: "In favour of the latter (Hamburgh) is it's vicinity to Georgetown, which puts it in the way of deriving aids from it in the beginning, and of communicating in return an increased value to the property of that town."[29] In other words, the site's proximity to the amenities of Georgetown had emerged as an important advantage.

On January 24, 1791, Washington announced his choice for the ten-square-mile site of the Federal District. Soon after, Andrew Ellicott was sent to survey and mark the forty-mile-long boundary.[30] This still left undecided the actual site of the city. In late January L'Enfant was contacted and asked to proceed to Georgetown. The letter of instruction given to him by the President has unfortunately been lost. However, two specific details of these instructions may be deduced from subsequent events and related correspondence. First, there is a letter from Jefferson to the Commissioners of the Federal District, who, under the terms of the Residence Act of 1790, were authorized to survey and define the ten-square-mile district under the direction of the President.[31] Dated January 29, 1791, it states: "The President, having thought Major L'Enfant peculiarly qualified to make such a Draught of the Ground [topographical survey] as will enable himself to fix on the Spot for the public Buildings; he has been written to for that Purpose, and will be sent on, if he chuses to undertake it."[32] The letter confirms that Jefferson and Washington assumed that these two tasks, surveying the site and choosing locations for public buildings, were sequential and not directly related to each other. Jefferson anticipated that the new city would have a straightforward grid plan that could be staked out with little or no concern for its three-dimensional qualities.

Second, a letter of instruction from Jefferson to L'Enfant,

dated March 2, 1791, states that L'Enfant was to survey only the area around Carrollsburg. Jefferson was very specific:

The special object of asking your aid is to have drawings of the particular grounds most likely to be approved for the site of the federal town and buildings. You will therefore be pleased to begin on the Eastern branch, and proceed from thence upwards, laying down the hills, vallies, morasses, and waters between that, and the Patowmac, the Tyber, and the road leading from George town to the Eastern branch, and connecting the whole with certain fixed points on the map Mr. Ellicott is preparing.[33]

The letter contains no mention of sites for public buildings, and the peremptory tone suggests a desire to limit L'Enfant's role to merely that of a surveyor.

In a letter to William Deakins, Jr., and Benjamin Stoddert, also dated March 2, 1791, Washington describes L'Enfant's responsibilities more comprehensively:

Majr. L'enfant comes on to make such a survey of the grounds in your vicinity as may aid in fixing the site of the federal town and buildings. his present instructions express those alone which are within the Eastern branch, the Potowmac, the Tiber, and the road leading from George town to the ferry on the Eastern branch. he is directed to begin at the lower end and work upwards, and nothing further is communicated to him. The purpose of this letter is to desire you will not be yourselves misled by this appearance, nor be diverted from the pursuit of the objects I have recommended to you.[34]

The last sentence refers to a subterfuge by which Washington and Jefferson hoped that the presence of L'Enfant surveying around Carrollsburg would convince the Georgetown and Hamburgh landowners that the Eastern Branch site had been selected for the new city and federal buildings and that perhaps this would induce them to be more reasonable in setting prices for their land in and around Hamburgh. At Washington's request Deakins and Stoddert were negotiating possible purchases of land in and around Hamburgh as if on their own behalf, but in fact for the nation. In his letter to the agents of February 3, 1791, the President had stressed the need for secrecy.[35] Later, writing to L'Enfant, Washington noted that "no offer, worthy of consideration, would come from the Land holders in the vicinity of Carrollsburg."[36] From this it may be surmised that property owners in and around Carrollsburg were demanding negotiators or, more likely, were harboring exaggerated expectations about the value of their land as well as of the resources the President had at his disposal.

This secret strategy is confirmed by later correspondence, for it appears that L'Enfant exceeded the bounds of his instructions. On March 16, a chagrined Washington wrote to Jefferson, asking: "What steps had I best take to bring matters to a close . . . by declaring at once the site of the public buildings, prevent some inconvenience which I see may arise from the opinions promulgated by Mr. L'Enfant? as much probably from complaisance as judgement."[37] It appears that L'Enfant's actions or words had suggested to local landowners that more than one site was being considered. The next day Jefferson wrote to L'Enfant with instructions to survey both the Carrollsburg and Hamburgh sites. He further cautioned L'Enfant that "It is the desire that the public mind be in equilibrio between these two places till the President arrives, and we shall be obliged to you to endeavor to poise their expectations."[38]

L'Enfant's misstep likely resulted from a combination of three separate misunderstandings. First, he was not informed of the President's subterfuge and of the need for secrecy. Ignorant of the strategy by which Washington was hoping to limit property cost, he had no idea that his every action and word would be scanned by property owners of both the Carrollsburg and Hamburgh factions for hints of the President's intentions so that they could use the information to further their own interests.

The second misunderstanding stemmed from the confusingly general way in which Jefferson and Washington construed L'Enfant's duties. In his letter to L'Enfant of March 2, 1791, Jefferson instructed him to survey land "on

the Eastern branch, and proceed from thence upwards [northwards] . . .[to] the Patowmac, the Tyber, and the road leading from George town to the eastern Branch."[39] In his letter to Deakins and Stoddert, written on the same day, Washington repeated these instructions. L'Enfant apparently took the instructions seriously. On March 11, he informed Jefferson that he had arrived at Georgetown late in the evening of March 9. The next day he introduced himself to the Mayor, as Jefferson had asked him to do, and learned that Jefferson had neglected to inform the Mayor of his visit. Despite rain and fog he began his work on the 10th and 11th, exploring the site. He inspected some of the area around Carrollsburg and reported" riding over it [the site] on horseback as I have already done yesterday . . I rote from the easterne branch towards georgetown up the heights and down along the side of the bank of the main river and along side of goose and Rock creeks as far up as their Springs."[40] This route covered the territory he was to survey. But by riding the banks of the river and two creeks that form the perimeter of Hamburgh, L'Enfant may have inadvertently set in motion the rumor that this was to be the site of the new city.

L'Enfant believed that he was merely conducting a routine exploration of the site, which could prove useful if the inclement weather prevented him from completing a proper survey with instruments and chains. In that case he could fall back on "making a rough draft as accurat as may be obtained by viewing the ground in riding over it on horseback." This practice would have been common when he was serving as an engineer in the Revolutionary army, and an impending march or battle did not allow time for accurate surveys: it remained standard well into this century. Jefferson, however, did not serve in the army during the revolution and may not have understood what L'Enfant was trying to achieve. Had the President and Secretary of State simply cautioned L'Enfant not to venture near the Hamburgh area, this misunderstanding could have been avoided.

The third and perhaps most fundamental cause of

L'Enfant's mistake is that he interpreted his instructions far more broadly than did Jefferson and Washington. They assumed he was going to make a topographical survey of the site and advise them on locations for public buildings. L'Enfant described a very different mission. In his letter to Jefferson of March 11, he saw his charge as planning "the intended city on that grand Scale on which it ought to be planned." Two weeks later, in an undated report, thought to have been prepared for the President's visit and submitted to him on or about March 26, L'Enfant outlined his approach in more detail:

considering how in process of time a city so happily situated will extend over a large surface of ground, much deliberation is necessary for to determine on a plan . . . to render the place commodious and agreeable to the first settler, [while] *it may be capable of . . .* [being] *enlarged by progressive improvement . . . which should be foreseen in the* first delineation in a grand plan of the whole city combined with the various grounds it will cover and with the particular circumstance of the country all around.[41] (emphasis added)

L'Enfant went on to recommend the Carrollsburg area as ideal for the "First Setlement of a gr[a]nd city," for its harbor could be "in Every respect prefered to that of the potowmack toward Georgetown." He also suggested constructing a bridge over the Anacostia, below Evans Point, and another over the Potomac near Georgetown. By connecting these bridges with "a direct & large avenue . . . with a middleway paved for heavy carriage and walks on each side planted with double Rows of trees," development would be promoted "on the banks of the eastern branch." L'Enfant had also studied the land for sites for public buildings and drew the President's attention to a ridge running from Jenkins' Hill westwards, parallel to the Potomac, where "Every grand building would rear with a majestick aspect over the Country all round and might be advantageously seen From twenty miles off." And he spelled out his dislike for gridiron street plans: "Such a regular plan in deed however answerable as

they appear on paper . . . become tiresome and insipide."

This was a more sophisticated approach to city planning than Jefferson, or most of the other persons concerned with the new capital, had envisioned. It recognized the importance of planning for both present and future needs and in relation to surrounding geography and communities. It considered the city as a coherent entity at all times, with an economic base and a dynamic, reciprocal relationship between the plan, topography, and sites of important buildings. L'Enfant's report was a far more realistic and ambitious statement of what should be done than the instructions handed down by the President and Secretary of State. And L'Enfant believed, quite reasonably, that to undertake this work, he had to familiarize himself with all the surrounding land forms in order to assess the best site for the city and its public buildings. As he listened to L'Enfant talk and as he read his reports, Washington must have heard echoes of his own ambitious plans for Mount Vernon.

Jefferson had not seen L'Enfant's report when, in late March, he submitted to Washington a second design for a plan for the "Federal City."[42] This new plan showed a town of some 650 acres situated on land overlooking the Potomac south of Georgetown—encompassing Hamburgh as well as the present sites of the White House and State Department (fig. 9). The new town was considerably larger than either Carrollsburg (170 acres), Hamburgh (110 acres), Georgetown (135 acres), or Williamsburg (280 acres), but it was smaller than the 1,500 acres Jefferson had proposed as the necessary area six months before.[43] Despite the reduced size, the plan's configuration and siting ingeniously allowed the city to expand over time, to the north by 500 acres and to the south by 800 acres, thereby increasing to a total area of nearly 2,000 acres.[44] Jefferson's notes on the plan clearly state that the initial plat would be 650 acres, with the remainder available "to be laid off in the future." About half of the land was set aside for government use so that the actual size of the development was only a little larger than in his Carrollsburg plan.

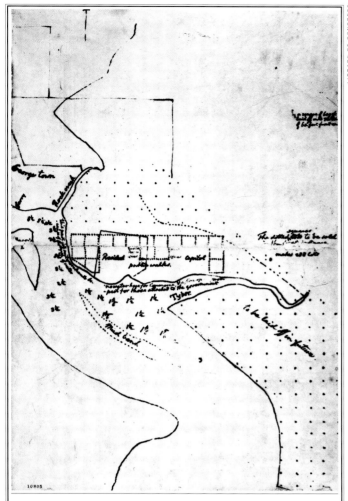

FIG. 9 *Jefferson had not seen L'Enfant's report when, in late March 1791, Jefferson submitted to Washington a second design for a plan for the "Federal City." Jefferson's plan showed a town of 650 acres situated south of Georgetown on land overlooking the Potomac. It encompassed Hamburgh and the present sites of the White House and State Department.*

The President arrived in Georgetown on March 28. The crucial events of the next two days are recorded in his diary for 28–30 March, 1791. On the 28th he was met by the "principal Citizen[s]," including landowners representing both the Georgetown and Carrollsburg interests, who were competing to have their property selected as the venue for the major government buildings in the new capital. Like Washington and Jefferson, both groups envisaged the capital as a town too small to encompass both areas. Washington also examined the partially completed surveys of the site prepared for him by L'Enfant and Ellicott. The next day he

rode over the site together with L'Enfant, at which time they were most likely to have discussed the latter's ideas for a "grand plan." Washington must have endorsed L'Enfant's support of a much larger new capital encompassing both Carrollsburg and Hamburgh, for that evening the President met with the competing landholders and proposed "That neither the offer from George town, or Carrollsburgh, separately, was adequate . . . That both together did not comprehend more ground nor would afford greater means than was required for the federal City; and that, instead of contending which of the two should have it they had better, by combining more offers make a common cause of it . . ."[45] On March 30, the opposing groups voted to accept the President's plan. The next day Washington informed Jefferson that he had been able "to reconcile the contending interests" and wished to carry out the plan "on an extensive and proper scale."[46] With this decision the capital ceased to be the small Virginia speculative development that the Secretary of State had been advocating and became a substantial city of many square miles.

A few days later, on April 8, 1791, L'Enfant summarized these events in a letter to Alexander Hamilton, Secretary of the Treasury: "Niether of the tow [two] offer[s] singly taken appeared to me of a sufficient extant to answer the grand object in view . . . I vantured the chance and gave imagination its full Scope in invading all the propriety of all, on a supposed more extensive location . . ."[47] The implication is clear: L'Enfant was proposing a larger city that included both Hamburgh and Carrollsburg. The letter continues: "I vantured some remarks thereon the which I submitted to the President on his arrival at this place and was fortunate enough to see meet with his approbation."

That the idea for this bold scheme, encompassing both areas, originated with L'Enfant is reinforced in a letter the President wrote to Jefferson on March 31. There he outlined a plan to acquire more land and he changed the project's schedule, "the enlarged plan of this agreement having done away with the necessity and indeed postponed the propriety, of designating the particular spot, on which the public buildings should be placed. . ."[48] In this letter he specified an area of 3,000 to 5,000 acres.

Washington was referring to the Georgetown visit as an occasion to designate the sites of public buildings. Aside from proposing the larger and more ambitious land plan, L'Enfant must also have convinced Washington to postpone any other decision. Only after his Georgetown meetings with L'Enfant did Washington appear to understand, for the first time, that surveying the site, designing a plan, and selecting sites for buildings were all interdependent choices — essential to creating an integrated and three-dimensional city plan.

L'Enfant reported the details of his meetings with Washington to Secretary of State Jefferson on April 4, 1791. He stated that the President had ordered him to continue "the delineation of a grand plan for the local distribution of the City, to be done on principle conformable to the ideas which I took the liberty to hold before him as the proper for the Establishment . . ."[49] This was a major achievement for the young city planner.[50] Once it was presented to him, Washington immediately understood the significance of L'Enfant's proposal, which served a number of his own ends. The idea for a large capital city buttressed Washington's confident vision of the future. It also enabled him to reconcile the two groups of contending landowners by incorporating both Hamburgh and Carrollsburg in the area to be purchased by the government. He warned both groups that any new strife would merely encourage those who supported keeping the capital in Philadelphia.

In this context it is important to note, again, that the President chose not to try to acquire property by condemnation. The Residence Act allocated no funds for purchasing land for the nation, which meant that land acquisition had to be negotiated.[51] The legislatures of Maryland and Virginia had appropriated monies for this purpose, which were put, with some restrictions, at the President's disposal. Washington's plan was to have the landowners deed their land to the United States. When the final plan had been established, these landowners would receive half of the lots in the new city, the specific proportion to be determined by the extent of their land. Other lots would be sold by the federal government to raise money for constructing public buildings. The land that would be kept under federal ownership would be paid for at a predetermined rate. On March 30, both the Carrollsburg and Georgetown factions voted to accept the President's new plan, which now encompassed L'Enfant's vision of the federal city. Four days later Washington wrote to L'Enfant from Mount Vernon instructing him to use "as much ground . . . as there is any tolerable prospect of obtaining" in order to avoid "those blotches which otherwise might result from not comprehending all the lands that appear well adapted to the general design."[52]

The sheer scale of the plan Washington approved for the capital — more comprehensive and ambitious in its scope and iconography than ever before attempted in the creation of a new city — may well have appeared contrary to common sense. He went on in the same letter to describe a site that comprised 6,400 acres, or more than ten times the initial area of Jefferson's 660-acre second plan. Even this was considerably smaller than the area encompassed by L'Enfant's eventual design, from which we may surmise again that, while the President wished to realize a great capital, L'Enfant was the first to envision its real dimensions.

The city depicted by L'Enfant in his final plan of August 1791 is approximately 11 square miles. This was an enormous area for its time. In 1800, London was the largest city in Europe with a population of 1 million occupying approximately 9 square miles; Philadelphia, the largest city in the U.S., had a population of 68,000 in 1800, in an area of just over 1 square mile.[53] L'Enfant and Washington clearly embraced the potential for immense growth. With eight times the area of Philadelphia, the new city could house a population of half a million to a million at the same density, or a population of more than a million at the density of

London. To provide a context within which to perceive the scale, Washington noted that "Philadelphia stood upon an area of three by two miles, and that, if the metropolis of *one State* occupied so much ground, what ought that of the United States to occupy?"[54]

Another aspect of Washington's concern with the scale and character of the new capital city may have been a desire to refute the assertions of some European biologists, including the Count de Buffon and the abbé Raynal, that animals and humans declined in strength and intelligence in the New World.[55] It was to disprove these accusations of biological inferiority that Jefferson had begun work on his *Notes on Virginia*. Alexander Hamilton responded in *The Federalist* that ". . . Americans disdain to be the instruments of European greatness! Let the thirteen States, bound together in a strict and indissoluble Union, concur in erecting one great American system, superior to the controul of all transatlantic force or influence, and able to dictate the terms of the connection between the old and the new world!"[56] In 1787 a writer in *The American Museum* urged Americans to "explode the European creed that we are infantile in our acquisitions, and savage in our manners, because we are inhabitants of a new world."[57] Citing a variety of American accomplishments, the author asserted that "art, then, was to be fostered . . . because it would demonstrate anew that America had entered the family of civilized states, and that she possessed an attachment to refined forms, the fruits of progress." It was a commonplace that art was somehow an expression of national greatness, and surely Washington's vision of a great new capital was partly inspired by the monumental language of architecture and city planning.[58]

Unsympathetic, then, to Jefferson's far more modest conception, Washington aligned himself with L'Enfant's vision—to plan a capital city appropriate to his sense of the United States as "a vast Empire" of thirteen states acting as one nation, and occupying an area larger than any European state except Russia. In retrospect, it is likely that an under-

standing between the two men began with Washington's receipt of L'Enfant's first letter about the new capital. On September 11, 1789, L'Enfant wrote that "the plan should be drawn on such a scale as to leave room for that aggrandizement & embellishment which the increase of the wealth of the Nation will permit it to pursue at any period however remote."[59] This vision coincided with Washington's hopes for the nation's growth and development. A shared sense of the future defined the task of planning the new capital city as "political," in Wren's sense of the word, as it "establishes a nation, draws people and commerce; makes the people love their native country."

A UNIQUE PLAN. Beyond the consideration of scale, Washington believed that only a new and unique city plan could adequately embody the ideals of the unprecedented federal democratic republic. We have no known record of Washington's ideas for the character of the plan, but his actions, and his letters of instruction, indicate how he did *not* want to see the capital evolve. Above all, he wished to avoid just another orthogonal subdivision, typical of the land development projects in Virginia or Maryland. As a young man of seventeen, Washington had assisted the surveyor John Page, Jr., to survey and lay out just such a plan for Alexandria, Virginia, as depicted on the "Plan of Alexandria and Belhaven" of 1749 (fig. 10).[60]

Like Madison, Jefferson, and other politicians involved in planning the federal city, Washington had extensive property holdings and knew how to survey. In fact, land surveying was part of the social fabric of his time. "Many ambitious young men were moving ahead of actual settlement and were buying up some of the best of the lands. That was so natural a way of making money that [they] never became conscious of reaching any formal decision to share in current land speculation."[61] Both Washington and Jefferson were competent surveyors. Jefferson's father, Peter, along with Joshua Fry had prepared an authoritative survey of Virginia in 1751. Washington earned his livelihood as a surveyor for a number of years, and he surveyed or annotated more than a hundred maps.[62]

Washington's close collaborators Jefferson and Madison, and his friends David Stuart, Thomas Johnson, and Daniel Carroll, whom he appointed Commissioners of the federal city, all appeared to be supremely confident of their ability to plan the new capital.[63] The typical Virginia settlement of the time was a few hundred acres and had a grid plan. Many such settlements had been built during the preceding century, of which Yorktown (1691), Fredericksburg (1721), and Alexandria are typical examples. In such plans, the surveyor selected the site for development, determined typical block size, and then designated land for public use. These three decisions were generally made independently of one another. It is unlikely that any of Washington's associates, with the possible exception of Jefferson, who had spent time in Europe, could have conceived of another approach.

This point of view was clearly articulated by Madison. In response to the passage of the Residence Act on July 9, 1790, he advised Jefferson on the steps necessary to realize the new Federal District: "prescribe the place"; obtain a "survey of the district," which the President "shall ultimately elect"; define the extent of the district; secure the "requisite quantity of ground"; and "fix the site for the public buildings."[64] The plan itself was not even mentioned, because it was assumed to be implicit in the tasks of surveying and defining the district. Madison's advice outlines procedures for acquiring land and laying out the standard Virginia settlement of a few hundred acres with a gridiron plan. Jefferson, too, followed this approach in preparing his plan proposals of August and September 1790.

In rejecting this assumed procedure, Washington differed from all his closest associates. As we have seen, he and Jefferson followed Madison's sequence of steps until the third and fourth tasks. Here they stalled, because at this point, in late March 1791, L'Enfant and Washington met for the first time to discuss their ideas for the new capital. Once

L'Enfant presented his plan for a larger city, which broke precedent by offering more than simply a diagram for subdividing city blocks, the direction of the project immediately changed. Washington worked closely with the young planner until August, when L'Enfant's final plan was approved. Jefferson and Madison, and even the Federal District Commissioners who were charged by Congress with superintending the realization of the federal city, were relegated to the status of observers.

If Washington had ever been interested in following his closest associates' advice, he would have been able to call on at least three able men to realize a plan expeditiously. All came highly recommended to him. The first, Andrew Ellicott, surveyed and marked the boundary of the ten-square-mile federal district. A professional surveyor, he could easily have staked out a gridiron plan. His father, Joseph Ellicott, had been a founder of the settlement of Ellicott's Lower Mills, Maryland, and Andrew Ellicott would have been familiar with the procedures for planning a new town. Trained in mathematics, astronomy, and other sciences, as well as clock-making, his father's trade, the younger Ellicott soon became one of the new nation's most important astronomers and makers of scientific instruments.[65] His work on the boundary between Virginia and Pennsylvania, the western boundary of Pennsylvania, and the state survey of New York gained him a reputation as the leading surveyor and cartographer in America.[66] It is unlikely, however, that he could have designed a city plan that was more than a straightforward grid much less one that possessed a particular symbolism. Unable to envision a city on the proposed site, he wrote that the land "bears no more proportion to the Country around Philadelphia, and Germantown, for either wealth or fertility, than a Crane does to a stall-fed Ox!"[67]

If Washington were looking for a more accomplished designer, one of the most skilled was Joseph Clark. Born in England, Clark lived nearby in Annapolis and was among the region's most important architects.[68] In 1785–88 he had

FIG. 10 *The* Plan of Alexandria and Belhaven *of 1749 was the work of George Washington, at the time a young man of seventeen, assisting surveyor John Page, Jr.*

rebuilt the Maryland Statehouse's roof and designed and erected its remarkable new lantern (fig. 11). In 1790 he designed Wye Hall for William Paca, one of four Marylanders who had signed the Declaration of Independence. Like Washington at Mount Vernon, Clark was one of the first architects to use the five-part house plan that was to become fashionable in Maryland and the South.[69] He was eager to work on the new capital. Alexander Contee Hanson, a prominent Annapolis lawyer and chancellor of the state of Maryland, as well as a man whom Washington was set to appoint District Judge for Maryland, wrote two enthusiastic letters to the President on Clark's behalf. Washington

endorsed both letters, but answered neither. Eventually Clark did submit a plan for the federal city to Washington. Sadly, it has been lost.[70]

The President's third option was to use the plans prepared by Jefferson. Without seeming to have been aware that Washington was searching for someone to execute a large-scale vision and unusual iconography, the Secretary of State submitted two thoughtfully wrought, modest grid plans. Like others, Jefferson simply assumed that the city would be built on a grid. His "Draft of Agenda for the Seat of Government," dated August 29, 1790, proposed a plan with a 200-square-yard block size. On September 14, in a second

FIG. 11 *Between 1785 and 1788 architect Joseph Clark rebuilt the roof of the Maryland Statehouse, designed and erected its remarkable new lantern, and added the entrance porch. The inviting new building soon became a home to all citizens of the state.*

report for the President, he included a sketch of this grid plan for the city on a site facing the Eastern Branch. In March 1791, Jefferson handed Washington his second design for the federal city. This new plan was another orthogonal grid. It was beautifully sited, at Hamburgh, overlooking the Potomac and the Tiber (refer to fig. 9). A precinct of government buildings set in three public squares—two for the President's House, offices, and gardens, and one for the Capitol—looked south across the Potomac to Alexandria. A market occupied one square, and nine squares were set aside for "the Public Walks." Jefferson developed this scheme of public areas from his earlier ideas for the new Virginia State capital at Richmond, which was also based on a grid. It was similar to earlier grid plans in Virginia, but may

also have been influenced by the plan of Philadelphia, or by features of some Moravian towns such as Savannah, Georgia, and Salem, North Carolina—cities characterized by the subtle use of grids, the provision for expansion, and a layout around central squares.[72]

In land area, Jefferson's plans were only a fraction of the 11 square miles envisioned by L'Enfant and even a small portion of the "ten miles square" land area (100 square miles) for the new capital called for in the Constitution.[73] Washington expressed no interest in either of the Secretary of State's two designs. In a letter of April 4, 1791, to L'Enfant, transmitting Jefferson's second plan together with another plan—probably Clark's—Washington noted, "I do not conceive that you will derive any material advantage from an examination of the enclosed papers."[74]

While Washington lacked Ellicott's brilliance in astronomy and cartography, he was probably as skilled as Ellicott, Clark, or L'Enfant at staking out a grid development. There is no record, however, that he himself even attempted to sketch a plan for the capital. This fact is remarkable because the city needed to be realized quickly in order to forestall any counter-legislation to have Philadelphia remain the capital. Washington knew first-hand just how easy it would have been to design a grid plan of his own and then have Ellicott or Clark survey the site and stake it out. Alternatively he could have adopted Jefferson's thoughtful second plan and enlivened it with groups of public squares, such as the ones Jefferson envisioned, or those that Philadelphia and Savannah used. This approach was precisely what all his associates expected and would have applauded. Yet at no time did Washington evince even the slightest interest in a subdivision by grid.

L'ENFANT'S QUALIFICATIONS AS PLANNER. The problem Washington faced was that he did not know precisely what type of plan to use instead of a grid. This is why, from the outset, he wanted the services of someone who understood the importance of planning the new capital on a large scale, someone who, in the words of L'Enfant, could conceive a plan that would impart to posterity "a grand idea of the patriotic interest which prompted it."[75] However diffusely and intuitively, Washington sensed that L'Enfant would understand his vision of the capital's scope. For this reason L'Enfant was selected to plan the new city. No record exists of any conversation the two might have had at Valley Forge in the winter of 1777–1778 when, at the request of Lafayette, L'Enfant drew the General's portrait, or in New York prior to Washington's inauguration. Perhaps it was only the sentiments L'Enfant expressed in his letter of September 11, 1789, asking to be appointed to plan the capital, that caught the President's attention.[76] In any case, it was L'Enfant who was able to articulate all of Washington's goals with a proposal that reflected their depth and breadth.

L'ENFANT'S TRAINING. L'Enfant had studied at the Académie Royale de Peinture et de Sculpture in France. His father, Pierre L'Enfant, was a professor there and an important "documentary painter" of battles. These artists, the predecessors of the next century's combat photographers, were assigned to accompany military campaigns and paint scenes of battles.[77] Documentary painters also served as cartographers to draw plans of battle tactics, logistics, and strategy. In the French army, the *Ingénieur-Géographe,* or topographical engineer, reconnoitered and surveyed terrain to map enemy positions and defenses, battlefield maneuvers, itineraries of column marches, campsites, fortifications, and battle histories.[78] L'Enfant's father was a likely source of L'Enfant's early knowledge of engineering and military affairs. This included skill in surveying and depicting city plans, and an understanding of fortifications and military maneuvers.

Although the young L'Enfant was not a trained military engineer, it is important to remember that the barriers between mathematics, architecture, art, physics, and engineering were not then as firmly drawn as they are today. Michelangelo planned fortifications, and Wren and Robert Boyle worked as easily in architecture as they did in astron-

omy and physics. Nevertheless, L'Enfant's knowledge of surveying and engineering was far more comprehensive than that of most officers in the Continental Army. An organization of non-professionals, the army suffered from a desperate shortage of trained engineers—a major concern of General Washington, who frequently mentioned the dearth of officers capable of drawing and using fortification plans.[79] Congress remedied the deficiency by recruiting foreign specialists, and in 1777 Louis Le Bègue Duportail, a French engineer trained in the scientific approach of the army school of Mézières, was appointed commandant of the army's Corps of Engineers, with three French engineers under him.[80] They were soon joined by another group of foreign officers, which included Tadeusz Kosciuszko and Pierre-Charles L'Enfant.

In the Corps of Engineers, the basic skills L'Enfant had acquired in France would have been supplemented by experience in the field and by his passionate will to learn. He assisted Baron von Steuben in preparing a manual of military training and improved his skills in surveying, basic engineering, and the design of fortifications. His military experience may also have included education in the layout of military camps; the study of cities' plans for purposes of defense, attack, or billeting troops; an understanding of the relationship of urban form to geography, topography, and military strategy; and the study of cartography, which was an important component of training at Mézières (fig. 12).[81]

L'Enfant must have been an excellent military engineer, for after the war he was commissioned to design Fort Miflin, Pennsylvania, and Fort Washington, Maryland (fig. 13). He was also offered a professorship in engineering at West Point. However, his direct experience in city planning was limited; his training in art and architecture at the Academy had prepared him to create buildings and cities in paint rather than in masonry and mortar, and he had never planned a new city. Nevertheless, L'Enfant was better prepared to design the new federal city than either Christopher

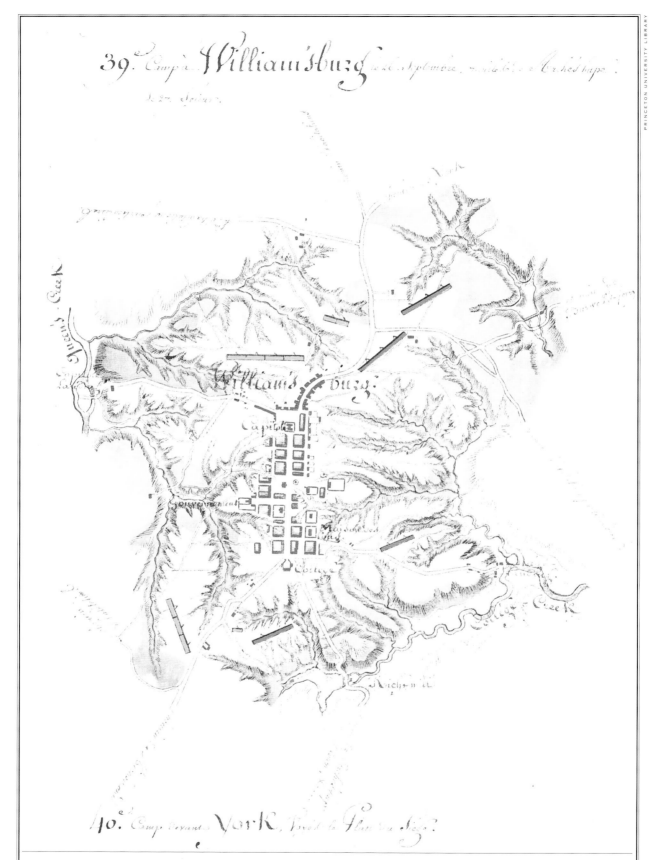

FIG. 12 *This plan, the* Thirty-Ninth Camp at Williamsburg, Virginia *(September 1781), is typical of the survey and cartographic work of a well-trained military engineer. Such plans would be used for organizing military camps and battle tactics and billeting troops.*

FIG. 13 *Fort Washington, Maryland (1815–1824) was designed by L'Enfant to guard access to the new capital from the Potomac River.*

Wren or John Evelyn had been to replan London after the fire of 1666. And his knowledge was far more comprehensive than that of the surveyors and engineers who planned new colonial settlements; certainly it exceeded the preparation of the many renaissance architects who, though trained as painters or sculptors, planned towns, parts of cities, and engineering projects.[82]

L'ENFANT'S EARLY WORK IN ARCHITECTURE AND ICONOGRAPHY. As we have noted, Washington first met L'Enfant at Valley Forge, where the young officer — then only 23 — had drawn Washington's portrait. Their next encounter was at a reception at the French Legation in Philadelphia in September 1782, to celebrate the birth of the Dauphin. It

was held in a beautiful pavilion that L'Enfant had designed for the event. Two of the several emblems decorating the walls were described in the journal of Comte de Clermont-Crèvecoeur: "The room was beautifully decorated. At the east end of the room was a rising sun surmounted by thirteen stars (the arms of America) with an Indian watching the sunrise and apparently dazzled by its rays."[83] L'Enfant's talents must have been well known by this time, for the French envoy, the Chevalier de La Luzerne, had written to Washington specifically requesting permission to use his services to plan the legation's pavilion.[84] Another observer, the Baron de Closen, an aide to the Comte de Rochambeau, noted in his journal: "One cannot imagine a building in better taste; sim-

FEDERAL HALL

The Seat of CONGRESS

Printed & Sold by A Doolittle New-Haven 1790

FIG. 14 *The Old City Hall in New York was used for meetings of the Continental Congress. In 1788, L'Enfant was commanded to remodel it as a venue for the new government of the United States. The illustration shows Washington, on the balcony of this building, taking the oath of office as the new nation's first President on April 30th, 1789.*

plicity is there united with an air of dignity."[85]

In 1783 L'Enfant designed the Insignia and Diploma of Membership for the Society of the Cincinnati, an association of officers who fought in the Revolution. Washington was elected the first president of the organization and approved the allocation of funds for L'Enfant's travels and for the designs. L'Enfant's Insignia, like Charles Thompson's design for the Great Seal a year earlier, was based on the American bald eagle (a bird he described as "peculiar to this continent") and on a thirteen-pointed star.[86] The eagle was also an ancient Roman symbol of the alliance of government and the gods; rendered in silver, the Cincinnati insignia recalled the silver eagle that was the standard of a Roman legion under the Republic.[87]

The young officer's reputation grew quickly. When, in 1788, New York decided to plan a banquet for six thousand people "in honor of the Constitution of the United States," L'Enfant was commissioned to design the pavilions and other facilities. His plan had ten pavilions, one for each state that had ratified the Constitution.[88] He also designed the Glory over the altar at St. Paul's Chapel in New York, where Washington and his family often attended services when New York served as the capital.[89] A few months later he was commissioned to remodel Federal Hall in New York for meetings of the Continental Congress (Fig. 14). The new building was pronounced "superior to any . . . in America" because of its design and innovative and patriotic decorative themes.[90] These included a frieze "ingeniously divided to admit thirteen stars in the metopes"; the "American Eagle and other insignia in the pediment"; the "tablets over the windows, filled with the 13 arrows and the olive branch united"; the interior of the "Representatives' room" with carvings of "trophies . . . and the letters U.S. in a cipher, surrounded with laurel"; an intended statue of a woman representing Liberty to be set over the speaker's chair; a special architectural order in the Senate chamber with a star and rays set amid foliage and a small medallion with "U.S." in a

FIG. 15 *The wrought iron balcony railing of Federal Hall was decorated with thirteen arrows representing the first thirteen states that voted to accept the Constitution.*

cipher suspended by drapery; and a ceiling ornamented with a sun and thirteen stars.[91] It was on the balcony of L'Enfant's building that Washington took the oath of office, standing in front of a railing decorated with thirteen arrows (fig. 15). For the occasion, he wore a jacket cut from fabric made in the United States, with silver buttons decorated with an eagle that was inspired by L'Enfant's design for the Cincinnati.[92] Writing in 1944, the architectural historian Talbot Hamlin called L'Enfant's Federal Hall "as far removed from the French style as it is from any English precedent . . . In this building the French L'Enfant was already American."[93]

Indeed, the young French-born designer embraced his adopted land with pride. Wishing to celebrate democracy, he invented new ornaments based on the history of the United States, many of which are still employed today. As he searched for a talented architect and planner to build the federal city, Washington must have understood that he would be hard put to find anyone with L'Enfant's distinctive talents. He had passed over Ellicott, Clark, and Jefferson. Neither Bulfinch, who was engaged in his first commissions in Boston, nor Samuel McIntire, who had been designing houses in Salem for a decade, was as inventive in architecture and design or as experienced in engineering and sur-

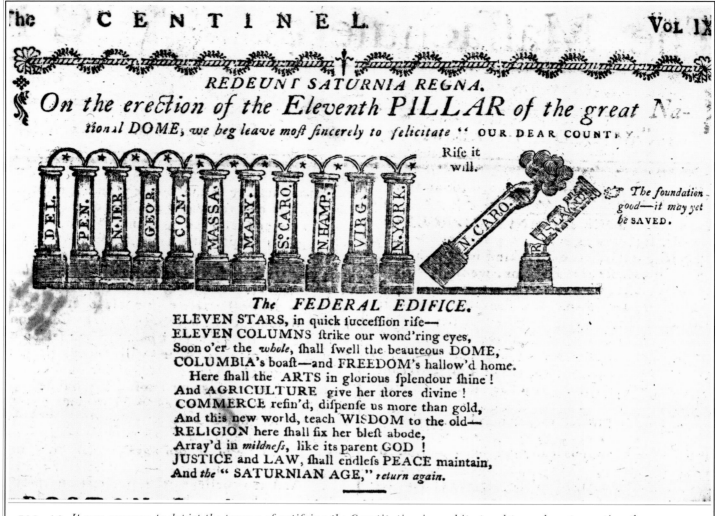

FIG. 16 *It was common to depict the process of ratifying the Constitution in architectural terms by representing the new country as a temple with individual columns signifying which states supported the Constitutional edifice.*

veying. Other French architects, such as J. J. Ramée and M. I. Brunel, worked in a modified Louis XVI style and in Washington's eyes may have been regarded as less relevant and innovative than L'Enfant.[94]

POLITICAL IDEALS EXPRESSED
IN ART AND CITYSCAPE

Washington must have particularly admired the way L'Enfant was able to give physical form to the new nation's ideals by using architectural symbols. The President was aware that representing republican ideals was a challenge being explored in the arts. When the states were voting to accept the Constitution, it was common to depict the process in architectural terms by representing the new country as a temple with individual columns signifying which states supported the Constitutional edifice (fig. 16). Columns shown under construction represented states that were still to vote; demolished columns symbolized those opposed to ratification. Perhaps this concept of a federation as a classical building inspired the President to express the nation's ideals in the plan of its capital city. In his first inaugural address, Washington himself referred to America's future in terms of staking out a building prior to construction, stating that "the destiny of the Republican model of Government, [is] justly considered as *deeply*, perhaps *finally* staked, on the experiment entrusted to the hands of the American people." (emphasis added)[95]

PAINTING. Washington also knew of Benjamin West's

innovative use of accurate modern costume in paintings like *The Death of General Wolfe* (1771). Writing to Jefferson in Paris, on August 1, 1786, regarding the portrait statue that Jean-Antoine Houdon had been commissioned to carve by the Commonwealth of Virginia for its Capitol, the President stated his preference for "modern costume" (an idea "introduced in painting by Mr. West") rather than "a servile adherence to the garb of antiquity."[96] Jefferson seemed to concur. In a letter to Washington, dated August 14, 1787, he cites not

LIBRARY OF VIRGINIA

FIG. 17 *Houdon's statue of Washington presents the president in modern military uniform with the jacket unbuttoned, signifying that he has just resigned his commission and is returning to his farm. The sculptor was not the first to associate Washington with Lucius Quinctius Cincinnatus, who left his farm to lead Rome to victory and then, refusing all honors, returned to it.*

only West, but also painters John Copley, John Trumbull, and Mather Brown in support of "modern costume."[97]

SCULPTURE. As executed, Houdon's statue shows Washington in military uniform, but with the jacket unbuttoned, signifying that he had just resigned his commission and was returning to his farm (fig. 17). The unbuttoned jacket may also have suggested modesty, wisdom, and discerning judgment. Washington is holding a walking stick but retains his sword and army coat on a nearby bundle of thirteen fasces that surround an axe with a projecting blade—a Roman symbol of confederation. A plough, the symbol of farming, appears next to him. The association of Washington with Lucius Quinctius Cincinnatus, who left his farm to lead Rome to victory and then, refusing all honors, returned to it, had already been made by L'Enfant in 1783 in his design of the medal of the Society of the Cincinnati (fig. 18). Cincinnatus was also evoked a year later by Charles Willson Peale in his 1784 portrait of Washington at the surrender of Yorktown.[98] Perhaps Houdon learned about the Society medal directly from L'Enfant, or from Peale's painting, which was received by Jefferson in Paris in early 1785. The plough motif may have been taken directly from L'Enfant's medal.[99]

Houdon wished to achieve a likeness that encompassed the character and inner spirit of his subject. For this reason he traveled to the United States to meet Washington in his own milieu, agreed to show him in modern garb, and modeled the statue to life size rather than the more conventional grander scale. All three decisions were appropriate enlightenment responses to the challenge of finding an iconography for the leader of a democratic republic. Surely Houdon could have far more easily created his sculpture in Paris, using a life-mask of Washington and relying on detailed measurements of his body. Instead, he withdrew from a commission offered by the Empress of Russia in order to make the long and dangerous journey across the Atlantic, in the company of Benjamin Franklin, to observe the "colonial rebel" in all the circumstances of his daily life.

In a letter to Washington from Paris on December 10, 1784, Jefferson confirmed that Houdon "thinks it [the statue] cannot be perfectly done from a picture . . . and offers to go himself to America for the purpose of forming your bust from life."[100]

The question of who proposed the size of the sculpture is complicated. Jefferson expressed his ambivalent views in a letter to Governor Benjamin Harrison: "We are agreed in one circumstance, that the size shall be precisely that of life. Were we to have executed a statue in any other case, we should have preferred making it somewhat larger than life; because as they are generally a little elevated, they appear smaller (than life size) . . ."[101] Jefferson went on to explain that

we think it important that some one monument should be preserved of the true size as well as figure, from which all other countries (and our own at any future day when they shall desire it)

FIG. 18 *The Insignia of the Society of the Cincinnati was designed by L'Enfant in 1783. The use of the eagle to represent the United States had been seen earlier in the design of the Great Seal.*

may take copies . . . We are sensible that the eye, alone considered, will not be quite as well satisfied; but connecting the consideration that the whole, and every part of it presents the true size of the life, we suppose the beholder will receive a greater pleasure on the whole.

Jefferson appeared to endorse a life-size sculpture even at the cost of realizing a less significant work of art. A simpler and cheaper way to obtain "the true size of life" for future generations to use as a model would have been to make a life mask and a body cast.[102] In fact, Jefferson continued to be troubled by both the use of "modern costume" and the life-size scale of Houdon's sculpture. He addressed these questions again, thirty-one years later, in a letter to Nathaniel Macon, a Senator from North Carolina, noting that "every person of taste in Europe, would be for the Roman [dress] the effect of which is of a different order. Our boots and regimentals have a very puny effect." He spoke disparagingly of the scale of the sculpture as being "only the size of life. Yours [a reference to another project for a statue of Washington] should be something larger. The difference it makes in the impression can scarcely be conceived."[103]

It is possible that in 1784–1785 Jefferson may have been showing off his newly acquired expertise in European art and that Houdon may not have shared his ambivalence about the size of the sculpture. Houdon himself may have preferred to make the figure of Washington life-size; there is no record of a dispute about the statue's scale, and the sculptor's prestige was so great that someone would have noted his dissent on such a vital question. There was also ample precedent for the sculpture's size. A few years earlier the Comte d'Angiviller, Louis XIV's Director General of Buildings, who intended to transform the Louvre, a royal palace, into a vast public museum, had commissioned a series of "lifesize statues of the great men of France" for the collection.[104] Houdon's recently completed "Voltaire Seated" (1781), at the Comédie-Française, was also sculpted to life size. Finally, there was the plan to use white marble for the Washington sculpture. It was widely believed that the color subtly suggested greater size.[105]

Houdon did complain about the length of the proposed inscription that Madison composed for the sculpture. Jefferson communicated Houdon's apprehension to Madison: "He called on me the other day to remonstrate . . . He says it is too long to be put on the pedestal."[106] The sculpture had a low plinth, on which Houdon had carved the simple words "George Washington." Thus his objection probably was based on visual concerns, and not, as Jefferson thought, literary ones. He may have been worried about the extent to which an additional pedestal, whose size would have to be large enough to house a long inscription, would raise the sculpture to a greater height than he intended, transforming Washington from an exemplary fellow-citizen into a monarch or aristocrat looming above the viewer's gaze. Garry Wills has argued that Houdon wished to have the life-size sculpture stand on the ground of Virginia without a pedestal.[107] This would have allowed the viewer to stand toe-to-toe with Washington and feel his presence more powerfully. Although the force of the image is indeed intensely felt at ground level, such a decision would have violated a long tradition of placing life-size effigies, with engraved plinths, on pedestals.[108] Because Houdon's complaint addressed the length and not the presence of an inscription, it is likely that he accepted that such sculptures were a public tribute and needed an explanatory text.

Houdon's pursuit of "liveliness and naturalness" was important to those commissioning the statue, who wished to present Washington as an ideal republican.[109] This initiative was also apparent in L'Enfant's plan of

Washington, D.C., submitted to the President in August 1791. Proposing a series of squares in the city, each dedicated to one of the founding states and decorated with statues of leading citizens who had helped create the new republic, L'Enfant intended these statues to serve as exemplars of citizen-leaders for future generations.[110]

The planner and sculptor shared humble origins as well as French ancestry. It is likely that they also discussed questions related to the particular challenge for artists and designers of representing a leader of a democratic republic. Houdon must have been curious about L'Enfant's more intimate knowledge of the President and his experience during the revolutionary war.[111] Part of the thrill of the Virginia commission for Houdon, and the reason he neglected the more lucrative and, in Europe at least, more prestigious Russian commission, was the opportunity to establish new precedents for the ages. This challenge also lured the Italian sculptor Giuseppe Ceracchi and the English architect Benjamin Henry Latrobe to the new republic to create monuments to its political ideals. Because Houdon spoke no English, L'Enfant wrote to Charles Thompson, Secretary of the Continental Congress, on his behalf regarding the commission for another likeness of Washington, an equestrian statue called for by a Congressional Act of 1783.

ARCHITECTURE AND DESIGN. In architecture and urban design, Jefferson's innovative new Virginia State Capitol in Richmand (based on an ancient Roman temple) and Joseph Clark's "house-like" improvements to the Maryland Statehouse, were the first proposed responses after the Revolution to the question of the appropriate architectural form for a statehouse (refer to figs. 4 and 11). Similarly, between 1776 and 1782 many mottos and symbols were proposed for the Great Seal. John Adams, Thomas Jefferson, and Benjamin Franklin, among others, contributed to this process, subjecting each concept to great scrutiny in order to ensure that its meaning was an appropriate and adequate expression of the young nation's ideals. Designs for the Seal in 1782 by William Barton and Charles Thompson were the first to use the eagle—the white and the American eagle respectively—as a symbol of the new nation. And the addition of the motto *Novus Ordo Seclorum*, a new order for the ages, defined both its political and aesthetic goals.[112]

When it came to embodying republican ideals in a city rather than a work of art or architecture, Washington was at a loss. How to plan and build a great capital city from scratch? The only immediate precedent in Europe to which Washington might have looked for guidance was St. Petersburg, which was established as Russia's capital in 1703 by Peter the Great. Washington, who had never traveled outside of the United States, probably knew little or nothing about it. There is no mention of St. Petersburg in his correspondence or diaries, or, for that matter, in those of Jefferson. L'Enfant was probably not aware of the Russian Capital either, despite the key role in its planning played by another Frenchman, Jean Baptiste Alexander Leblond (fig. 19).[113] In his September 11, 1789, letter to Washington, L'Enfant wrote: "No nation had ever before the opportunity offered them of deliberately deciding on the spot where their Capital City should be fixed. . ."[114] Had L'Enfant been aware of such an important precedent, it is likely he would have cited it to Washington, if only because of its vast size. Leblond's St. Petersburg plan encompassed approximately eight square miles, and its site on the banks of the Neva River, its goal of furthering the development of the Russian economy and hinterlands, and its defensive function also gave it much in common with Washington's aspirations for the new federal city.[115]

The capitals of Europe—Milan, Florence, Paris, London—began as settlements that simply grew in increments over time. Many such cities first had been established as colonies by the ancient Greeks and Romans, just as New

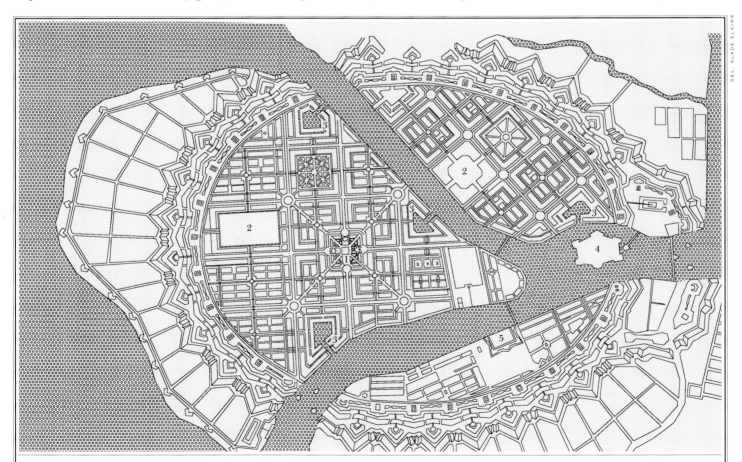

FIG. 19 *One of the few precedents for a capital city Washington might have looked to for guidance was St. Petersburg, Russia, created in 1703 by Peter the Great and planned by Jean Baptiste Alexander Leblond. Like Washington, D.C., St. Petersburg was sited along a river. Its street system uses both diagonal and orthogonal grids. 1. Palace. 2. Market Square. 3. Harbor. 4. Fortress. 5. Admiralty.*

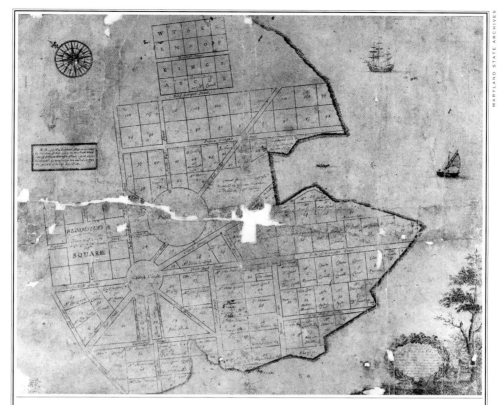

FIG. 20A *In 1693, Governor Francis Nicholson designed the new Maryland State capital at Annapolis with an unusual combination of grid and diagonal roads. The State House and the church are sited in two circles as the focal points of radial avenues.*

FIG. 20B *Although Annapolis has grown, and the State House has a large addition at the rear, this street pattern remains fundamentally unchanged.*

York, Boston, and Philadelphia had developed from small Dutch and English settlements. In imagining the new capital, Washington may have lacked a sense of the possibilities by which a grid plan could become, over time and in the hands of fine architects, a great city like Florence. In such cases America did not look with favor on European capitals. Jefferson believed that the "city of London, tho' handsomer than Paris, is not so handsome as Philadelphia."[116] And the town of Versailles was an adjunct to the Palace, a grid, and too small to have elicited Washington's interest. More to the point was the contempt many Americans felt for the court at Versailles. Jefferson described courtiers as having an "imposing exterior" that concealed "the weakest and worst part of mankind." He compared the court to a "menagerie."[117] And surely the "Sun King" symbolism that is at the core of the plan for Versailles would not have appealed to Washington, or to most Americans, as a model.

Washington wanted the federal city to be a coherent artifact whose meaning could be readily understood by everyone from the outset. As we proposed, he believed that some degree of coordination between the city plan and its buildings was necessary, and two examples of city plans may in fact have influenced his vision. Both were close at hand and were familiar to him: Governor Francis Nicholson's unusual plan for the new Maryland state capital at Annapolis (1693) and the plan Nicholson also designed for the Virginia state capital at Williamsburg (1699) (figs. 20 a & b & 21).

Nicholson's plan for Annapolis was inspired by the designs of Christopher Wren and John Evelyn for London after the Great Fire of 1666. Here statehouse and church were situated in *rond-points* appropriately called the "Public Circle" and the "Church Circle." They were linked by a street on which King William's School, the forerunner of Saint John's College, was located, underlining the prominent role assigned to education in the colony. On one side was a 350-foot-wide residential square and a 100-foot-wide market square. The plan also provided sites for public landings and common lands.[118]

Williamsburg, Virginia, was founded in 1699 when Nicholson moved the capital there from Jamestown. Its plan was centered on a three-quarter-mile-long principal axis, the Duke of Gloucester Street, with the College at the west end and the Capitol, set in a square 475 feet wide, at the east end. The street occupies a divide between two rivers. At the time, the plan's emphasis on representative government and public education must have contrasted dramatically with the expression of the dual authority of church and palace in most European capitals. The Williamsburg Capitol has a tripartite "H" plan. Its central connecting space is an open, arcaded loggia for the gathering of citizens, with the House of Burgesses on one side and the General Court on the other; their apsidal rooms recall the ancient Roman civil basilica, which also housed a hall of justice and a public meeting place.[119] Nicholson's was probably the first use of the term "Capitol" since antiquity. It was the source of Jefferson's later application of the word to the statehouses at Richmond and Washington.[120]

Williamsburg was designed for a population of two thousand. Midway along its principal axis is the Market Square, an agora-like space that articulates the right of public assembly (fig. 22). It is also the site of the Magazine and the later Courthouse (built in 1770). These buildings assert respectively the citizen's right to bear arms and to defend life and property; they also testify to the importance of local government. Just beyond the west side of the Market Square is the church and the cross axis, which extends out on one side of the Duke of Gloucester Street. This area, the Palace Green, is 200 feet wide and 1,000 feet long. The Governor's Palace terminates the vista on one side, and there is no terminal vista in the opposite direction, at the intersection. The city's plan expressed the three-pronged separation of government powers in a triangular relationship. It was a clear precedent for L'Enfant's plan for Washington. Nicholson's location of Bruton Parish Church without an axis or vista reflected the reduced role of religion in democratic public life, and the future separation of church and state.

The unusual characteristic that the plans for Annapolis and Williamsburg share is their three-dimensional quality. In each, the architecture of the principal buildings was coordinated with the city plan to form an integrated composition.[121] By contrast, as John Reps notes about the more typical settlement plans of Virginia and Maryland,

one can scarcely contend that the surviving plats indicate any great skill in or attention to the planning of towns. Furthermore, all evidence points to the conclusion that their planners scarcely considered the third dimension of architecture at the time of their layout . . . It is just this lack of noteworthy features in early tidewater towns that makes so remarkable the achievement of planning the capital cities of the two colonies . . .[122]

Washington was familiar with both Annapolis and Williams-

burg, and it is possible that their three-dimensional planning, particularly at Williamsburg, as well as the use of axes and vistas to buildings, suggested how a well-wrought city plan could express the character of the new republic's unique system of government. His subsequent actions all point to this recognition: He retained the services of L'Enfant and immediately approved of the plan he designed.

THE AMERICAN BALANCE OF PRECEDENT AND INVENTION. L'Enfant possessed an eye and mind skilled in the classical architectural tradition. To express meaning through the creation and organization of beautiful elements, he was able to draw on a complex language of form. This language enabled him to make distinctions of great importance by his subtle design and placement of related buildings; to conceive of a series of gear-like squares set in a street system

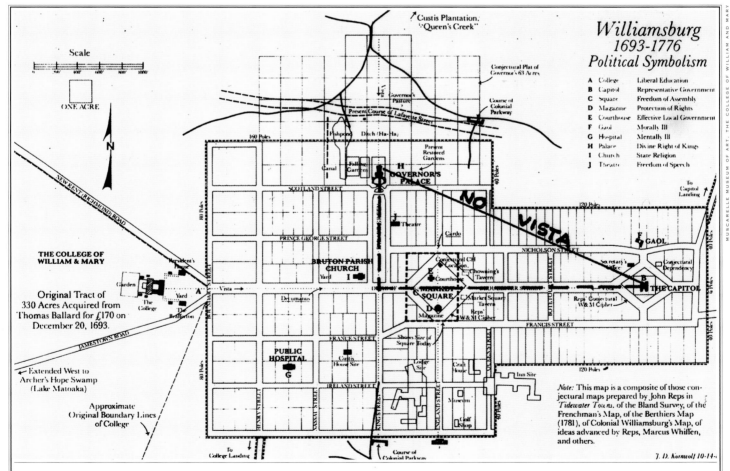

FIG. 21 *In 1699, Nicholson designed the Virginia State capital at Williamsburg. This plan uses a grid and cross-axial arrangement of the two main streets. The Capitol and College of William and Mary are located at either end of the main axis. The Governor's Palace is at one end of the cross axis.*

FIG. 22 *The Market Square, an agora-like space that articulates the right of public assembly, is located near the crossing of the axes in the center of Williamsburg.*

of superimposed diagonal and orthogonal grids; to create a variety of public squares and parks; and to imbue the entire design with artful and complex iconography. But it is the special genius of L'Enfant and his great client that they were able to take architectural forms and ideas that had previously been used to assert the ancient prerogatives of kings, aristocrats, and bishops, and to transform and expand their meanings to express the tenets of the young democracy. In L'Enfant's vision, a new sense of beauty and meaning of form were fused into a grand plan that still, after two hundred years, animates the organization of the city. Against the sprawling metropolitan area that has grown up around it during the past decades, the strength and integrity of this vision still stand out.

The classical tradition is passed on in each generation by creative minds that integrate the unique circumstances of the present with the best models of the past. Because he was French-born and academically trained, L'Enfant was steeped in European sources from which he no doubt drew inspiration. But the American founders were launching a new nation and a new type of government. As the representatives of this republic drafted and ratified the Constitution, they intended a very different balance between the use of precedent and invention than the one practiced by their English and European counterparts, and this perspective colored the approach of the most perceptive artists, architects, and patrons to architectural design and city planning. The contrasting attitudes of the first great architect of the republic, Benjamin Henry Latrobe, and of James Madison, architect of the Constitution, serve to illustrate some of the ways in which tradition was broached.

When Latrobe addressed the Society of Artists of the

United States in 1811, he predicted that the design of America's future towns, cities, and buildings would continue to be based on classical ideals: "The days of Greece may be revived in the woods of America and Philadelphia become the Athens of the western world."[123] The analogy of Athens, the first democratic city-state, suggests that Latrobe saw architecture as emerging from the heritage of ancient Greece, a past recreated in his mind both by records of the ruins and by graphic reconstructions. To acknowledge the Athenian ancestry of American democracy was the conventional Greek-revival viewpoint, which Latrobe shared with other English and European architects, as well as with essayists, poets, and philosophers. The past was a lens for viewing the future.

Very different and much more challenging was Madison's vision as outlined two decades earlier in *The Federalist* in 1787: "Is it not the glory of the people of America, that, whilst they have paid a decent regard to the opinions of former times and other nations, they have not suffered a blind veneration for antiquity, for customs, or for names, to overrule the suggestions of their own good sense, the knowledge of their own situation and the lessons of their own experience?" Madison was challenged by situations for which no paradigms existed, such as the struggle to establish a new form of government:

Had no important step been taken by the leaders of the Revolution for which a precedent could not be discovered, no government established of which an exact model did not present itself, the people of the United States might . . . at best have been laboring under the weight of some of those forms which have crushed the liberties of the rest of mankind. Happily for America, happily, we trust, for the whole human race, they pursued a new and more noble course. They accomplished a revolution which has no parallel in the annals of human society: They reared the fabrics of governments which have no model on the face of the globe.[124]

Madison's understanding of the past was more radical than Latrobe's. He saw it as a wellspring of experience, to be con-

sulted for guidance. Thus he and Hamilton analyzed the role of the Amphictyonic Council in ancient Greece to better understand "the tendency of federal bodies rather to anarchy among the members, than to tyranny in the head."[125]

L'Enfant's similar point of view emerges in a letter he wrote to Jefferson on April 4, 1791. He wished to compare well-resolved designs with "deffective ones," to "unite" the "useful with the commodius," and to recognize local customs. In his touchingly strained English, he explained:

I would reprobate the Idea of Imitating and that contrary of Having this Intention it is my wish and shall be my endeavour to delineate on a new and original way the plan the contrivance of which the President has left to me without any restriction soever. Yet the contemplation of what exists of well improved situation, [g]iven the parrallel of these with deffective ones, may serve to suggest a variety of new Ideas and is necessary to refine and strengthen the Judgement particularly in the present instance when having to unite the useful with the commodious and agreeable viewing these will by offering means of comparing enable me the better to determine with a certainty the propriety of a local which offer Extensive field for combinations.[126]

L'Enfant's method of "uniting" various qualities to create new "combinations" is strikingly similar to Madison's description, in *Federalist* No. 37, of the founder's task as one of combining various qualities of government that had been unsuccessfully melded in past models. This is why, he explains, the past should not be idealized or copied but studied and critically evaluated.[127]

For L'Enfant, the methodological choice was between "imitating," or basing the design on known and relevant models, and delineating in "a new and original way." Even if a novel approach were taken, the design should nevertheless be tested by comparison with both successful and unsuccessful examples of similar projects in order "to refine and strengthen . . . Judgement." For this reason he asked Jefferson to lend him copies of plans of other cities. Jefferson clarified his own ideas about the use of approved models from former epochs in his reply to L'Enfant on April 10, 1791:

Whenever it is proposed to prepare plans for the Capitol, I should prefer the adoption of some one of the models of antiquity, which have had the approbation of thousands of years; and for the President's House I should prefer the celebrated fronts of modern buildings, which have already received the approbation of all good judges.[128]

For major public buildings, Jefferson believed a model that stood the test of centuries was essential. Lesser buildings permitted a greater range of aesthetic speculation. Regarding new projects for which no direct precedent existed, aesthetic freedom was, of course, inevitable. Twenty-five years later, when he was planning his architectural masterpiece, the "academical village," Jefferson adopted a more Madisonian approach to using models from the past.

L'ENFANT AND PRECEDENT. It was in the Madisonian spirit of exploring new realms and ideals, while sustaining the conventions, traditions, and language of classical architecture and city planning, that L'Enfant approached the design of the new federal city. The past offered guidance and inspiration, but not specific answers or much support. As we have noted, there were only three American models to which Washington and L'Enfant could turn for the expression of political ideals in a city plan. The most important was Governor Francis Nicholson's 1699 plan of Williamsburg, Virginia, with its expression of the separation of powers set in a triangular relationship and the Market Square articulating the right of public assembly (refer to fig. 22). A clear forerunner of what L'Enfant would plan for Washington, Williamsburg had been an outgrowth of Nicholson's earlier design for Annapolis of 1694, where *rond-points* were used as sites for statehouse and church.[129] These buildings, as opposed to open space, became the focal points of the city's plan in which the use of symbolism to integrate form and meaning made Nicholson unique as an urban designer. A

third precedent was Jefferson's first plan for the complex of state government buildings at Richmond, a design that proposed a series of public squares, with separate buildings for the General Assembly and for the governor of the state.[130]

A dearth of precedent put L'Enfant in a position similar to that of the nation's new Supreme Court, which, as it began deliberating was compelled to create a conceptual base for its operation. In 1793, when the Court wrote its first substantial opinion, Justice James Wilson recognized that the Court could not appeal to any precedents built up from its own cases, and so he found it necessary to speak first about "the principles of general jurisprudence."[131] Similarly, L'Enfant had to chart new territory relying on the approbation of "good judges," though the achievements and errors of the past were also available for guidance. To a greater extent than Latrobe, Thomas Bulfinch, Thomas U. Walter, and the architects of the Capitol who succeeded them, L'Enfant understood the balance of precedent and invention that also inspired the Federalist papers and the Constitution. With the goal of visibly representing the latter document, he constructed his plan part by part. First, he explored the site in order to grasp its physical characteristics and to find prominent features that could be used for sites of the Congress House, President's House, and other key buildings. He then established the street system, locating the Mall, a canal, and a series of public plazas to form an armature on which buildings could be arranged. This skeleton was fleshed out with ideas drawn from L'Enfant's recollections of Paris, from French gardens such as those at Marly, and from his knowledge of other city plans. The force of his inspiration enabled him to transform French planning ideas—which typically expressed the centralization of royal power and, as such, would have been inappropriate in planning Washington, D.C.—to suit the new purpose of democracy. L'Enfant's life had followed a similar course. He had been a royalist in France, but later, in 1784, had described himself as "well impregnated with the spirit of republican government."[132] He became a citizen of the United States, and in a moving statement of his allegiance, signed his plan for the nation's capital city "Peter Charles L'Enfant."

L'Enfant may have relied on some European sources for the initial expression of his ideas, but we must look elsewhere for his fundamental inspiration. Except for the few letters written by Washington and Jefferson, L'Enfant's own notes and correspondence, and, most important, the plan itself, no documentation of sources or influences has been found. This investigation has tried to suggest that among the circumstances that fundamentally affected his thinking, four ideas dominated: the ideals of the statesmen who created the republic; President Washington's vision of a new capital city; the political role of architecture and city planning at the time; and the balance between precedent and invention that characterized the American mind after the Revolution.

◆

THE PLAN UNFOLDS

As we noted, the plan of Washington, D.C., is a physical embodiment of the Constitution, the "grand idea" that had been only recently adopted to unify the young nation and define its government. While L'Enfant understood this important programmatic issue at an early stage, his approach to planning the city had to be tempered by the realities of geography, geology, topography, landscape, aspect, and existing development. The government had only limited means and its leaders wished to establish the capital in a very short time. He could not alter the site in any significant way, as he lacked the resources to hire enough laborers. Thus, existing site conditions had to be exploited to maximum advantage.

On March 31, 1791, after meeting with local land-holders, Washington informed Jefferson that L'Enfant should begin planning the new capital: "the whole shall be surveyed and laid off as a city (which major L'Enfant is now directed to do)."[133] Having arrived in Georgetown just over three weeks earlier, on March 9, 1791, L'Enfant could complete his topographical survey map of the site and begin developing the plan based on ideas he and Washington had discussed on March 29 and 30.

L'Enfant described his approach in three documents: a report of March 26, 1791, prepared for his first meeting at the site with Washington; his letter to Washington of June 22, 1791, which described the early draft of the plan; and the text he wrote on the plan submitted to Washington in August. He would proceed first by studying the topography and character of the site or, in L'Enfant's odd wording, "the general distribution of the grand local." Then he would find prominent sites, "principal points to which I wished making the rest [of the city] subordinate," for locating important buildings and open spaces.[134]

The site was a rectangular area lying southwest of the higher land that formed the northern edge of L'Enfant's plan. Its original topography had a formative impact on what evolved into four distinct areas: the low river terrace of Tiber Creek, which became the Mall; Jenkins' Hill, adopted as the site of the "Congress House"; the irregular terraces on the north side of Tiber Creek, which L'Enfant described as a ridge at the Tiber "entrance" with a view "10–12 miles down the Potowmack" used for the "presidial palace"; and the lower area of the upper Tiber River valley[135] (figs. 23 a & b & fig. 24). The Tiber, often called Goose Creek, was a stream that ran parallel to the present Constitution Avenue.[136]

LOCATIONS OF PRINCIPAL BUILDINGS. L'Enfant now required only one more item of basic information to begin his plan: a list of essential buildings. To this end, he wrote Jefferson on April 4, 1791:

I Shall in the mean while, sir, beg for Every information respecting all what may in your jugement appear of most immediate importance to attend to as well as relating to Every desirable Establishement which it will be well to foresee, although delaying or perhaps leaving the Execution thereof to a natural succession of time to Effect . . . The number and nature of the publick building with the necessary appendix I Should be glad to have a Statement of as speedily as possible.[137]

DON HAWKINS

FIGS. 23 A & B *The original topography of the site of the new capital has been recreated by Don Hawkins based on survey maps used to lay out the streets. The topography had a formative impact on L'Enfant's plan. (a) There are four distinct areas: the low river terrace of Tiber Creek, which became the Mall; the high point of the site, Jenkins Hill, which evolved into the site of the Capitol; and the ridge on the north side of Tiber Creek, which was used for the White House. The fourth zone is the lower area of the upper Tiber Creek (b).*

Although there is no record of Jefferson's response, it may be assumed that L'Enfant was given the information and that he probably discussed the placement of important buildings with Jefferson and Washington.

Now L'Enfant started to work in earnest on the planning. He outlined his method in a report to the President dated June 22, 1791:

My whole attention was given to the combination of the general distribution of the grand local . . . having first determined some principal points to which I wished making the rest subordinate I next made the distribution regular with streets at right angle north-south and east west but afterwards I opened others on various directions as avenues to and from every principal places wishing by this not merely to contrast with the general regularity . . . but principally to connect each part of the city with more efficacy by . . . making the real distance less from place to place in menaging on them a reisprocity [reciprocity] of sight and making them thus seemingly connected promot a rapide stellement [settlement] over the whole.[138]

First he established "the principal points," or main features of the plan, and from these he selected the suitable sites for major buildings. The prominence of each site, its views to other sites and to surrounding physical features, and its relative importance in the overall plan were the prime factors that determined suitability. In an undated note thought to have been given to the President at the end of their March meeting in Georgetown, L'Enfant observed, "The most desirable positions offer for to erect the Publique Edifices thereon—from these height very grand build[i]ng would rear with a majestic aspect over the Country round and might be advantageously seen From Twenty mile off."[139] This approach is confirmed by L'Enfant's note to the text on his final plan describing his working method. His "Observations explanatory of the Plan," at 1, state: "The positions for the different Grand Edifices and for the several Grand Squares or areas ... were first determined on the most advantageous ground commanding the most extensive prospects ..."

The location of the "Grand Edifices" was worked out in collaboration with Washington. In his diary for June 28, the President wrote: "I went out with Majrs. L'Enfant and Ellicott to take a more perfect view of the ground, in order to decide finally on the spots on which to place the public buildings." The next day, the diary continues: "I called the Several subscribers [property owners] together and made known to them the Spots on which I meant to place the build-

FIG. 24 *Andrew Ellicott, who surveyed the boundaries of the federal city, drew this version of L'Enfant's plan in 1793. It shows how well the new city nestles into the area between the surrounding hills, to the north and east, and the Potomac and Anacostia Rivers, to the south and west.*

ings for the P. & Executive departments of the Government and for the Legislature ... and in the removal of the Presidents house more westerly for the advantage of higher ground."[140] A year later Washington was still preoccupied with these matters and corresponded with David Stuart, one of the commissioners, expressing concern that the size of the square allotted to the President's House not be diminished.[141]

CAPITOL AND WHITE HOUSE. L'Enfant selected sites for the Capitol, the White House, and the Department of State. His report to the President of June 22, 1789, described "the west of Jenkins Heights which stands as a pedestal waiting for a monument" as the best site for the "congressional building." He added, "I am confident, were all the wood cleared from the ground no situation could stand in competition with this (fig. 25). Some might require less labor to be rendered agreeable but after all assistance of arts none ever would be made so grand and all others would appear but of secondary nature."[142] It is important to note that on his final plan L'Enfant designated the Capitol as the "Congress

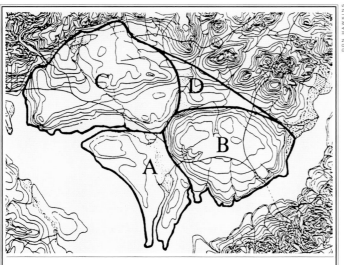

FIG. 23B *Map showing four distinct geographical areas (see figure 23a).*

House." The specific domestic connotation, growing out of colonial experience, was modified after his services were terminated. On the later version of L'Enfant's plan, prepared and signed by Andrew Ellicott, it is named the Capitol, most likely at Jefferson's insistence.[143]

L'Enfant recommended the "ground on the west side of the Tiber entrance," which would "stand to the view of the whole city," as the site of the Presidential residence. This decision effectively established the size and site of the Mall. His report then described the location of "three grand Departments of State contiguous to the principal Palace and on the way leading to the Congressional House" (fig. 26). Also on his final plan, L'Enfant replaced the designation

"Palace" with "House" for the President's residence. In doing so, he was expressing the idea that citizenship in a constitutional government is the prime political office.[144] All other offices are secondary, and office-bearers, whether elected or appointed, serve for a limited period of time. We may talk of changing administrations, but the ideals of government by the people remain unchanged. Thus, Lincoln would never tire of saying that his role was that of a servant to those who elected him.

STREET SYSTEM. Using the sites of prominent buildings as fixed points, L'Enfant developed a grid of streets that created the city's north-south and east-west axes (fig. 27). A system of diagonal streets was superimposed on the orthog-

FIG. 25 *L'Enfant described Jenkins Hill as a pedestal waiting to receive a monument. This quality is aptly illustrated in a painting by William D. McCleod, ca. 1844. The new Capitol on its hill is seen from the site of present-day Union Station. The sparse development on the north side illustrates Charles Dickens' comment in 1842 that Washington was a "City of Magnificent Intentions."*

FIG. 26 City of Washington From Beyond the Navy Yard *(1833), by George Cooke, shows the Capitol on Jenkins Hill, the White House, and the developing city. The artist is looking across the Anacostia River. The Navy Yard occupies a prominent site on the river.*

onal grid to "connect each part of the city with more effi-cacy . . . *and making the real distance less from place to place*" by taking advantage of reciprocal views from one site to another. These streets also gave unity to the city plan. As important features of the plan, L'Enfant noted the canal, Mall, market, harbor, cascade, squares, a national church, naval column, Mount Vernon Square, navy yard, naval hos-pital, and Washington Circle. He also mentioned the impor-tance of connecting his new road system to existing roads leading to surrounding towns across the Anacostia ferry, Bladensburg, and Georgetown.

The topography of the site may have played an impor-tant role in the development of the combined orthogonal and diagonal street system. For example, the Georgetown-Anacostia ferry road, now Pennsylvania Avenue, is parallel to the line of hills that form the northern edge of L'Enfant's plan (refer to fig. 24). This initially may have established the alignment of one set of the diagonal avenues. A second road, symmetrical about the Capitol's axis, now Maryland Avenue, starts in the east at the Bladensburg Road and fits neatly into the Tiber valley as it turns in a northeasterly direction. In an attempt to document L'Enfant's thought process, William T. Partridge has asserted that two roads existing at the time suggested to L'Enfant the placement of the two most impor-tant thoroughfares: Pennsylvania and Maryland avenues.[145] The latter was developed from the main road to Bladensburg, which entered the city site at what is now the intersection of Maryland Avenue and Fifteenth Street, N.E., continued in

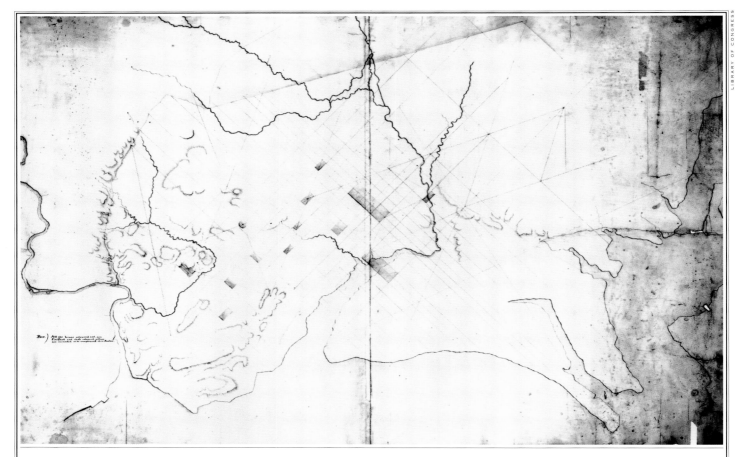

FIG. 27 *The Street System. An early sketch by L'Enfant shows how he used the Capitol, White House, and other prominent places as fixed points in the new city. From this beginning he developed a grid of streets that set up the city's north-south and east-west axes and the open space that became the Mall.*

the direction of Jenkins' Hill, which it skirted, and then proceeded north of Carrollsburg to the Potomac. Similarly, the existing road between Georgetown and the Eastern Branch drawbridge suggested to L'Enfant the location for Pennsylvania Avenue. These two diagonal roads met on the east-west axis of the Capitol, intersecting it at the same angles.

As these two roads are forced to negotiate their way around Jenkins' Hill, using the valley formed by St. James Creek and the Tiber, they each form a crank. Elaborating this crank by developing a set of ten more radial streets to focus on the Capitol provided a design feature that could then be repeated at the White House and other important sites. L'Enfant integrated the diagonal avenues into the plan by using them to connect important buildings and places, like dowels binding together the two grid systems. The Mall, which forms the plan's spine, occupies the flat land of the

Tiber valley from the front of the Capitol extending all the way to the Potomac. By integrating topography and using pre-existing routes, river ferries, and fords, L'Enfant respected existing communities as he built for the future. He also reduced development costs for the fledgling government.

SEPARATION OF POWERS. The concept of separation of powers is embodied in the spatial relationship L'Enfant planned between the Capitol and White House. The two buildings do not face each other. Rather, their primary axes interact at right angles on the Mall, a symbolic reflection of the mandate that these two seats of power not be connected directly, but only through the spine of the Constitution. Pennsylvania Avenue provided a direct link, 1.6 miles long, between the Capitol and White House. The orientation of these two buildings did not recognize this important diagonal route, as if to express the difficult nature of communications between the branches of government they represent and the separateness of their roles. As befits its representational function, the Capitol was centralized; because the President is elected independently, by the nation at large, the White House is less strategically placed.

It was appropriate that such a cornerstone of the Constitution as the separation of powers should be a key component expressed in L'Enfant's design. Separation of powers ensured that the executive branch could not manipulate or assume in whole the responsibilities of the judiciary or the legislature. Washington would stress this balance in his farewell address of 1796: "It is important . . . that the habits of thinking in a free Country should inspire caution in those entrusted with its administration, to confine themselves within their respective Constitutional spheres; avoiding in the exercise of the Powers of one department to encroach upon another. The spirit of encroachment tends to consolidate the powers of all departments in one, and thus to create . . . a real despotism."[146]

President Washington wanted the offices of the executive branch to be near the White House for convenience, and believed that a location too near the Capitol would result in inefficiency, as staff would be at the beck and call of Congress. Although the text accompanying the plan noted that provision had been made for executive departments near the Presidential mansion, no actual site was designated. This failure to provide land suggests that both Washington and L'Enfant believed it was best to leave the final selection of the site to future presidents and commissioners. As a modern commentator would observe, "The failure of the community plan to define clearly a place for the administrative units . . . finds its parallel in the ambiguity of the Constitution itself regarding the place of these units."[147]

MALL. The Mall represented the Constitution, binding the independent states and the separate branches of government into one nation. Without it, the plan would have lacked a strong central focus, as if representing the loosely knit feder-

ation of states under the Articles of Confederation. In his Memorandum of August 19, 1791, which accompanied the plan, L'Enfant referred to the "public walk from under the Federal House to the Potomac" as giving to the "city from the very beginning a superior charm over most of those of the world." He then raised the idea of "appropriating several squares to be allotted to each of the several states. . . ," noting that "these ideas . . . met with your approbation at the beginning."[148] The points may have been discussed at the late March meeting and thus were possibly part of L'Enfant's thinking soon after his arrival at Georgetown. As we have seen, L'Enfant was not satisfied to set aside one or more squares of a grid as park land for public buildings, as Jefferson had done at Richmond and had proposed in his own plan for the federal city. Instead, the idea for a tree-lined public promenade on the axis of the Capitol must have been in his mind from the outset, and he employed the Mall as the plan's unifying element and main axis, distinct in all aspects from the rest. The scale severely limited his choice of its site as well as those of the Capitol and President's House. He wrote:

The gardens [of the President's house] *. . . are connected with the publique walk and avenue to the Congress house in a manner as most* [must] *form a whole as grand as it will be agreeable and convenient to the whole city which form the distribution of the local will have an early access to this place of general resort and all along side of which may be placed play houses, room of assembly, accademies and all such sort of places as may be attractive to the learned and afford diversion of the idle.*[149]

Given the Mall's great sweep, it is difficult to imagine it in any other location. The south side of the White House was bounded by the Potomac River. If the Mall had been on the north side of the White House, this would have mandated placing the Capitol on Meridian Hill, thus removing it far from what was envisioned as the future commercial core of the city (fig. 28). Even more important, the axes of the Mall and the Capitol would have lost their sense of infinite westward extension and, thereby, their important symbolic linkage with the vast American hinterland.

L'Enfant's June 22 report described the Mall as a "grand and majestic avenue," starting at the base of the "congress building," where a cascade 40 feet high and "more than one hundred feet wide" would come "rolling down" and intersect at right angles "with the prospect from the palace at a point which being seen from both I have designated as the proper form to erect a grand equestrian figure." (Here he was referring to the statue of Washington that had been commissioned in 1783 by the Continental Congress.) This unusual arrangement may have been suggested to L'Enfant by André Le Nôtre's plan of the grounds at Chantilly, where two axes at right angles to each other—the old and new approach roads— intersect at an equestrian statue of Anne de Montmorency (fig. 29). By using Pennsylvania Avenue to connect the Capitol and White House, L'Enfant established the hypotenuse of the triangle that expresses the separation of powers.

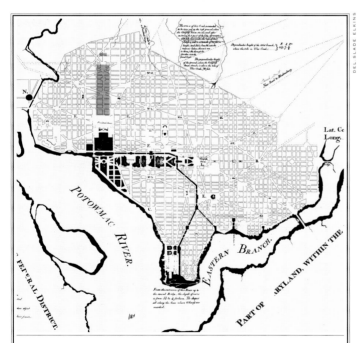

FIG. 28 *If the Mall had been on the north side of the White House, this would have mandated placing the Capitol on Meridian Hill, and the center of government would have been far removed from what L'Enfant envisioned as the future commercial core of the city.*

Presidents, it is instructive to note, are relegated to Pennsylvania Avenue for their inaugural parades, and the Mall's use for the past two hundred years as a venue for public demonstrations, celebrations, and meetings of national scale and significance has justified L'Enfant's aim that it be a "place of general resort." L'Enfant's Mall, which was smaller than it is now, was also intended to offer sites for important buildings facing Constitution and Independence avenues.

The equestrian statue of Washington that L'Enfant proposed for the Mall was to be placed at the crossing of the axes of White House and Capitol, the plan's fulcrum. This, too, is fitting: Washington was the commander of the Revolutionary Army, whose victory had made possible the creation of the United States; he was the first President and *pater patriae* of the nation, and the driving force behind the founding of the federal city. But as proposed, the scale of this statue was too small; it would have been a mere dot in the distance when viewed from the Capitol or White House. Because L'Enfant was a brilliant designer, it is possible to speculate that he might have changed the form of this monument had he not been dismissed soon after completing the plan. The executed monument, Robert Mills's obelisk, is more daring in form and suitable in scale, albeit strangely situated somewhat off the intersection of the axes of White House and Capitol (fig. 30).[150]

SQUARES. The "fifteen squares" in the plan represent the role of the thirteen original states and the first two additional ones. As L'Enfant noted in the text explaining the scheme:

The Squares colored yellow, being fifteen in number, are proposed to be divided among the several States of the Union, for each of them to improve . . . The center of each Square will admit of Statues, Columns, Obelisks, or other ornaments such as the different states may choose to erect: to perpetuate not only the memory of such individuals whose counsels or Military achievements were conspicuous in giving liberty and independence to this Country; but also those whose usefulness hath rendered them worthy of general imitation, to invite the youth of succeeding generations to tread in the paths of those sages, or heroes whom their Country has thought proper to celebrate.[151]

FIG. 29 *L'Enfant's unusual placement of an equestrian statue of Washington at the crossing of the axes of the Capitol and the White House may have been suggested by André Le Nôtre's plan of the grounds at Chantilly. Here two axes at right angles intersect at an equestrian statue of Anne de Montmorency.*

L'Enfant further noted on the plan that the squares would be most "advantageously and reciprocally seen from each other, and as equally distributed over the whole city district and connected by spacious avenues." This network was independent of the Mall and thereby reinforced the importance of each state's own sphere of authority under the Constitution (fig. 31). The system of streets and avenues is designed in relation to the Mall, but is also adjusted, with an organic asymmetry, to the contour of the land and rivers. The statues L'Enfant intended for the squares, as well as the later ones of Jefferson, Grant, and Lincoln in monuments on the Mall, and of Jackson in Lafayette Square, would be intimate in scale and immediate in impact, appropriate in commemorating citizens whose courage and exemplary conduct make them worthy of emulation.

CANAL. Principal sites and a road system in hand, L'Enfant went on to transform Tiber Creek into a canal from the Potomac to Jenkins' Hill, where it turned south to the Eastern Branch. Here he planned wharves and warehouses, with the canal encouraging commerce by providing convenient transport to markets and stores. He varied the width of the canal to establish water features on one side of the Mall, below the White House and Capitol, and at the foot of Eighth and Twelfth streets. A number of similar water features, related to fountains and squares, were specified for the southeast quadrant of the city.

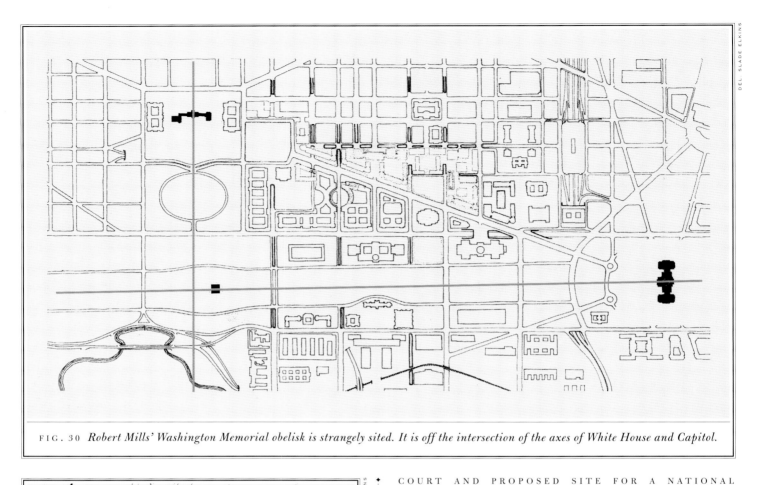

FIG. 30 *Robert Mills' Washington Memorial obelisk is strangely sited. It is off the intersection of the axes of White House and Capitol.*

FIG. 31 *L'Enfant planned a network of squares throughout the federal city and proposed that individual states erect statues of exemplary citizens to occupy them. This network was independent of the Mall as if to emphasize each state's own sphere of authority under the Constitution.*

COURT AND PROPOSED SITE FOR A NATIONAL CHURCH. In a memorandum to the President dated August 19, 1791, which probably accompanied the final plan that was to be engraved, L'Enfant described unspecified sites associated with squares for "Judiciary Courts, the National Bank, and grand Church, the playhouse, markets, and exchange."[152] L'Enfant proposed housing the Supreme Court in a building near Fourth Street between the White House and the Capitol, a position that reflected the judiciary's role as the third branch of government. The location was not so critical a component of the plan as Jenkins' Hill or the site of the White House; it reflected, perhaps, that the Justices, because they are appointed to permanent positions, are sheltered from pressure both from within and outside government. At the time, the role of the Supreme Court was not regarded as pivotal, which may explain why the Court was soon assigned space on the Capitol's ground floor rather than in a building of its own. This placement may also have been a response to then current ideas that judicial authority should be modest and inconspicuous in its overt claims. For example, Montesquieu stressed the use of the jury system as a means of avoiding the hatred that might be attached to the court's punitive function were it not made, in a sense, "invisible."[153] Hamilton referred to the judiciary's "silent influence" on the other branches of government, which may anticipate its resistance to unconstitutional projects. Only in our own century was the Supreme Court given prominent quarters on the east side of the Capitol, with a monumental building designed by Cass Gilbert and completed in 1935.

An important aspect of L'Enfant's plan that failed to win approval was his proposal for a national church. The notes on the plan, at References D, described it as a "Church . . . intended for National Purposes . . . and assigned to the special uses of no particular Sect or denomination, but equally open to all."[154] Further, in the memorandum of August 19, 1791, which accompanied the plan, the suggestion was made to provide "a free donation to every particular religious society of ground for a house of worship."[155] L'Enfant may not have fully understood all the implications of the Constitution's separation of church and state, and neither of these suggestions was given much weight by the commissioners who supervised building the federal city. We also should remember that he was working at breakneck speed, and that he never had an opportunity to revise the first complete draft of his plan. That no religious building would come to occupy a site of axial importance in the city was a fitting reflection of the separation of church and state, and the ascendancy of the idea of citizen's natural rights over the divine right of kings.

MANY CENTERS. L'Enfant's plan of Washington has numerous centers. The Capitol and White House are the most important; the Supreme Court, other government buildings, and the state squares are minor ones. The Mall and the grids of streets and state avenues facilitate communication, provide views to state squares and important buildings, and therefore serve as links of a metaphorical chain binding the nation together. They also extend to the edge of the plan, as if poised to penetrate the surrounding landscape and unite the expanding nation in a network of communication centered in Washington. Further, the street system ensures a sense of "equality of advantages" among the various parts of the city while emphasizing differences in aspect, topography, and character of landscape.

The Capitol on Jenkins' Hill, with its great dome, is the central feature of the plan. This accorded with Washington's view that "the election of the different branches of Congress by the freemen . . . is the pivot which turns the first wheel of government, a wheel which communicates motion to all the rest."[156] L'Enfant incorporated this metaphor by making the "Congress House" the "pivot" of twelve spoke-like radiating avenues. As a main gear locks into auxiliary gears and imparts motion to them, so the Congress activates the other departments and branches of government. These auxiliary gears are represented in the plan of the city by its many plazas and squares (fig. 32).

FIG. 32 *As a main gear locks into auxiliary gears and imparts motion to them, so the Congress activates the other departments and branches of government. These auxiliary gears are represented in the plan of Washington, D.C., by the intersection of important streets in the diagonal and orthogonal street system.*

FAÇADES AND INTERIORS TO AUGMENT THE PLAN'S ICONOGRAPHY. L'Enfant intended that the expression of fundamental political ideals extend beyond the plan of the city to the architecture of public buildings. Both he and the nation's founders believed that the exteriors and interiors of such buildings should inspire citizens to apply these ideals in their daily lives. In this way, architecture and city planning could help to realize the injunction, eloquently expressed by the Virginia Declaration of Rights, that "no free government, nor the blessings of liberty, can be preserved to any people, but by a firm adherence to justice . . . [and] by frequent recurrence to fundamental principles."[157] The subsequent design of the federal Capitol, its signature dome rising above the Washington skyline, was not only a hemisphere in the tradition of the ancient Roman Pantheon, but also a triumphant proclamation to all the world that in the United States the rights and prerogatives of Europe's kings, archbishops, and aristocrats belong to all citizens.

This concept would be understood by future architects of the Capitol. Its material form, as visualized by William Thornton, Benjamin Henry Latrobe, and Charles Bulfinch, and later redesigned by Thomas U. Walter, was not revolutionary or even especially innovative. Rather, it was the Capitol's new meaning that made it one of the most radical architectural statements in history. Unlike its predecessors, the Capitol rotunda shelters neither royal nor religious icons; instead it is an open space within which citizens may meet and discuss legislation to shape their future. The space was planned as the conceptual center of the new democracy, a notion Madison articulated when he asserted that the seat of government "shall be in a position from which it could contemplate with the most equal eye, and sympathize most equally with, every part of the nation."[158] The room was decorated with paintings illustrating the story of the republic's founding, the culmination of which is General Washington resigning his commission to return to his plantation as a private citizen. House and Senate chambers were placed to either side of the rotunda, off the Mall's main axis and on the Capitol's minor axis, embodying the concept that in a democracy, elected representatives do not constitute the government; rather, it is "We the People," the heart and soul of the nation, who occupy the center (fig. 33).

The rotunda's axes were integrated into L'Enfant's plan of Washington and extend north, south, east, and west to symbolize the unity of the nation and equal access for all to the heart of government. These ideas are reinforced by the twelve radial avenues that focus on the Capitol and lead to the building's many entrances, inviting citizens to observe House and Senate debates and to exchange views with congressional representatives. Jefferson would write to Latrobe on July 12, 1812, that the rotunda was "the first temple dedicated to the sovereignty of the people, embellishing with Athenian taste the course of a nation looking far beyond the range of Athenian destinies."[159] Earlier, Latrobe's plan of the Capitol designated the rotunda a "Hall of the People."[160] In passionate measures of stone and mortar, the architecture of the Capitol echoes the words of John Adams: "There is but one element of government, and that is the People."[161]

From the beginning, the significance of this extraordinary architectural iconography was sometimes ignored. Immediately after Washington's death, for example, William Thornton proposed that the first President be buried in a tomb below the crypt floor, one level beneath the rotunda.[162] Other such proposals would follow. But Washington had wisely chosen to be buried as a private citizen rather than as a mythical figure, almost a demigod. He knew well that the elevation of a mortal to such heights would threaten the foundation of democracy. Simply as Mr. Washington, he remains, to this day, a more potent ideal and a remarkable figure in American history.

A CITY DEVOTED ENTIRELY TO DEMOCRATIC GOVERNMENT. While L'Enfant located a harbor and naval yard in the plan, he set aside no specific areas for industry. Washington was conceived as a city whose raison d'être was

SECTION THROUGH DOME OF U.S. CAPITOL

FIG. 33 *The Capitol is planned with the House and Senate chambers on either side of the rotunda, on the building's cross axis but off the Mall's main axis. The Capitol Rotunda is a space for citizens to gather. Located at the intersection of the axes of city and Capitol, it embodies the concept that in a democracy it is "We the People" who are the heart and soul of the nation.*

democratic government. As such it was intended to be dependent on the rest of the nation, especially the West, for agriculture, industry, and commerce. In developing the ideas for the new Capital, L'Enfant also raised the issue of defense against foreign aggression. In the September 11, 1789, letter to Washington offering his services to plan the new city, he suggested that consideration be given to the creation of a series of coastal fortifications on the Atlantic. He first raised this subject in 1784 and even presented the idea to Congress.[163] Because one of the city's purposes was to unify the nation, it was believed that no provisions should be made for its defense against internal strife. This accorded with the founders' views, as well as those of the first Congress, for such barriers would have violated the very purpose of the city; its strength lay in its vulnerability, and in its major function, which was, as it remains, democratic government.

THE FUNCTION OF ARCHITECTURE IN A DEMOC-RACY. For Washington and L'Enfant, city planning was no mere exercise in the manipulation of urban form; it was the creation of what one recent commentator has called a

"great didactic machine."[164] Such a purpose may be realized when a city plan and the architecture of its public buildings serve to integrate political ideals into the daily lives of citizens, helping to unify the nation by celebrating the unique values on which it is founded. The expression in architecture and city planning of the principles of a democratic society, based on the rule of law, can reinforce traditional moral, ethical, and political beliefs. This function is especially important in a democracy, as authority is vested in the people and not in repressive forces such as military might, police power, terror, or divine right. For President Washington it was also important that the new capital be realized by an exemplary democratic planning process. His reliance on patient persuasion and tact, rather than expropriation, in acquiring the land and securing the cooperation of local landowners remains a model of the proper exercise of authority.

Washington, D.C., then, was intended as the first exemplar of the values of citizenship in a republic, and, as L'Enfant noted in his June 22, 1791, report to the President, the new Capital was to "serve as models for all subsequent undertak-

FIG. 34 *In 1902, the McMillan Commission presented a plan for the future of Washington, D.C. It was based on L'Enfant's forgotten plan of 1791. Additional vistas were added with the proposed memorials for Lincoln and Jefferson. This bird's-eye view of the general plan, from a point 4,000 feet above Arlington, was rendered in 1902 by F.L.V. Hoppin.*

ing[s]" in city planning.[165] One is apt to forget that the political freedom and economic opportunity we now take to be the rights of all citizens were at that time just beginning to be accepted, and on a scale never before contemplated in the history of humanity. It was this momentous change that was formalized in the city's plan.

L'ENFANT'S INFLUENCES. Many commentators have asserted that L'Enfant's plan is an outgrowth of the influence of French gardens and French urbanism—of Le Nôtre's plan of Versailles, the Tuileries Palace gardens, the Place de la Concorde, and what was then just the beginning of the Avenue des Champs-Élysées in Paris.[166] Before the scope of this influence can be properly evaluated, it is important to look more carefully at the claim and also to note how very different L'Enfant's plan is from these French prototypes.

The Capitol is the focus of twelve radial streets; the White House of nine. L'Enfant intended that these vistas from one important building to another reduce distance, avoid the monotony of a grid, and unify the city (fig. 34). At Versailles no avenues converge on the garden façade of the palace or on the buildings in the gardens. Even the Grand Trianon is pulled back so as not to interrupt the continuity of the avenues focused on its forecourt—except for the one forming its main axis. A circular, but empty, space just beyond the far end of the canal has nine avenues radiating out from it, and seven other avenues focus on the head of the canal itself. Thus the theme of converging radial avenues serves very different ends at Washington and at Versailles.

Further, study of the plan and seventeenth-and eighteenth-century perspectives of the garden at Versailles, as seen from the palace, show that the diagonals cut through the forest are barely discernible. They would have been even less evident to a person on the ground. No avenues converge on the palace's garden side. The plan shows a large grid of parterres forming an area of transition between palace and canal. The radial avenues focus on the head of the canal, and are restricted to the forests, which the grids relate to the

palace. Both remain separate elements in the plan. This, too, is very different from the plan of Washington, where a systematic lamination of orthogonal and diagonal streets is imposed over the entire area of the plan, and the avenues focus on buildings and other important elements. The central axis at Versailles created by the canal also differs greatly, in form and lack of integration into the architecture of the palace, from the way in which the Mall is locked into the plan of Washington and into the architecture of the Capitol and the White House.

The entrance court of Versailles has three short avenues converging on the gateway of the palace forecourt. L'Enfant used twelve radial avenues to focus on the center of his plan's most important buildings. Finally, one must ask if a garden layout can reasonably be compared to a city plan. L'Enfant and Washington looked across the site of the future city and saw rivers, farms, wilderness, and marsh but envisioned a great metropolis. It is difficult to believe that, as they were conceiving the plan for a great city, their imaginations were molded by the design of a palace garden and forest whose formal symbolism was abhorrent to their republican sensibilities.[167]

L'Enfant was acutely aware of the limited resources at his command and therefore probably imagined that relatively modest buildings, such as those he saw at Georgetown or Philadelphia, would define his plan's squares and streets. Consequently, the large scale of the Place de la Concorde and the Tuileries Palace gardens in Paris probably had more influence on the later plans for Washington prepared by the McMillan Commission than they did on L'Enfant.[168] So while we should prudently acknowledge the importance of L'Enfant's memories of Le Nôtre's gardens, particularly Marly and Chantilly; his appreciation for urban spaces in Paris and smaller French cities like Versailles and Richelieu; his familiarity with plans for fortified towns like Rocroi by Sébastien Le Prestre de Vauban, with their radial patterns of streets; and his recollections of Sixtus V's improvements to

Rome, we should take seriously L'Enfant's own description of his methodology. His precedents may be best understood by observing that residual ideas from Europe, in concert with ideas gleaned from Nicholson's city plans in America, were ready ingredients, waiting to be adapted and transformed into a startlingly new and original creation.

L'ENFANT IS DISMISSED

It had taken L'Enfant only a little more than three months, despite bad weather, to complete the survey and to prepare the first draft of the plan he presented to the President in June 1791—a remarkable achievement. A more refined plan, altered in response to Washington's comments, was completed by August 1791. Six months later, on February 27, 1792, L'Enfant's services were officially terminated.

Though several reasons have been advanced for his dismissal, this event is still difficult to explain. There had been many complaints, primarily from Jefferson and the Commissioners, about L'Enfant's conduct: that he had delayed in securing an engraved plan of the city for use at land sales;[169] that he was responsible for the demolition of a house without recourse to law;[170] that he hindered the commissioners responsible for superintending the realization of the city—all friends of the President—by removing surveyors' stakes because he was dissatisfied with his subordinate role;[171] that he slandered the Commission;[172] that he was uncooperative;[173] and that he refused to acknowledge the Commission's authority.[174] Yet in each of these cases, Washington exonerated L'Enfant after learning the full set of facts governing the situation and L'Enfant's explanation for his conduct.[175] Nevertheless, the cumulative effect of these complaints undercut the President's confidence in L'Enfant's ability. A crisis was precipitated when Commissioner David Stuart wrote the President an eight-page letter filled with accusations against L'Enfant, which, like most of the previous ones, were unsubstantiated. Stuart threw down the gauntlet by writing that the Commissioners at their last meeting had unanimously determined "to give up their enviable offices rather than to be any longer subject to his [L'Enfant's] . . . caprice."[176] This undated letter was probably written in late January or early February 1792, when L'Enfant had been at work for less than a year.

The critical factor in this confrontation was the difference between the vision of L'Enfant and Washington on the one hand and that of the commissioners and Jefferson on the other. Like many committees, the commission preferred to resolve conflicts by balancing interests. Its members resented having to adhere rigidly to the L'Enfant plan, which was to them a mere abstraction; they particularly resented being thwarted when they tried to accommodate its form to political expediency; and most of all, they deeply resented L'Enfant's access to the President. Indeed, the commissioners appear to have avoided any course of action that would have been construed as acceptance of L'Enfant's. They believed that Washington's unequivocal commitment to the L'Enfant plan, and his admiration for the man, made their own task impossible.

For his part, L'Enfant distrusted the commission's methods and believed it was imperative for him to communicate directly with the President. He felt intense loyalty to "my General" and to the integrity of his plan. A bond of mutual admiration between the two men had developed during their consultations and correspondence. It was strengthened by their rides together exploring the site and selecting locations for buildings, as well as by the knowledge that their vision of a great capital was not shared by Jefferson and the others around the President.

Why Jefferson wished to have L'Enfant removed is a more difficult question. As we have noted, Jefferson's vision of the federal city was of a small town at the center of an agrarian nation, a conception that was totally at variance with the L'Enfant plan.[177] He may have taken umbrage at the rejection of his design, or perhaps he hoped to be able to remold the L'Enfant plan into a scheme that would be more to his liking.[178] It is probable that Jefferson did not even see L'Enfant's plan until the end of August, when it was in final form, and that finding his own views so ignored may have added insult to injury. Regardless of what motivated him, his intention can be deduced from the care he exercised to appear unbiased, while never coming to L'Enfant's aid; his acceptance of the commission's unsubstantiated complaints; and his failure to solicit L'Enfant's own version of events.

Jefferson's behavior in the entire matter was hardly that of a Secretary of State with the power to control events; instead he served as the transmitter of tidings between L'Enfant, his accusers, and the President. In this role he raised the issue that ultimately led to L'Enfant's downfall. On November 6, 1791, he wrote to Washington proposing that the commissioners, and not the President, were solely responsible for superintending the realization of L'Enfant's plan: ". . . will not the present afford you a proper occasion of assuring the Commissioners that you leave everything respecting L'Enfant to them."[179] The letter and its subject were unusual, for until then the record suggests that the commissioners had worked amicably with L'Enfant.[180] Further, there was nothing in the enabling legislation, "An Act for Establishing the Temporary and Permanent Seat of the Government of the United States" of July 16, 1790, to support Jefferson's position. Apparently the Secretary of State conveniently forgot that he had worked closely with Representative Madison and the President to establish the precise location and boundaries of the new capital—without informing the commissioners.[181] Nevertheless, Jefferson's letter eventually drove a wedge between patron and planner, and L'Enfant's subsequent woes developed from it.

Jefferson knew that Washington's loyalty to the commissioners, who were politically powerful as well as his close friends and appointees, was stronger than even his great admiration and respect for L'Enfant. Such an understanding is evident from the fact that after L'Enfant's dismissal, Jefferson wrote to Commissioner Thomas Johnson: ". . . there was never a moments doubt about parting with Major L'Enfant rather than with a single Commissioner."[182] This appears to confirm that Jefferson may have been L'Enfant's implacable enemy and that the Secretary's superior understanding of bureaucratic maneuvering had set in motion the events leading to L'Enfant's downfall. In his *Reminiscences*, Benjamin Perley Poore wrote that L'Enfant "was a favorite with Washington, but Jefferson disliked him on account of his connection with the Society of the Cincinnati, and availed himself of his difficulty with the Commissioners to discharge him."[183]

L'Enfant, overwhelmed by work and politically somewhat naive, was unable to defend himself. Most of the time he was not even aware that he was under attack. We do not know why he did not ask Hamilton, for example, for help.[184] Washington appears to have been his only powerful supporter. In addition to his difficult task of establishing the President's office, Washington was compelled between November 1791 and March 1792 to attend to a series of crises. On November 4, 1791, on the northern frontier, General Arthur St. Clair's expeditionary army had been defeated by a coalition of Indian tribes including the Miami, the Wabash, the Delaware, and the Wyendots.[185] The ensuing investigation by the House of Representatives was the first of its kind and posed constitutional problems that the President was forced to address. Jefferson and Hamilton were vying for control of the postal system; there was financial panic in March; and then came the news that Jefferson had decided to resign as Secretary of State at the end of the President's first term. Washington also faced the challenges of creating the long-sought, federally supervised militia recently authorized by Congress; of acting on Hamilton's Report on Manufactures; and of deciding whether he should present himself again for office. It was probably both difficult and tedious for him to address the seemingly endless, and to him trivial and exasperating, quarrels between the commissioners and L'Enfant.

Did Washington fail to adequately support the man

whose work he so admired? It is doubtful that he was ever fully informed of the precise sequence of events that led to L'Enfant's dismissal, or even that he was able to follow the events closely enough to determine responsibility for them. Indeed, Washington's memory of his dealings with L'Enfant may have been distorted by the day-to-day pressures of office; by his fears that L'Enfant's unreasonable behavior, as described by the commissioners' complaints, could delay and jeopardize the entire project; and by his own quick temper, which often caused him to misinterpret certain actions by associates as slights. Such a flaring of temper had led to Hamilton's resignation from his staff in February 1781, though the President's anger usually abated quickly as the facts of a situation came to the fore, and he would apologize or take action to reestablish equilibrium.[186] This kind of misunderstanding may have accounted for Washington's loss of sympathy for L'Enfant's plight during the crucial period from January to March 1792. If so, given the importance of the project and the extraordinary quality of L'Enfant's plan—which so precisely met the President's unusual brief—one cannot help feeling that Washington should have taken the time to ascertain the facts of the situation. By December 1791 the President appeared to have forgotten how closely he and the young artist/engineer had worked together for most of the year, and that it had been he himself, and not L'Enfant, who had periodically presented the fruits of their labor to the commission.[187]

The final indignity was that L'Enfant's name did not appear as author on the published engraving of the plan of Washington, D.C. This omission was allowed to occur despite Washington's instruction to Jefferson on February 22, 1792, that "The Plan I think, ought to appear as the Work of L'Enfant."[188] Washington's wishes were ignored, and L'Enfant's associate, Andrew Ellicott, who had been commissioned by Jefferson to secure the engraving, attached his own name.

L'Enfant left the site of the Federal City and moved to New Jersey to plan the new city of Paterson. It was to be a center for manufacturing. Due to the financial failure of one of the plan's sponsors, L'Enfant then moved to Philadelphia where he was asked to design the house of financier Robert Morris. The latter's bankruptcy led to the abandonment of the incomplete house—a double blow to L'Enfant, who had lent Morris money. Resisting the encouragement of Secretary of State James Monroe, L'Enfant declined an offer made in 1812 of appointment as superintendent of West Point. He did, however, accept the commission to build Fort Mifflin in Philadelphia in 1798 and Fort Washington, on the Potomac south of Alexandria, in 1814. L'Enfant lived in Prince Georges County, Maryland, from 1815 until his death in 1825. He died a poor man.

THE VALUE OF L'ENFANT'S PLAN

In the midst of the disputes over L'Enfant's role, Washington wrote the Commissioners that "I have no scruple in declaring to you (though I do not want him to know it) that I know not where another is to be found, who could supply his place."[189] The Commission's resentment and arrogance drowned out Washington's plea for patience and tolerance. A year later, during the search for a superintendent to realize the plan for the new capital, the President asked, "But where, you may ask, is the character to be found who possesses these qualifications? I frankly answer I know not! Major L'Enfant (who it is said is performing wonders at the new town of Patterson) . . . is the only person . . . that I think fit for it."[190] Washington's deep regret at the loss of his brilliant planner is as obvious as his pride in his protege's accomplishment.

L'Enfant's great achievement was to embody the organizing principles of the Constitution into the skeleton and sinews of his design of the new capital city. The extraordinary growth and vitality of Washington, D.C., testify to the strength of the concepts underlying his plan. It has accommodated the changing needs of the community and nation for two centuries without substantive alteration of its internal matrix. The plan is remarkable for its architectonic brilliance, its integration with its site, and its comprehensive iconography. L'Enfant understood that the duty of the architect or city planner is to articulate not only form, but meaning.

President Washington's written approval of the plan showed the extent to which he concurred with L'Enfant's vision of the new capital, which so gratifyingly reflected his own wishes. The President wrote of L'Enfant on November 20, 1791:

Since my first knowledge of the Gentleman's abilities in the line of his profession, I have viewed him not only as a scientific man, but received one who added considerable taste to professional knowledge; and that, for such employment as he is now engaged in; for projecting public works; and carrying them into effect, he was better qualified than anyone who had come within my knowledge in this Country, or indeed in any other the probability of obtaining whom could be counted upon. I had no doubt, at the same time, that this was the light in which he considered himself; and of course he would be tenacious of his plans as to conceive they would be marred if they underwent any change or alteration . . . Should his services be lost, I know not how to replace them.[191]

The passage of time has proved Washington's confidence to be fully justified. The plan for Washington, D.C., is one of the great benchmarks in the history of city planning. Even though it has been implemented and modified by L'Enfant's successors and by generations of planners, politicians, and administrators, it preserves even now its original structure and meaning. Some observers have claimed, correctly, that closing streets and avenues and implementing other changes to the original plan have diluted its conceptual and aesthetic power.[192] Sadly, this process continues even today. But like the authors of *The Federalist*, L'Enfant understood that his plan for the federal city should not merely satisfy immediate needs. They asserted:

[W]e must bear in mind that we are not to confine our view to the present period, but to look forward to remote futurity.

Constitutions of civil government are not to be framed upon a calculation of existing exigencies, but upon a combination of these with the probable exigencies of ages, according to the natural and tried course of human affairs.[193]

When L'Enfant produced his extraordinary plan, with its configuration of the Mall as spine and organizing element, with Congress House and President's House sited to express the separation of powers, with public squares set like gears and cogs connected by radiating avenues and a system of grid streets, it must have seemed to Washington that a sublime vision was suddenly given physical reality. Supreme realist that he was, Washington understood that the federal city he envisioned would have to remain incomplete until "a century hence, if the Country keeps united . . . will produce a City, though not as large as London, yet of a magnitude inferior to few others in Europe . . ."[194] This prediction, part of a letter he wrote to Sarah Fairfax in 1798, proved correct, for in 1902, 104 years later, the McMillan Commission plan restored L'Enfant's plan and created the modern city we see today. Clearly, both Washington and L'Enfant had their eyes fixed on a point far in the future. Their plan remains so powerful that the meaning of its forms still rings out as loud and clear after the passage of two hundred years as at any time in the past.

An early version of this paper was presented at the symposium The Mall in Washington 1791–1986 *held at the National Gallery of Art, Washington, D.C., in 1987. A shorter version,* "L'Enfant, Washington, and the Plan of the Capital," *was published in* The Magazine Antiques, *July 1991, 112–123. I am indebted to Pamela Scott, James Kornwolf, Willam Allen, and Carroll William Westfall for their criticism and advice.*

Allen, William C. *The Dome of the United States Capitol: An Architectural History.* Senate Document, 102nd Congress, 1st Session. Washington, D.C.: GPO, 1992.

Bennett, George Fletcher. *Early Architecture of Delaware.* Wilmington: Historical Press, 1932.

Bobrick, Benson. *Angel in the Whirlwind.* New York: Simon & Schuster, 1997.

Boyd, Sterling. *The Adam Style in America, 1770-1820.* New York: Garland, 1985.

Brownell, Charles E. and Jeffrey A. Cohen. *The Architectural Drawings of Benjamin Henry Latrobe.* New Haven: Yale University Press, 1994.

Brownell, Charles E., Calder Loth, William M. S. Rasmussen, and Richard Guy Wilson. *The Making of Virginia Architecture.* Charlottesville: University of Virginia Press, 1992.

Custis, George Washington Parke. *Recollections and Private Memoirs of Washington by His Adopted Son George Washington Parke Custis.* New York, 1860.

Eliot, T. S. *Poetry and Drama.* Cambridge, Mass.: Harvard University Press, 1951.

Ferguson, Robert A. *The American Enlightenment 1750-1820.* Cambridge, Mass.: Harvard University Press, 1994.

Ferling, John E. *The First of Men: A Life of George Washington.* Knoxville: University of Tennessee Press, 1988.

Freeman, Douglas Southall. *George Washington, A Biography.* New York: Scribner's, 1948.

Halfpenny, William. *The Practical Builder; or, Workingman's General Assistant.* London, 1774.

Harris, John, and Gordon Higgot. *Inigo Jones, Complete Architectural Drawings.* New York: Harper & Row, 1989.

Harris, John. *The Palladians.* London: Trefoil Books, 1981.

Isaac, Rhys. *The Transformation of Virginia 1740-1790.* Chapel Hill: University of North Carolina Press, 1982.

Jefferson, Thomas. *The Papers of Thomas Jefferson.* 29 vol. to date. Edited by Julian P. Boyd. Princeton, N. J.: Princeton University Press, 1954-.

Jones, Thomas. *History of New York During the Revolutionary War.* New York: Simon & Schuster, 1879.

Kimball, Fiske. *Domestic Architecture of the American Colonies and of the Early Republic.* New York: C. Scribner's, 1922.

Langley, Batty and Thomas Langley. *Ancient Masonry Both in the Theory and in the Practice.* London, 1734.

Langley, Batty and Thomas Langley. *The Builder's Jewel; or, The Youth's Instructor and Workingman's Remembrancer.* London: 1746.

Langley, Batty. *The City and Country Builder's and Workingman's Treasury of Designs: Or the Art of Drawing and Working the Ornamental Parts of Architecture.* London, 1750.

Latrobe, Benjamin Henry. *The Virginia Journals of Benjamin Henry Latrobe, 1795-1798.* Ed. Edward C. Carter II. New Haven: Yale University Press, 1977.

Lossing, Benson J. *George Washington's Mount Vernon.* New York, 1859.

Maccubbin, Robert P. and Peter Martin, Eds. *British and American Gardens in the Eighteenth Century.* Williamsburg, Va.: Colonial Williamsburg Foundation, 1984.

Marshall, William. *Planting and Rural Ornament.* London, 1796.

Martin, Peter. *The Pleasure Gardens of Virginia: From Jamestown to Jefferson.* Princeton, N. J.: Princeton University Press, 1991.

Mavor, William. *"Brissot's Travels," Historical Account of the Most Celebrated Voyages, Travels, and Discoveries from the Time of Columbus to the Present Period.* London, 1797.

McClatchy, J.D. *Twenty Questions.* New York: Columbia University Press, 1998.

McLaughlin, Jack. *Jefferson and Monticello, The Biography of a Builder.* New York: Henry Holt, 1988.

Middleton, Charles. *Designs For Cottage, Farm House, and Country Villas.* London, 1793.

Millar, John Fitzhugh. *The Architects of the American Colonies.* Massachusetts: Barre Publishers, 1968.

Morris, Robert. *Lectures on Architecture.* Farnborough, England: Gregg International Publ., 1971

Morris, Robert. *Select Architecture.* London, 1755; New York: Da Capo Press, 1970.

Morrison, Hugh. *Early American Architecture from the First Colonial Settlements to the National Period.* New York: Oxford University Press, 1952.

Morse, Jedediah. *American Geography; or, A View of the Present Situation of the United States of America.* London, 1792.

Niemcewicz, Julian Ursyn. *Under Their Vine and Fig Tree: Travels through America in 1797-1799, 1805, with some further account of life in New Jersey.* Ed. and Trans. by Metchie J. E. Budka. Elizabeth, New Jersey: Grassman, 1965.

Owen, Scott Campbell. "George Washington's Mount Vernon as British Palladian Architecture." *Thesis presented to the University of Virginia,* 1991.

The Oxford Companion to Gardens. Eds. Susan and Sir Geoffrey Jellicoe. Oxford: Oxford University Press, 1986.

Pain, William. *The Practical Builder or Workingman's General Assistant.* London, 1774.

Palladio. *Four Books of Architecture.* Ed. Isaac Ware. New York: Dover Press, 1965.

Pogue, Dennis J. "Mount Vernon, Transformation of an Eighteenth Century Plantation System." *Historical Archaeology of the Chesapeake.* Eds. Paul A. Shakel and Barbara J. Little. Washington, D. C.: Smithsonian Institution Press, 1994.

Ragsdale, Bruce A. *A Planter's Republic, The Search for Economic Independence in Revolutionary Virginia.* Madison, Wisc.: Madison House, 1996.

Randall, Willard Sterne. *George Washington: A Life.* New York: Henry Holt & Co., 1997.

Rieff, Daniel D. *Small Georgian Houses in England and Virginia, Origins and Development through the 1750s.* Newark, Del.: University of Delaware Press, 1986.

Shakel, Paul and Barbara Little. *Historical Archaeology of the Chesapeake.* Washington, D.C.: Smithsonian, 1994.

Smith, William Loughton. *The Journals of William Loughton Smith, 1790-1791.* Ed. Albert Mathews. Massachusetts, 1917.

Summerson, John. *Inigo Jones.* Harmondsworth: Penguin, 1966.

Upton, Dell. *Holy Things and Profane: Anglican Parish Churches in Colonial Virginia.* Cambridge, Mass.: MIT Press, 1986.

Warville, Jacques Pierre Brissot de. *On America, New Travels in the United States of America Performed in 1788.* London, 1792.

Washington, George. *The Diaries of George Washington.* 6 vols. Eds. Donald Jackson and Dorothy Twohig. Charlottesville: University of Virginia Press, 1976-1979.

Washington, George. *The Papers of George Washington, Colonial Series.* 10 vol. Eds. W.W. Abbott and Dorothy Twohig. Charlottesville: University of Virginia Press, 1983-1995.

Washington, George. *The Papers of George Washington, Confederation Series.* 6 vols. Ed. by W.W. Abbott. Charlottesville: University of Virginia Press, 1992-1997.

Washington, George. *The Papers of George Washington, Revolutionary War Series.* 7 vols. Ed. Dorothy Twohig. Charlottesville: University of Virginia Press, 1985-1997.

Washington, George. *The Writings of George Washington from the Original Manuscript Sources, 1745-1799.* 39 vols. Ed. John C. Fitzpatrick. Washington, D.C.: GPO, 1939-1944.

Waterman, Thomas Tileston. *The Dwellings of Colonial America.* Chapel Hill: University of North Carolina Press, 1950.

Waterman, Thomas Tileston. *Mansions of Virginia.* Chapel Hill: University of North Carolina Press, 1946.

West, Thomas G. *Vindicating the Founders: Race, Sex, Class, and Justice in the Origins of America.* Lanham, Md.: Rowman & Littlefield, 1997.

Wells, Camille, Ed. *Perspectives in Vernacular Architecture II.* Columbia, Mo.: University of Missouri Press, 1986.

Wilstach, Paul. *Mount Vernon, Washington's Home and the Nation's Shrine.* Garden City, N.Y.: Doubleday, 1916.

SELECTED BIBLIOGRAPHY: PART TWO

Adams, Henry. *History of the United States of America during the Administrations of Thomas Jefferson.* New York: Library of America, 1986.

Adler, Mortimer. *We Hold These Truths.* New York: Macmillan, 1987.

Allen, William C. *The Dome of the United States Capitol: An Architectural History.* Washington, D.C.: GPO, 1992.

Arkes, Hadley. *First Things.* Princeton: Princeton University Press, 1986.

Bedini, Silvio A. *Thomas Jefferson, Statesman of Science.* New York: Macmillan, 1990.

Bowling, Kenneth R. *Creating the Federal City, 1774-1800: Potomac Fever.* Washington, D.C.: AIA Press, 1988.

Brown, Roger H. *The Republic in Peril: 1812.* New York: Columbia University Press, 1971.

Bryan, John M., Ed. *Robert Mills, Architect.* Washington, D.C.: AIA Press, 1989.

Caemmerer, H. Paul. *The Life of Pierre Charles L'Enfant.* New York: Da Capo, 1970.

Carroll, John and Mary Ashworth. *George Washington, First in Peace: Volume Seven of the Biography by Douglas Southall Freeman.* New York: Scribner's, 1957.

Ceaser, James W. *Reconstructing America, The Symbol of America in Modern Thought.* New Haven: Yale University Press, 1997.

Egorov, Iurii Alekseevich. *The Architectural Planning of St. Petersburg, Its Development in the 18th and 19th Centuries.* Ed. and Trans. by Eric Dluhosch. Athens, Ohio: Ohio University Press, 1969.

Ferrand, Max, Ed. *The Records of the Federal Convention of 1787.* Rev. ed. New Haven: Yale University Press, 1937.

Flexner, James Thomas. *George Washington and the New Nation: 1783-1792.* Boston: Little Brown, 1969.

Freeman, Douglas Southall. *George Washington.* New York: Scribner's, 1948.

Garvan, Beatrice B. *Federal Philadelphia 1785-1825.* (Exhibition catalog, Philadelphia Museum of Art). Philadelphia: The Museum, 1987.

Gutheim, Frederick and Wilcomb E. Washburn. *The Federal City: Plans & Realities.* Washington, D.C.: Smithsonian Institution, 1976.

Hamilton, Alexander. *The Papers of Alexander Hamilton.* Ed. Harold C. Styrett. New York: Columbia University Press, 1965.

Hamilton, Alexander, John Jay and James Madison. *The Federalist.* Introduction by Edward Mead Earle. New York: Modern Library, 1937.

Hamlin, Talbot. *Greek Revival Architecture in America.* New York: Oxford University Press, 1944.

Harley, J. B., Barbara Bartz Petchenik, and Lawrence W. Towner. *Mapping the American Revolutionary War.* Chicago: University of Chicago Press, 1978.

Harris, Neil. *The Artist in American Society, The Formative Years 1790-1860.* Chicago: University of Chicago Press, 1982.

Hitchock, Henry-Russell and William Seale. *Temples of Democracy, The State Capitols of the U.S.A.* New York: Harcourt, Brace, Jovanovich, 1976.

Jefferson, Thomas. *Jefferson, Writings.* Ed. Merrill D. Peterson. New York: Viking, 1984.

Jefferson, Thomas. *The Papers of Thomas Jefferson.* 29 vol. to date. Eds. Julian P. Boyd, et al. Princeton: Princeton University Press, 1954-.

Jeffferson, Thomas. *The Writings of Thomas Jefferson.* 15 vols. Ed. Albert Ellery Bergh. Washington D.C.: Thomas Jefferson Memorial Association, 1907.

Kimball, Fiske. *American Architecture*. Indianapolis and New York: Bobbs Merrill, 1928.

Kite, Elizabeth S. *L'Enfant and Washington, 1791-1792*. Baltimore: Johns Hopkins Press, 1929.

Kornwolf, James D. *"So Good a Design": The Colonial Campus of the College of William and Mary: Its History, Background, and Legacy* (Exhibition catalog, Joseph and Margaret Muscarelle Museum of Art). Williamsburg: College of William and Mary, 1989.

Kostoff, Spiro. *The City Shaped, Urban Patterns and Meanings through History*. Harmondsworth: Penguin, 1991.

Kouwenhoven, John A. *Columbia Historical Portrait of New York*. Garden City, N.Y.: Doubleday, 1953.

Levey, Michael. *Painting and Sculpture in France 1700-1789*. New Haven: Yale University Press, 1993.

Longstreth, Richard, Ed. *The Mall in Washington, 1791-1991*. Washington, D.C.: National Gallery, 1991.

Malone, Dumas, Ed. *Dictionary of American Biography*. New York: Scribner's, 1961.

Matson, Cathy D. and Peter S. Onuf. *A Union of Interests, Political and Economic Thought in Revolutionary America*. Lawrence, Kan.: University of Kansas Press, 1990.

McDonald, Forrest. *Alexander Hamilton: A Biography*. New York: Norton, 1979.

McDonald, William L. *The Pantheon, Design, Meaning, and Progeny*. Cambridge, Mass.: Harvard University Press, 1976.

Mitchell, B. R. *European Historical Statistics in 1750-1975*. New York: Columbia University Press, n.d.

Murtagh, William J., *Moravian Architecture and Town Planning*. Chapel Hill: University of North Carolina Press, 1967.

Nettleship, Henry and J. Sandys, Eds., and Oscar Seyffret, Trans. *Dictionary of Classical Antiquities*. London, 1894.

Novotony, Fritz. *Painting and Sculpture in Europe 1780-1880*. Harmondsworth: Penguin, 1990.

Patterson, Richard S. and Richardson Dougall. *The Eagle and the Shield, A History of the Great Seal of the United States*. Washington, D.C.: 1976.

Peets, Elbert. *On the Art of Designing Cities: Selected Essays of Elbert Peets*. Ed. Paul D. Spreiregen. Cambridge, Mass.; MIT Press, 1968.

Price, Richard. *Richard Price and the Ethical Foundations of the American Revolution*. Ed. Bernard Peach. Durham: N.C.: Duke University Press, 1979.

Reps, John William. *The Making of Urban America*. Princeton: Princeton University Press, 1965.

Rice, Howard C., Jr., and Anne S. K. Brown, Eds. and Trans. *The American Campaigns of Rochambeau's Army 1780, 1781, 1782, 1783*, 2 vols. Princeton: Princeton University Press, 1972.

Scully, Vincent. *Architecture: The Natural and the Man Made*. New York: St. Martin's, 1991.

Seldes, George. *The Great Quotations*. Secaucus, N.J.: Carol Pubs. Group, 1983.

Stephenson, Richard W. *"A Plan Whol(l)y New:" Pierre Charles L'Enfant's Plan of the City of Washington*. Washington, D.C.: Library of Congress, 1993.

Van Every, Dale. *Ark of Empire, The American Frontier 1784-1803*. New York: Morrow, 1963.

Washington, George. *The Diaries of George Washington*, 6 vols. Eds. Donald Jackson and Dorothy Twohig. Charlottesville: University of Virginia Press, 1976-1979.

Washington, George. *The Writings of George Washington from the Original Manuscript Sources, 1745-1799*. 39 vols. Ed. John C. Fitzpatrick. Washington, D.C.: George Washington Bicentennial Commission, 1931-1944.

Wilford, John Noble. *The Mapmakers*. New York: Knopf, 1982.

Wills, Garry. *Cincinnatus: George Washington & the Enlightenment*. Garden City, N.Y.: Doubleday, 1984.

Wren Society London. *Catalogue of Sir Chr. Wren's . . . (work) at All Souls, St. Paul's Library*. Oxford: Printed for the Wren Society at the University Press, 1924-1943.

Young, James Sterling. *The Washington Community 1800-1828*. New York: Columbia University Press, 1966.

ENDNOTES: PART ONE

1. By the middle of the nineteenth century, Mount Vernon was visibly falling into ruins because Washington's heirs were unable to maintain the property. The estate had been sub-divided among them. Dismayed by the neglect of what she believed was an important part of our cultural heritage, Anne Pamela Cunningham, a near invalid from South Carolina, organized the Mount Vernon Ladies Association. By April 6, 1858, the association raised money to purchase the house, immediate gardens, and some of the surrounding farm. They immediately set about the task of repairing and restoring its fabric, and maintaining it for the nation. The success of this exemplary endeavor speaks for itself: every year almost one million visitors explore George and Martha Washington's house and surrounding gardens.

2. These include Parliament's tax proposals of 1769 and the Coercive Acts of 1774.

3. Thomas Jefferson, *The Papers of Thomas Jefferson*, ed. Julian P. Boyd, vol. 10 (Princeton: Princeton University Press, 1954-) 27. Additional Questions of M. de Meusnier with Jefferson's Answers [ca. Jan.-Feb. 1786]. [Series hereafter referred to as Boyd].

4. For example, see Washington to George Mason, April 3, 1769, in George Washington, *The Papers of George Washington, Colonial Series*, eds. W. W. Abbott and Dorothy Twohig, vol. 8 (Charlottesville: University of Virginia Press, 1983-1995) 177-180.

5. Washington to Robert Cary & Co., September 20, 1765, *Papers, Colonial Series* 7: 400-401.

6. Willard Sterne Randall, *George Washington: A Life* (New York: Holt, 1997) 212-213.

7. Bruce Ragsdale observes that "throughout the revolutionary era, from the earliest resistance to imperial policy in the 1760s to the debate on ratification of the Federal Constitution in 1788, Washington pursued a vision of economic independence that he considered a prerequisite for the liberty, security, and prosperity of Virginia." Bruce A. Ragsdale, *A Planter's Republic, The Search for Economic Independence in Revolutionary Virginia* (Madison, Wis.: Madison House, 1996) xi.

8. Ragsdale 43-110.

9. Camille Wells, "The Planter's Prospect: Houses, Outbuildings, and Rural Landscapes in Eighteenth-Century Virginia," *Winterthur Portfolio* Spring 1993: 1-9 and Tables 3 and 6.

10. Dennis J. Pogue, "Archaeology at George Washington's Mount Vernon: 1931-1987," *Mount Vernon Ladies' Association* (Mount Vernon, Va.: Archaeology Department) file report 1, 1988, 1: 4-7. It may also reflect an unusual radial plan to plant trees at the entrance to Gunston Hall. This unexecuted plan suggests an interest in using angles and radials in site planning.

11. Letter from Dennis J. Pogue to the author, January 14, 1998.

12. "Memorandum of Carpentry Work to Be Done," June 1791, in George Washington, *The Writings of George Washington from the Original Manuscript Sources, 1745-1799*, ed. John C. Fitzpatrick, vol. 31 (Washington, D.C.: GPO, 1939-1944) 307-309. [Series hereafter referred to as Fitzpatrick].

13. George Washington to Lund Washington, August 19, 1776, in George Washington, *The Papers of George Washington, Revolutionary War Series*, ed. Dorothy Twohig et al, vol. 6. (Charlottesville: University of Virginia Press, 1985-1997) 84-86.

14. George Washington, "Memorandum," November 5, 1796, Fitzpatrick 35: 260.

15. George Washington, "Memorandum," November 5, 1796, Fitzpatrick 35: 259-266.

16. Benjamin Henry Latrobe, July 19, 1796, in Benjamin Henry Latrobe, *The Virginia Journals of Benjamin Henry Latrobe, 1795-1798*, ed. Edward C. Carter II, vol. 1 (New Haven: Yale University Press, 1977) 162-163 [hereafter referred to as Latrobe]. Although he is commonly referred to as Benjamin Latrobe, Latrobe usually signed his name B. H. Latrobe or B. Henry Latrobe.

17. Sally Foster Otis to Mrs. Charles W. Apthorp, January 13, 1801, in The Mount Vernon Ladies Association of the Union, *Annual Report, 1961* (Mount Vernon, Va.: The Association, 1961) 35 [hereafter referred to as MVLA]. The original is at the Massachusetts Historical Society, (PS-168), in Boston, Mass. Sally Otis was a niece by marriage of James Otis, one of the signers of the Declaration of Independence.

18. Edward G. Williams, ed., "Samuel Vaughan's Journal or 'Minutes made by S. V., from Stage to Stage, on a Tour to Fort Pitt,'" *Western Pennsylvania Historical Magazine* 44 nos. 1-3 (1961): 274.

19. John Pintard, *Diaries* 1, transcribed by J. Stoddard Johnston. The typescript is in the Mount Vernon Ladies' Association Library. The original manuscript is at the New-York Historical Society, New York, NY. Pintard visited the house on July 31, 1801.

20. There may have been a series of entrance gates to the farm complex. In his journal, written during a visit to Mount Vernon on February 4, 1799, Joshua Brookes, a young Englishman visiting the United States on business, wrote: "Two miles before you reach the house is the first gate, four of which you pass through, very indifferent ones except the last which is painted white." Joshua Brookes, "A Dinner at Mount Vernon-1799," From the Unpublished Journal of Joshua Brookes (1773-1859) *New-York Historical Society Quarterly* April 1947: 22.

21. "Mr. and Mrs. Samuel Powel at Mount Vernon- 1787," in MVLA *Journal*, vol. MCMXLII (1942). The full original of "Samuel Powel's *Journal*" is in the Bringhurst, Claypoole, Evans, Faulke, and Parker papers in the files of the Genealogical Society of Pennsylvania in Philadelphia, Pa.

22. Edward Hooker, *Diary*, December 8, 1808. The typescript is at the Mount Vernon Ladies' Association. The original is at Sterling

Library, Yale University, New Haven, Conn.

23. Julian Ursyn Niemcewicz, *Under Their Vine and Fig Tree: Travels through America in 1797-1799, 1805, with some further account of life in New Jersey,* trans. and ed. Metchie J. E. Budka (Elizabeth, N.J.: Grassman, 1965) 95.

24. Niemcewicz 95.

25. Niemcewicz 95 and 98.

26. Sally Foster Otis to Mrs. Charles W. Apthorp, January 13, 1801.

27. Vaughan's plan shows the blacksmith's forge and House for Families slave quarter in the wrong place. The Mansion House elevation is also incorrect; it is shown as symmetrical and with an extra window.

28. Samuel Vaughan's *Journal* 273.

29. "American Advices," Philadelphia, April 19, 1791, *Osborne's New Hampshire Spy,* 04 May 1791: 10.

30. Latrobe 1: 163. Latrobe's less than positive assessment may be the result of having approached the house via the south lane and the stables. Powel, on the other hand, approached through the Bowling Green, as Washington intended.

31. Ibid.

32. Between 1793 and 1796 the north dependency was used as quarters for William Pearce, the farm manager.

33. The thinness of the column shafts and the use of recessed panels may have been inspired by the elevation of a greenhouse using cruciform-shaped columns. This is illustrated on plate LXXIX in William Pain's *The Practical Builder or Workingman's General Assistant* (London, 1774). Plate LXXVIII of this handbook shows the elevations of a house with an open colonnade between house and dependencies. I am indebted to Calder C. Loth for this suggestion made in a letter to me dated September 8th, 1997. The most serious study of possible design sources for the arcade, and Mount Vernon, is the Master of Architecture thesis presented to the faculty of the University of Virginia by Scott Campbell Owen: "George Washington's Mount Vernon as British Palladian Architecture" 1991, 30-32.

34. For planting of scarlet or "French" honeysuckle (the native *Lonicera sempervirens*), see the entry for March 31, 1785, in George Washington, *The Diaries of George Washington,* eds. Donald Jackson and Dorothy Twohig, vol. 4 (Charlottesville: University of Virginia Press, 1976-1979) 110-111, and George Washington to George Augustine Washington, July 29, 1787, in George Washington, *Papers, Confederation Series* ed. Dorothy Twohig, vol. 5 (Charlottesville: University of Virginia Press, 1997) 276-277.

35. The door and pediment may be an inch or two off center. These dimensions are by the author, using the measured drawings prepared in 1937 by Morely Jeffers Williams, Office of Research and Restoration, Mount Vernon Ladies' Association.

36. George Washington to George Augustine Washington, June 3, 1787, Fitzpatrick 29: 228.

37. Because the cupola is depicted in more detail than the rest of the elevation, Charles Brownell suggests that the drawing may be a study of the cupola design. See Charles E. Brownell, "Mount Vernon," in Charles E. Brownell, Calder Loth, William M. S. Rasmussen, and Richard Guy Wilson, *The Making of Virginia Architecture* (Charlottesville: University of Virginia Press, 1992) 206. [Hereafter referred to as *Virginia Architecture*].

38. Samuel Powel's *Journal,* October 6, 1787.

39. George Washington to William Thornton, December 30, 1798, Fitzpatrick 37: 79.

40. George Washington to Lund Washington, September 30, 1776, in *The Papers of George Washington, Revolutionary War Series,* ed. Dorothy Twohig et al, vol. 6 (Charlottesville: University of Virginia Press, 1994) 442.

41. George Washington to Lund Washington, August 20, 1775, *Papers, Revolutionary War Series* 1: 337.

42. Latrobe 1: 163.

43. Washington to William Thornton, October 1, 1799, Fitzpatrick 37: 387. See also George Washington, "Memorandum," dated November 5, 1796, Fitzpatrick 35: 263-264, in which Washington discusses the preparation of the sand and how to apply it to the paint, and "Restoration Painting," MVLA *Annual Report,* 1956 15.

44. Ibid. 16. Test results by the Forest Products Laboratory, U.S. Department of Agriculture, note that "sand inhibits checking of the paint film, which, in consequence lasts longer."

45. I am indebted to Calder C. Loth for suggesting that Shirley Place may have been the source of Washington's rustication at Mount Vernon.

46. Washington also knew Governor Shirley's son, who was killed serving under General Braddock in July 1755. See Douglas Southall Freeman, *George Washington, A Biography,* vol. 2. *Young Washington* (New York: Scribner's, 1948) 23 and 71 n49.

47. Freeman, *Young Washington* 164-165.

48. Hugh Morrison, *Early American Architecture From the First Colonial Settlements to the National Period* (New York: Oxford University Press, 1952) 484-485.

49. Freeman, *Young Washington* 163.

50. It is an interesting coincidence that at about the same time as Washington was embellishing Mount Vernon with rusticated siding, Sir William Chamber was designing and building the Orangery at Kew Gardens (ca. 1757), which also uses "V" jointed rustication. The Orangery is a stone building.

51. John Summerson, *Inigo Jones* (Harmondsworth: Penguin, 1966) 55-56. In a letter to the author, dated November 2, 1997, Charles Brownell suggests the Banqueting Hall and the Palazzo Thiene as possible sources for the rustication at Mount Vernon. Palladio's *Four Books of Architecture* was published in Venice in 1570. The first English translation was published in 1715. The later publication of 1738 by Isaac Ware is the edition referred to in this text. It was

reprinted in New York in 1965. Professor Brownell also notes that plate 57 of William Kent's *Design of Inigo Jones* of 1727 has designs for "Rustic" doors in which voussoirs interrupt the entablature. He believes that this may have inspired some of Batty Langley's door designs (see plate XXXIII in *The City and Country Builder's and Workingman's Treasury of Designs*), the likely source for the central door on Mount Vernon's west façade.

52. Jones's Doric gateway at Beaufort House, which is now at Chiswick House, London, and his Tuscan carriage gateway for Haton House, London, have "V" joints. These are illustrated in John Harris and Gordon Higgot, *Inigo Jones, Complete Architectural Drawings* (New York: Harper and Row, 1989) 129 and 135. According to Harris and Higgot, an inspiration for the latter design may be Domenico Fontana's unexecuted design for the Porta Exquilina (see pp. 135-136). At p. 149, there is an early sketch for the Queen's House by Jones that shows the rusticated base with a "V" joint. Jones's design for other gates, at Arundel House, at the Privy Garden of St. James's Palace, and at the Vineyard at Oatlands Palace, also use the "V" joint. See John Harris, *The Palladians* (London: Trefoil Books, 1981) 48-49. The ultimate source for Jones and Washington may be Palladio's Palazzo Thiene. Palladio's drawing of the palazzo's base shows a "V" joint. See Book 2, plates IX and X in Isaac Ware's translation of the *Four Books*. The base of the building, which Jones saw, but Washington did not, has the "V" joint.

53. See the Fourth Book, plates LII and LIII. Ware's edition of Palladio was published in London in 1738. The ancient Roman Temple of Mars the Avenger in Rome also uses rustication on all elevations and a similar cornice with block modillions. See Matthew John Mosca, "The House and its Restoration," in *The Magazine Antiques: Mount Vernon*, February 1989: 464. The modillion is illustrated on plate X of Ware's edition of Palladio.

54. I am indebted to Charles Brownell and Owen (1991) for this information.

55. Batty and Thomas Langley, *The Builder's Jewel or, The Youth's Instructor and Workingman's Remembrancer* (London, 1746) plate 75.

56. Daniel D. Rieff, *Small Georgian Houses in England and Virginia, Origins and Development through the 1750s* (Newark, Del.: University of Delaware Press, 1986) proposes that the drawing of the Killigrew House is by John Webb although the design is by Inigo Jones. He also lists houses with coved cornices. These include Thorne Abbey House (1660-1662), Cambridgeshire; Parsonage House (ca. 1670), Stanton Harcourt, Oxfordshire; the 1680 wing at Mompesson House, Salisbury, Wiltshire; Malmesbury House (1710) also in Salisbury; and Mothecombe House (1710), Devon. See pp. 101, 105, 107, 108, 110-111, 113, 116, and 119.

57. For St. Anne's and the Amstel House (also called the Nicholas van Dyke House) in Delaware see George Fletcher Bennett, *Early Architecture of Delaware* (Newark, Del.: University of Delaware Press, 1932) 36 and 60. For the cove cornice in Greater Philadelphia see John Fitzhugh Millar, *The Architects of the American Colonies* (Barre, Mass.: Barre Pubs., 1968) 123-124. In England, in the nineteenth century, Eden Nesfield designed coved cornices for the lodges at Kew Gardens (1866), and Richard Norman Shaw for lodges at Shavington Hall (1885) and Hartwell House. In this century Sir Edwin Lutyens designed a coved cornice at the Salutation (1911) and Ednaston Manor (1912).

58. The designs of a pulpit (plate CXVI), cistern (plate LX), and obelisk (plate CXXXI) all feature coves. Batty Langley, *The City and Country Builder's and Workingman's Treasury of Designs: Or the Art of Drawing and Working The Ornamental Parts of Architecture* (London, 1750).

59. Latrobe 1: 165-166.

60. Niemcewicz 97.

61. William Loughton Smith, *The Journals of William Loughton Smith, 1790-1791*, ed. Albert Matthews (Cambridge, Mass., 1917) 63, and quoted in Peter Martin, *The Pleasure Gardens of Virginia* (Princeton: Princeton University Press, 1991) 141-142.

62. Abigail Adams to Mrs. Richard Cranch [her sister], December 21, 1800, in MVLA, *Annual Report,* 1957 44. The original is at the Massachusetts Historical Society in Boston.

63. Peter Martin, *The Pleasure Gardens of Virginia: From Jamestown to Jefferson* (Princeton, N.J.: Princeton University Press, 1991) 141.

64. "American Advices," Philadelphia, April 19, *Osborne's New Hampshire Spy,* 4 May 1791: 10.

65. Samuel Vaughan's *Journal* 274.

66. Latrobe 1: 165-166.

67. In his book, *Planting and Rural Ornament*, vol. 1 (London, 1796) 136, William Marshall refers to a hang as terrain that is "too steep to be cultivated conveniently with the common plow. . ." The entry for "hanging wood" in *The Oxford Companion to Gardens,* eds. Susan and Sir Geoffrey Jellicoe (Oxford: Oxford University Press, 1986) 244, notes: "It was generally agreed by 18th-c. commentators that it was desirable to look at the wood from below, preferably so that the brow of the hill (if naked) was not visible."

68. John E. Ferling, *The First of Men: A Life of George Washington* (Knoxville: University of Tennessee Press, 1988) 4 and Latrobe 165. Latrobe writes that the trees were trimmed in order not to obstruct the view to the river. From this we may deduce that the trees also obstructed the view to the house from the river.

69. The deer park drawing is in the manuscript Collection at the Library of the Mount Vernon Ladies' Association. It is dated October 1798. This date is problematical according to Note 60, Fitzpatrick 36: 525.

70. Winthrop Sargent's diary. Typescript is at the Mount Vernon Ladies' Association. The microfilm edition of the diary is at the Ohio Historical Society in Columbus, Ohio.

71. The land between the wall and the river has been subjected to considerable erosion.

72. There are numerous building types with features influenced by the piazza at Mount Vernon. These include the following houses: the Breese House (1898) in Southampton, New York, by McKim Mead & White; the James Dickey House (1914) in Atlanta, by Neil Reid; the Collier Residence (ca. 1920) in Wickatunk, NJ, by John Russell Pope; the Smither House (ca. 1920) in White Plains, NY, by Donn Barbor; the Godfrey Residence (ca. 1920) in Bridgeport, CT, by Burrall Hoffman; "Albemarle" (1922) in Princeton, NJ, by Harrie T. Lindeberg; and Robert Venturi and Denise Scott Brown's proposed Brant House (1980) in Greenwich, CT. Other building types include the clubhouse of the Piping Rock Country Club (1921) in Locust Valley, NY, by Guy Lowell; the East Feliciana Court House (1839) in Clinton, LA, by J. S. Savage; the Virginia Building at the World's Columbian Exposition of 1893 in Chicago by Edgerton Rogers; and the Mount Vernon Memorial Park (date unknown) in Sacramento, CA.

73. Jay Edwards, "The Complex Origins of the American Domestic Piazza-Verandah-Gallery," *Material Culture* Summer 1989: 2-58. This is the most thorough survey of the possible origins of the piazza.

74. *Diaries* 2: 134 and 3: 12.

75. Andrea Palladio, *The Four Books of Architecture,* ed. Isaac Ware New York: Dover, 1965) Book Three 54-55 and plate 49.

76. William Pain, *The Practical Builder or Workingman's General Assistant* (London 1774). I am indebted to Calder C. Loth for this suggestion.

77. Langley *City and Country Builder's* 2, Prob. V.

78. At one time there may have been two small pavilions (probably privies) placed on the mounds at the outside edge of the hollow to frame the view. They were probably built in 1760 and connected the north and southeast corners of the house with wood fences. We know that the one to the south was removed in 1796, but the existence of the one to the north has not been established. I am indebted to Dennis J. Pogue for this information.

79. Rev. John E. Latta's account of his visit to Mount Vernon in the summer of 1799 was read by Mrs. Mary L. Dubois at a meeting of the Bucks County Historical Society, in Doylestown, PA, on January 26, 1915. The typescript is at the Mount Vernon Ladies' Association. Washington notes in his diary that "a Parson Lattum from Pennsylvania dined here & left it in the afternoon." See *Diaries* 6: 355.

80. Washington to Lund Washington, August 19, 1776, *Papers, Revolutionary War Series* 6: 84-85.

81. Niemcewicz 95. Niemcewicz mentions locust trees in both the north and south groves, as does B. Henry Latrobe. See *Virginia Journals* 1: 165. Washington writes of locusts only in the north grove, with flowering trees in the south.

82. Latrobe 1: 165-166.

83. *Osborne's New-Hampshire Spy,* 4 May 1791: 10-11. This description parallels that of Jedediah Morse, who described the house and surrounding buildings as a "rural village" in the account of his visit on November 2, 1786, in Jedediah Morse, *American Geography; or A View of the Present Situation of the United States of America* (London, 1792) 381.

84. *Diaries* 4: 103.

85. Washington to Anthony Whiting, October 14, 1792, Fitzpatrick 32: 182.

86. Washington to Anthony Whiting, December 16, 1792, Fitzpatrick 32: 265-266.

87. Washington to Anthony Whiting, January 13, 1793, Fitzpatrick 32: 300.

88. Washington to Anthony Whiting, December 2, 1792, Fitzpatrick 32: 248.

89. Washington to Anthony Whiting, March 3, 1793, Fitzpatrick 32: 365.

90. Washington to William Triplett, September 25, 1786, *Papers, Confederation Series* 4: 268.

91. Washington to William Pearce, November 22, 1795, Fitzpatrick 34: 369-74.

92. Washington to Anthony Whiting, October 14, 1792, Fitzpatrick 32: 179-180.

93. Washington to William Pearce, March 13, 1796, Fitzpatrick 34: 496.

94. Washington to William Pearce, May 22, 1796, Fitzpatrick 35: 66.

95. Perhaps Washington shared Alexander Pope's opinion that "All gardening is landscape-painting. . . . Just like a landscape hung up." Pope's remark was made in 1734 and is quoted in Martin xxiii.

96. Niemcewicz 100.

97. Ragsdale 67-68.

98. *Diaries* 1: xxvi-xxviii.

99. Washington to Capel and Osgood Hanbury, September 20, 1765; Washington to James Gildart, September 20, 1765; and Washington to Robert Cary & Co., September 20, 1765, in *Papers, Colonial Series* 7: 393-394, 397, and 398-402. See also Ragsdale ix.

100. *Diaries* 1: xxxi.

101. *Diaries* 1: xxxi.

102. Washington to George William Fairfax, June 30, 1785, in *Papers, Confederation Series* 3: 90.

103. For example, he paid salaries to managers rather than allotting them a percentage of the crop. Because his experiments were not always successful he thought a salary was a fairer form of remuneration. He also understood that the percentage system focused managers' attention on seeking short-term gain and offered no incentive to them to improve the soil. Washington believed that conducting agricultural experiments was an important responsibility of landowners with substantial resources.

104. Quoted in J.D. McClatchy, *Twenty Questions* (New York: Columbia

University Press, 1998) 92.

105. Jacques Pierre Brissot de Warville, *On America, vol. 1, New Travels in the United States of America performed in 1788* (London, 1792, reprinted New York: A.M. Kelley, 1970) 428. See also William Mavor, "Brissot's Travels," *Historical Account of the Most Celebrated Voyages, Travels, and Discoveries from the Time of Columbus to the Present Period,* vol. 19 (London, 1797) 308.

106. Orlando Redout V and John Riley, "George Washington's Treading Barn at Dogue Run Farm: Documentary and Architectural Analysis" February 1993 (unpublished paper in the library at Mount Vernon) 16. There is no visual record of the appearance of the barn. However, Washington's sketch for the stable complex, which was added to the rear of the barn, is described in Fitzpatrick 32: 287-291. Arthur Young replied to Washington's request for advice on the plan of an ideal barn on February 1, 1787.

107. The relationship between the barn and adjacent stables in discussed in Redout and Riley, Appendix Two 84-92.

108. Washington to Arthur Young, December 12, 1793, Fitzpatrick 33: 177.

109. Redout and Riley 18.

110. Redout and Riley 23.

111. For a description of the treading process, see Redout and Riley 24-25.

112. Washington to Henry Lee, October 16, 1793, Fitzpatrick 33: 133.

113. Washington to William Pearce, March16 [-17], 1794, Fitzpatrick 33: 296.

114. Niemcewicz 102.

115. Current research at Mount Vernon is restudying the room names assumed to be used by Washington in the inventory of his brother's estate at Mount Vernon. As this research progresses, the current designation of rooms may be altered.

116. I am indebted to Dennis J. Pogue and Marc A. Le François for this information.

117. Diaries 1: 258. The entry for Thursday, March 27, 1760, reads: "Agreed to give Mr. William Triplet, £18 to build the two houses in the front of my House (plastering them also) and running Walls for Pallisades to them from the Great house & from the Great House to the Wash House and Kitchen also." The "two houses in the front" may refer to the two buildings, possibly outhouses, on the east side of the piazza. Dennis J. Pogue, "Mount Vernon, Transformation of an Eighteenth-Century Plantation System," in *Historical Archaeology of the Chesapeake,* eds. Paul A. Shakel and Barbara J. Little (Washington, D.C.: Smithsonian Institution, 1994) 105.

118. Mesick, Cohen, Waite, Architects, *Historic Structure Report,* 3 vols. 1993, prepared for the Mount Vernon Ladies' Association, 2: 297 and 303. The location of this arch or similar form may be marked by the false beam that currently divides the room. [Volumes hereafter referred to as *Historic Structure Report*].

119. The modillion in the cornice may have been derived from plate X, Book Four, in Palladio's *Four Books of Architecture. The Historic Structure Report* posits plate 75 in Batty Langley, *Builder's Jewel* (London, 1757) as the source. Neither book was in Washington's library.

120. Mark R. Wenger, "The Central Passage in Virginia: Evolution of an Eighteenth Century Living Space," in Camille Wells, ed., *Perspectives in Vernacular Architecture, II* (Columbia, Mo.: University of Missouri Press, 1986) 139.

121. Writing in 1732, William Hugh Grove referred to the "manner of Building" in Virginia with a "broad Stayrcase with a passage thro the house in the middle which is the Summer hall and Draws the air." Gregory Stiverson and Patrick H. Butler III, eds., "Virginia in 1732: The Travel Journal of William Hugh Grove," *Virginia Magazine of History and Biography,* 85 (1977): 28. Quoted in Wenger 139.

122. George Washington's inventory of Lawrence Washington's estate lists "household items in the Mansion." Under the heading "Passage & Parlour" are three tables ("1 Large Table," another "1 large Black Walnt Table," "1 Large old Fash[ioned] Table") and "12 Russian Leather Chairs." This suggests that there were large tables in both rooms.

123. *Historic Structure Report* 2: 297 and 302.

124. I am indebted to Charles Brownell and Owen (1991) for information the use of Palladio's capital rather than Scamozzi's design. Palladio's full Ionic was readily available in pattern books, which may account for its use at Mount Vernon. The source of the door design has been attributed to plate 349, in Batty and Thomas Langley, *Ancient Masonry Both in the Theory and in the Practice* (London, 1734 or 1735). I concur with Owen, page 7, and Brownell (in a letter to the author, dated November 2, 1997) that this attribution is not convincing.

125. Matthew John Mosca, "The House and its Restoration," *The Magazine Antiques, Mount Vernon,* February 1989: 468.

126. George Washington Parke Custis, *Recollections and Private Memoirs of Washington by His Adopted Son George Washington Parke Custis* (New York, 1860) 527-528.

127. Samuel Powel's *Journal,* October 6, 1787.

128. Washington to Mary Ball Washington, February 15, 1787, in *Papers, Confederation Series* 5: 35.

129. William Pain, *The Practical Builder or Workingman's General Assistant* (London 1774) plate LXII. I am indebted to Calder Loth for this possible design source.

130. Lund Washington to George Washington, November 12, 1775 in *Papers, Revolutionary War Series* 2: 356.

131. Washington to John Rawlins, August 29, 1785, Fitzpatrick 28: 237.

132. Owen 10.

133. Robert Morris, *Lectures on Architecture* (London, 1739, reprinted Farnborough, Eng.: Gregg Publishers, 1971) 73-74. I am indebted

to Owen 10-11, for this reference.

134. The serliana is illustrated on plate LI. The text explaining the proper use of the feature is on page 18.

135. Washington to Lund Washington, September 30, 1776, *Papers, Revolutionary Series* 6: 442.

136. Washington to Joseph Rakestraw, July 25, 1787, Fitzpatrick 29: 250.

137. Washington to George Augustine Washington, August 12, 1787, in *Papers, Confederation Series* 5: 287.

138. I am indebted to Marc A. Le François for this information. See Marc A. Le François, *A History of Shutters at Mount Vernon* (Mount Vernon, Va.: MVLA, 1996).

139. Wenger 142.

140. de Warville XIX: 307.

141. Roger Griswold to Fanny Griswold, December 1, 1800. Typescript in Mount Vernon Ladies' Association. The original is at Yale University.

142. Abigail Adams to Mrs. Richard Cranch, December 21, 1800.

143. Sally Foster Otis to Mrs. Charles W. Apthorp, January 13, 1801, MVLA, *Annual Report,* 1961 35. The original is at the Massachusetts Historical Society.

144. Owen 42-45, discusses this as part of a design program based on the Tuscan order.

145. T. S. Eliot, *Poetry and Drama* (Cambridge, Mass.: Harvard University Press, 1951) 42.

146. Rudolf Wittkower, "English Neo-Palladianism, the Landscape Garden, China and the Enlightenment," *Palladio and English Palladianism* (London, 1974) 177–190, and James D. Kornwolf, "The Picturesque in American Gardens and Landscape before 1800," in Robert P. Maccubbin and Peter Martin, eds., *British and American Gardens in the Eighteenth Century* (Williamsburg: Colonial Williamsburg Foundation, 1984) 93-106.

147. Martin, *The Pleasure Gardens of Virginia* 136.

148. *Diaries* 4: 78.

149. *Diaries* 4: 104.

150. *Diaries* 4: 107.

151. Washington to Sir Edward Newenham, April 20, 1787, Fitzpatrick 29: 205.

152. Custis 371.

153. "General Washington and Mount Vernon, From the Diary of Robert Hunter, Jr.," entry for Thursday November 17, 1785, MVLA, *Annual Report,* 1945 24.

154. Samuel Powel's *Journal* October 6, 1787.

155. Washington to Samuel Vaughan, November 12, 1787, Fitzpatrick 29: 313.

156. Peter Martin notes that "the opening was like the lens of a camera letting in a variety of images from the distance." Washington used trees to screen Mount Vernon from the immediate countryside in order to "create a feeling of concealment and privacy in a natural way with groves cut through with twisting paths" and "vistos" to and from distant points. Most other plantations in Virginia were more exposed to the views from the surrounding area. *The Pleasure Gardens of Virginia* 137.

157. The inventory of his estate showed that the single book on architectural design in his library was Charles Middleton, *Designs for Cottage, Farm House, and Country Villas* (London, 1793). The book was written and acquired too late to influence any architecture at Mount Vernon. Although we lack verification, it is possible that Washington may have given away or loaned his books on architecture before his death. He may also have borrowed books, as he needed them, from friends such as his neighbor, George Mason, who possessed a fine library.

158. Owen and the *Historic Structure Report* are the most comprehensive historical studies of Mount Vernon's architecture. They are indispensable tools for scholars. Benson J. Lossing, *George Washington's Mount Vernon* (New York, 1859) and Paul Wilstach, *Mount Vernon, Washington's Home and the Nation's Shrine* (Garden City, N.Y.: Doubleday, 1916) established the basic history of the house; Fiske Kimball's *Domestic Architecture of the American Colonies and of the Early Republic* (New York: Scribner's, 1922) located it in its historical context; Sterling Boyd's *The Adam Style in America, 1770-1820* (New York: Garland, 1985) relates Mount Vernon's decoration to the Adam style; Thomas Tileston Waterman, *The Dwellings of Colonial America* (Chapel Hill: University of North Carolina Press, 1950) and *Mansions of Virginia* (Chapel Hill: University of North Carolina Press, 1946) trace architectural details to handbooks and other sources. Dennis J. Pogue's important studies are cited throughout these notes.

159. Dell Upton, *Holy Things and Profane: Anglican Parish Churches in Colonial Virginia* (Cambridge: MIT Press, 1986) 28.

160. Upton 28.

161. Jack McLaughlin, *Jefferson and Monticello, The Biography of a Builder* (New York: Henry Holt, 1988) 57.

162. Robert Morris, *Select Architecture.* I am indebted to Camille Wells for suggesting this possible connection between Mount Vernon, Mount Airy, and Battersea.

163. Rhys Isaac, *The Transformation of Virginia 1740-1790* (Chapel Hill: University of North Carolina Press, 1982) 305.

164. Washington to William Thornton, December 30, 1798, Fitzpatrick 37: 79.

165. See Washington to the Commissioners of the District of Columbia, July 23, 1792, January 31, 1793, and March 3, 1793; and Washington to the Secretary of State, June 30, 1793, Fitzpatrick 32: 93, 324-325, 363-364, and 510-512.

166. Thomas Jones, *History of New York During the Revolutionary War* (New York, 1879) quoted in Benson Bobrick, *Angel in the Whirlwind* (New York: Simon and Schuster, 1997) 312.

167. Washington to Benjamin Vaughan, February 5, 1785, and Washington to Samuel Vaughan, February 5, 1785, in *Papers, Confederation Series* 2: 325-326. Charles Brownell has commented that these letters are "two of the earliest documents connecting architecture with an ideal of importance . . . the "republican style" of living . . ." *Virginia Architecture* 204.

168. de Warville 429.

169. Niemcewicz 98.

170. This address is also called the "Circular to the States:" It is discussed in Thomas G. West, *Vindicating the Founders: Race, Sex, Class, and Justice in the Origins of America* (Lanham, Md.: Rowman & Littlefield, 1997) 169 and Robert A. Ferguson, *The American Enlightenment* 1750-1820 (Cambridge: Harvard University Press, 1994) 38-41.

171. Wendell Garrett, "Editorial," *The Magazine Antiques: Mount Vernon,* February 1989: 453.

172. As Secretary of State, Jefferson edited Peter Charles L'Enfant's plan of the new Federal City prior to its publication. He deleted the references to "Congress house" and substituted the word "Capitol" in its place. I am indebted to William C. Allen, Architectural Historian of the U. S. Capitol, for this information.

173. On his drawing of the "Plan of the Principal Story of the capital. US," Latrobe penciled a note of possible uses for this rotunda: it was intended for citizens to gather for "Impeachments, Inaugu[r]ations, Divine Service, General access to the building" and for other purposes like lobbying for future legislation. Jeffery A. Cohen and Charles E. Brownell, *The Architectural Drawings of Benjamin Henry Latrobe* (New Haven: Yale University Press, 1994) 416 and drawing D41.

174. William C. Allen, *The Dome of the United States Capitol: An Architectural History,* Senate Document, 102nd Congress, 1st Session (Washington, D. C.: GPO, 1992) 55.

175. Willaim B. Rhoads, "Franklin D. Roosevelt and the Architecture of Warm Springs," *Georgia Historical Quarterly,* Spring 1983: 70-87. President Roosevelt worked with the architect Henry Toombs to realize the building at Warm Springs.

ENDNOTES: PART TWO

1. Sir Christopher Wren, "Of Architecture; and Observations on Antique Temples, Etc.", Wren Society London, *Catalogue of Sir Christopher Wren's...(work) at All Souls, St. Paul's Library,* tract I (Oxford: Wren Society at the University Press, 1924-1943) 19: 126.

2. Peter Charles L'Enfant, "Plan of the City, intended For the Permanent Seat of the Government of the UNITED STATES, Projected agreeable to the direction of the President of the United States, in pursuance of an Act of Congress passed the sixteenth day of July MDCCXC, establishing the Permanent Seat on the banks of the Potomac." (Washington, D.C.: Library of Congress) August 1791. See text on plan at References, M.

3. William C. Allen, *The Dome of the United States Capitol: An Architectural History* (Washington, D.C.: GPO, 1992) 1.

4. Fiske Kimball, *American Architecture* (Indianapolis and New York: Bobbs Merrill, 1928) 73.

5. I am indebted to William C. Allen, former Architectural Historian of the United States Capitol, for this information.

6. H. Paul Caemmerer, *The Life of Pierre Charles L'Enfant* (New York: De Capo, 1970) 123-125 and 250-251.

7. John Carroll and Mary Ashworth, *George Washington, First in Peace: Volume Seven of the Biography by Douglas Southall Freeman* (New York: Scribner's, 1957) 433.

8. George Washington to Henry Lee, September 22, 1788, in George Washington, *The Writings of George Washington from the Original Manuscript Sources, 1745-1799,* ed. John C. Fitzpatrick (Washington, D.C.: George Washington Bicentennial Commission, 1931-1944) 30: 96. [Series hereafter referred to as Fitzpatrick].

9. Roger H. Brown, *The Republic in Peril:* 1812 (New York: Columbia University Press, 1971) 4.

10. Washington to John Jay, August 1, 1786, Fitzpatrick 28: 503. Also quoted in Brown 5.

11. Turgot to Dr. Richard Price, March 22, 1778, Richard Price, "Observations on the Importance of the American Revolution" (originally published 1785), in Richard Price, *Richard Price and the Ethical Foundations of the American Revolution,* ed. Bernard Peach (Durham, NC: Duke University Press, 1979) 222. Quoted in Cathy D. Matson and Peter S. Onuf, *A Union of Interests, Political and Economic Thought in Revolutionary America* (Lawrence, Kan.: University of Kansas, 1990) 1.

12. Mortimer Adler, *We Hold These Truths* (New York: Macmillan, 987) 12-20.

13. Washington to Governor Benjamin Harrison, October 10, 1784, Fitzpatrick 27: 475.

14. Henry Adams, *History of the United States of America During the Administrations of Thomas Jefferson* (New York: Library of America, 1986) 22.

15. Jefferson to James Monroe, June 17, 1785, Thomas Jefferson, *The Papers of Thomas Jefferson,* ed. Julian F. Boyd et al (Princeton, N.J.: Princeton University Press, 1953) 8: 229. [Series hereafter referred to as Boyd].

16. Elbert Peets, "The Background of L'Enfant's Plan," Elbert Peets, *On the Art of Designing Cities: Selected Essays of Elbert Peets,* ed. Paul Spreiregan (Cambridge, Mass.: MIT Press, 1968) 5.

17. Thomas Jefferson to George Rogers Clark, December 4, 1783, Boyd 19: 58 n175.

18. Dale Van Every, *Ark of Empire, The American Frontier 1784-1803* (New York: Morrow, 1963) 1-8; Kenneth R. Bowling, *Creating the Federal City, 1774-1800: Potomac Fever* (Washington, D.C.: AIA

Press, 1988) 39-61; and James Thomas Flexner, *George Washington and the New Nation: 1783-1792* (Boston: Little Brown, 1969) 73-82.

19. Washington to William Irvine, October 31, 1788, Fitzpatrick 30: 123.

20. Washington to Harrison, October 10, 1784, Fitzpatrick 27: 475.

21. Boyd, "Editorial Note," Boyd 19: 6.

22. Manasseh Cutler, "An explanation of the Map which delineates that part of the Federal Lands comprehended between Pennsylvania West Line, the rivers Ohio and Sioto, and Lake Erie" (Newport, 1788) 40, quoted in Boyd 19: 6 n5.

23. George Walker, "A Description of the Situation and Plan of Washington: Established as the Permanent Residence of the Congress after the year 1800." Broadside, London, 1793. Geography and Map Division, Library of Congress. I am indebted to Iris Miller for this reference. Henry Adams 5 also refers to activity on this route.

24. Washington to Stuart, April 8, 1792, Fitzpatrick 32: 19.

25. Washington to Arthur Young, December 12, 1793, Fitzpatrick 33: 176.

26. Boyd 17: 460-461. This manuscript is undated. Boyd argues that it was written in August 1790 and not November 1790, as suggested by Saul Padover in Thomas Jefferson, *Thomas Jefferson and the National Capital...1783-1818.* Ed. Saul K. Padover (Washington, D.C.: GPO, 1946).

27. Boyd 17: 461-463.

28. The precise location of the site Jefferson intended for his plan is not clear. His drawing and written description suggest it is the narrow strip of land west of Carrollsburg, between St. James Creek and the Potomac. John Reps believes that it is on the site of Carrollsburg. See John William Reps, *The Making of Urban America* (Princeton, N.J.: Princeton University Press, 1965) 246. This position is supported by the fact that Jefferson's plan and that of Carrollsburg are both nine blocks long by four blocks wide.

29. Boyd 20: 73.

30. Jefferson to Andrew Ellicott, February 2, 1791, Boyd 19: 68-69.

31. Their responsibilities also included providing public buildings for Congress and the executive and judicial branches "as the President shall approve."

32. Jefferson to Commissioners of the Federal District, January 29, 1791, Boyd 19: 67-68.

33. Jefferson to L'Enfant, March 2, 1791, Boyd 19: 355-356 and Elizabeth S. Kite, *L'Enfant and Washington, 1791-1792* (Baltimore: Johns Hopkins Press, 1929) 35.

34. Washington to William Deakins, Junior, and Benjamin Stoddert, March 2, 1791, Fitzpatrick 31: 226-227. Kite notes that no mention is made of a plan for the city in this letter. It is mentioned in Jefferson's letter, of January 29, 1791 to the Commissioners. See Kite 33.

35. Washington to Deakins and Stoddert, February 3, 1791, Fitzpatrick 31: 208.

36. Washington to L'Enfant, April 4, 1791, Fitzpatrick 31: 271.

37. Washington to Thomas Jefferson, March 16, 1791, Boyd 20: 78.

38. Jefferson to L'Enfant, March 17, 1791, Boyd 20: 80.

39. Jefferson to L'Enfant, March 2, 1791, Boyd 19: 355-356.

40. L'Enfant to Thomas Jefferson, March 11, 1791, Boyd 20: 77.

41. "Note relative to the Ground laying on the eastern branch of the River Potowmack & being Intended to parallel the severals position proposed within the limits between tha[t] branch & Georgetown for the Seat of the Federal city," Papers of Pierre Charles L'Enfant, Manuscript Division, Library of Congress. Endorsed on page 8, "Report on the District of Columbia as Suitable for a City by l'Enfant. No. 1. (PB&G) 1791. Enclosure." A note attached to the report states that "The above was personally handed to the Executive on his arrival at Georgetown at that time." Kite dates it March 26, 1791 for it continues to evaluate the site. It follows the train of thought L'Enfant began in his report of March 11 to Jefferson. Both Kite and Reps believe the report was prepared for Washington's visit to Georgetown. See Kite 47, Reps 243-245, and Richard W. Stephenson, *"A Plan Whol[l]y New:" Pierre Charles L'Enfant's Plan of the City of Washington* (Washington, D.C.: Library of Congress, 1993) 22 and n54. Professor Pamela Scott, who kindly discussed this matter with me, concurs with Kite.

42. The plan is referred to in Washington to L'Enfant, April 4, 1791, Fitzpatrick 31: 270. This letter served as a transmittal by which Washington sent Jefferson's plan to L'Enfant.

43. Measurements by author.

44. Jefferson's Draft of Agenda for the Seat of Government, dated August 29, 1790, and Jefferson's Report to Washington on Meeting held at Georgetown, dated September 14, 1790, are in Boyd 17: 460-463.

45. George Washington, *The Diaries of George Washington,* eds. Donald Jackson and Dorothy Twohig (Charlottesville: University of Virginia Press, 1979) 6: 103-106. See also James Thomas Flexner, *George Washington and the New Nation, 1783-1792* (Boston: Little Brown, 1969) 325-345. Flexner was one of the first to fully appreciate the pivotal role played by Washington in the design of the new capital.

46. Washington to Jefferson, March 31, 1791, Fitzpatrick 31: 256.

47. L'Enfant to Hamilton, April 8, 1791, Alexander Hamilton, *The Papers of Alexander Hamilton,* ed. Harold C. Syrett (New York: Columbia University Press, 1965) 8, 254.

48. Washington to Jefferson, March 31, 1791, Fitzpatrick 31: 257.

49. L'Enfant to Jefferson, April 4, 1791, Kite 41, and Boyd 20: 83.

50. Fiske Kimball stated that L'Enfant "stimulated Washington to enlarge the size of the area acquired . . ." See Kimball's text on L'Enfant in Dumas Malone, ed., *Dictionary of American Biography* (New York: Scribner's, 1961) IV: 167.

51. This fact was noted by Madison in his "Advice on Executing the Residence Act." This report was probably prepared for Jefferson in July or August 1790. See Boyd 19: 58-60. In his letter to Deakins and

Stoddert, February 3, 1791, Washington notes that the States of Maryland and Virginia appropriated monies that may be used for this purpose.

52. Washington to L'Enfant, April 4, 1791, Fitzpatrick 31: 271.

53. Area of cities covered by buildings measured by the author from the following maps: Washington, D.C.: Peter Charles L'Enfant, August 1791, Library of Congress; Philadelphia: "To Thomas Mifflin Governor and Commander-in-Chief of the State of Pennsylvania. This Plan of the City and Suburbs of Philadelphia is respectfully inscribed by the Editor," 1794, Yale University Map Collection; London: "Published as the Act directs January 1st, 1791 by Robert Sayer, Map & Printseller, No. 53 Fleet Street," Yale University Map Collection. The population statistics are from B. R. Mitchell, *European Historical Statistics in 1750-1975* (New York: Columbia University Press, 1978).

54. Washington to Commissioners of the District of Columbia, May 7, 1791, Fitzpatrick 31: 287.

55. Neil Harris, *The Artist in American Society, The Formative Years 1790-1860* (Chicago: University of Chicago Press, 1982) 20-21. See also James W. Ceaser, *Reconstructing America, The Symbol of America in Modern Thought* (New Haven: Yale University Press, 1997) 19-65.

56. Alexander Hamilton, John Jay, and James Madison, *The Federalist,* intro. by Edward Mead Earle (New York: Modern Library, 1937) 11: 69.

57. Harris 20.

58. Harris 19-20.

59. Caemmerer 128-129.

60. At the time, Washington was a young man of seventeen and working as an assistant to the county surveyor, John West, Jr. See Reps 97, and John Noble Wilford, *The Mapmakers* (New York: Knopf, 1982) 179.

61. Douglas Southall Freeman, *George Washington* (New York: Scribner's, 1948) 1: 215.

62. Wilford 178-180. Jefferson was an experienced surveyor and wrote a tract on his techniques for students. See Silvio A. Bedini, *Thomas Jefferson, Statesman of Science* (New York: Macmillan, 1990) 510.

63. Dr. David Stuart was Washington's business manager, friend, and confidant. He lived in Alexandria and was married to Martha Washington's daughter; Daniel Carroll was a Maryland congressman who lived at Joseph's Park, a 4,000-acre estate on the Potomac in Montgomery County, northwest of Georgetown; and Thomas Johnson of Frederick, Maryland nominated Washington in 1775 to be Commander-in-Chief of the Continental Army. When Washington was elected President, he replaced him as head of the Potomac Company. All these men were Potomac Company investors. See William C. di Giacomantonio, "All the President's Men, George Washington's Federal City Commissioners," *Washington History, the Magazine of the Historical Society of Washington, D.C.* 3.1 (1991): 52-74.

64. "James Madison's Advice on Executing the Residence Act," Boyd 19: 58-60.

65. Silvio A. Bedini, "The Survey of the Federal Territory, Andrew Ellicott and Benjamin Banneker," *Washington History, The Magazine of the Historical Society of Washington, D.C.* 3.1 (1991): 76-95.

66. Ellicott was a friend of David Rittenhouse and Benjamin Franklin. He was brought to Washington's attention by James Madison. This led to an appointment from the President to survey the western boundary of New York.

67. Ellicott to Sarah Ellicott, June 26, 1791, Ellicott Papers (Curtis Collection), manuscript Division, Library of Congress. Quoted in Bedini 86.

68. Kym Snyder Rice, "Joseph Clark, Maryland Architect," *The Magazine Antiques* March 1979: 552-555.

69. Clark advertised his services in the Baltimore *Maryland Gazette* on April 7, 1785 describing himself as an architect and contractor as well as someone able to execute "surveys & plot lands." Quoted in Howard C. Rice, Jr. and Anne S. K. Brown, eds. and trans. *The American Campaigns of Rochambeau's Army 1780, 1781, 1782, 1783* (Princeton, N.J.: Princeton University Press, 1979) 552.

70. Stephenson 25-26 and n78.

71. Boyd 17: 460-463.

72. William J. Murtagh, *Moravian Architecture and Town Planning* (Chapel Hill: University of North Carolina Press, 1967) 9-21.

73. Constitution of the United States, Article I, Sec. 8, par. 17.

74. Washington to L'Enfant, April 4, 1791, Fitzpatrick 31: 270-271. Washington described the second plan as "taken up upon a larger scale, without any reference to any described spot."

75. L'Enfant, 1791, Plan, text at M, Caemmerer 165.

76. Caemmerer 127-130.

77. Pierre L'Enfant served on the staff of Jean-Baptiste Berthier, a topographical engineer in the French army. Berthier became head of the corps of *Ingénieur-Géographe,* designed the Ministry of War building in Versailles, and commissioned L'Enfant senior to decorate the building with scenes of victorious French campaigns. Berthier's two sons served as engineers in Rochambeau's army. Although they were the same age as Pierre Charles L'Enfant, and also spent part of their youth at Versailles, I have not found any indications that they knew each other.

78. Rice and Brown I: 111-117 and II: figs. 11-16.

79. Fitzpatrick 3: 322, 325; 4: 61, 196, 528; 5: 109, 117, 132, 154, 318; 6: 160-161, 214, 340, 400-401; and 7: 388. I am indebted to J.B. Harley, Barbara Bartz Petchenik, and Lawrence W. Towner, *Mapping the American Revolutionary War* (Chicago: University of Chicago Press, 1978) 157 for this information on the role of engineers in the Continental Army.

80. Harley, Petchenik, and Towner 49.

81. Harley, Petchenik, and Towner 52-53.

82. Boyd 20: 9-11. Jefferson presents a very different view of L'Enfant's

qualifications. He finds that L'Enfant lacks "those very qualities of character and professional discipline" essential for such an undertaking and that "while he had no experience in planning a city . . . he had some politically powerful friends." Alexander Hamilton, Henry Knox, and Robert Morris are cited as examples. He criticizes Washington for ignoring the recommendation of his friend Contee Hanson that Joseph Clark be retained. Yet Clarke had less experience in engineering and city planning than L'Enfant and was probably seen to be a less innovative architect by the President. Jefferson also ignores the fact that Washington never ceased to admire L'Enfant, never ceased to be pleased with his plan, and never ceased to miss his services after terminating his role in the project.

83. Comte de Clermont-Crèvecoeur, "Journal of Jean-François-Louis, Comte de Clermont-Crèvecoeur," September 1782, Rice and Brown I: 7 and n158.

84. La Luzerne to Washington, April 22, 1782, Washington Papers, Library of Congress. Washington agreed to loaning the officer and replied on April 27, 1782.

85. Kite 5.

86. L'Enfant to Baron von Steuben, June 10, 1783, Caemmerer 71-72. L'Enfant's design for the Society is discussed in Caemmerer 69-72. Charles Thompson's work together with that of Francis Hopkinson, who designed a thirteen-pointed star for the Great Seal, is discussed in Richard S. Patterson and Richardson Dougall, *The Eagle and the Shield, A History of the Great Seal of the United States* (Washington, D.C., 1976) 74-79, 83-88 and fig. 14. Thompson was the Secretary of the Continental Congress to whom L'Enfant wrote, on Houdon's behalf, regarding the proposed equestrian statue of Washington.

87. William L. McDonald, *The Pantheon, Design, Meaning, and Progeny* (Cambridge: Harvard University Press, 1976) 87, and Henry Nettleship and J. E. Sandys, eds., and Oscar Seyffert, trans., *Dictionary of Classical Antiquities* (London, 1894) 202.

88. John A. Kouwenhoven, *The Columbia Historical Portrait of New York* (Garden City, N.Y.: Doubleday, 1953) 81.

89. Caemmerer 98-100 and Jackson and Twohig 5: 452.

90. *Gazette of the United States* quoted in Caemmerer 177.

91. *Massachusetts Magazine*, June 1789, quoted in Caemmerer 113-117.

92. Flexner 185.

93. Talbot Hamlin, *Greek Revival Architecture in America* (New York: Oxford University Press, 1944) 7-8. Thomas Bulfinch, newly returned from Europe, thought so well of Federal Hall that he made a sketch of its façade. This sketch was published as a woodcut by the *Massachusetts Magazine*. His design for the Connecticut Statehouse in Hartford has been described as "an English version of Federal Hall." Henry-Russell Hitchcock and William Seale, *Temples of Democracy, The State Capitols of the U.S.A.* (New York: Harcourt, Brace, Jovanovich, 1976) 37-38.

94. Hamlin 8.

95. Fitzpatrick 30: 294-295. Washington's first inaugural address was delivered on April 30, 1789.

96. Washington to Jefferson, August 1, 1786, Fitzpatrick 28: 504-506 and John S. Hallam, "Houdon's Washington in Richmond: Some Observations," *The American Art Journal*, November 1978: 75.

97. Although Jefferson wrote to Washington on August 14, 1787, concurring with the decision to use modern garb, he retained his preference for the Roman toga. Hallam 76 and Boyd 11: 187-188.

98. Caemmerer 69-73 and Hallam 79-80.

99. Peale may also have been a source as posited by Hallam 76-78.

100. Jefferson to Washington, December 10, 1784, Boyd 7: 567. No other representation of Washington would be based on such meticulous observation of the living model.

101. Jefferson to Benjamin Harrison, January 10, 1785, Boyd 7: 599-601.

102. This approach would also avoid compromising the quality of the sculpture, which could then be made as large as was necessary. On September 1, 1784, St. John de Crèvecoeur had written to Jefferson with detailed instructions for making a face cast, a "Mould En Creux of his [Washington's] Face." See St. John de Crèvecoeur to Jefferson, September 1, 1784, Boyd 7: 413-414.

103. Jefferson to Nathaniel Macon, January 22, 1816, Thomas Jefferson, *The Writings of Thomas Jefferson*, ed. Albert Ellery Bergh (Washington D.C.: Thomas Jefferson Memorial Association, 1907) 13: 409-410. Also quoted in Gilbert Chinard, ed., *Houdon in America* (Baltimore, 1930 and 1979) 50. The General Assembly of North Carolina planned to commission a statue of Washington. Jefferson recommended that Antonio Canova receive the commission.

104. Michael Levey, *Painting and Sculpture in France 1700-1789* (New Haven: Yale University Press, 1993) 236.

105. I am indebted to Professor Suzanne Lindsay for this information.

106. Jefferson to James Madison, February 8, 1785, Boyd 9: 265-266.

107. Garry Wills, *Cincinnatus: George Washington & the Enlightenment* (Garden City, N.Y.: Doubleday, 1984) 237-240.

108. A sculpture without a pedestal would also have left Houdon's engraved inscription on the plinth at floor level and difficult to read. The question of the height of the sculpture mandates consideration of Washington's gaze. Unlike Houdon's Voltaire, which is more immediately engaging, the image of Washington may have been planned for viewing from a perspective that was slightly above the viewer's eye level. The sculpture itself seems to need the space between it and the viewer that a low pedestal—perhaps only half as high as the one used—would facilitate. Although the power of the toe-to-toe confrontation Wills eloquently describes cannot be denied, an equally strong case may be made that Washington is actually looking past the viewer and into the distance.

109. Fritz Novotony discusses Houdon's "liveliness and naturalness" which "could be reconciled with Classicism in the name of 'truth.'" Levey 377.

110. L'Enfant, 1791, Caemmerer 165.

111. Caemmerer 89.

112. Patterson and Dougall 90-91.

113. Spiro Kostoff asserts that L'Enfant was familiar with the plan for St. Petersburg. He cites no source for this statement, however. Spiro Kostoff, *The City Shaped, Urban Patterns and Meanings through History* (Harmondsworth: Penguin, 1991) 211.

114. L'Enfant to Washington, September 11, 1789, Kite 34.

115. Iurii Alekseevich Egorov, *The Architectural Planning of St. Petersburg, Its Development in the 18th and 19th Centuries,* ed. and trans. Eric Dluhosch (Athens, Ohio: Ohio University Press, 1969) Part I.

116. Jefferson to John Page, May 4, 1786, Thomas Jefferson, *The Writings of Thomas Jefferson,* ed. Merrill D. Peterson (New York: Viking, 1984) 853.

117. Jefferson to Mr. Rutledge and Mr. Shippen, June 3, 1788, Peterson 660.

118. Reps 105-108.

119. James D. Kornwolf, *"So Good a Design": The Colonial Campus of the College of William and Mary: Its History, Background, and Legacy* (Exhib. cat., Joseph and Margaret Muscarelle Museum of Art) (Williamsburg: College of William and Mary, 1989) 121-135 and Reps 108-114.

120. Kornwolf 126-127.

121. Reps 108-114.

122. Reps 103.

123. Beatrice B. Garvan, *Federal Philadelphia 1785-1825* (Exhib. cat., Philadelphia Museum of Art) (Philadelphia: The Museum, 1987) 39.

124. *The Federalist* 14: 85.

125. *The Federalist* 18: 112.

126. Kite 42.

127. *The Federalist* 37: 224-232. Madison's emphasis on the importance of learning and critically evaluating the past is discussed in *The Federalist* no. 14 and no.18.

128. Padover 59, and Caemmerer 149.

129. Kornwolf 22.

130. His plan is outlined in a draft of a bill to transfer the state capital to Richmond. It was presented to the Virginia House of Delegates on October 14, 1776.

131. Hadley Arkes, *First Things* (Princeton: Princeton University Press, 1986) ix.

132. Unpublished Memoir to Congress. Kite 7.

133. Washington to Jefferson, March 31, 1791, Fitzpatrick 31: 257.

134. L'Enfant Report, June 22, 1791, Caemmerer 151-154 and n3.

135. The original site of the federal city has been brilliantly analyzed by Don Alexander Hawkins, using survey maps of 1794 prepared by Nicholas King to prepare to lay out the street system. Don Alexander Hawkins, "Landscape of the Federal City," *Washington History,* 3.1 (1991): 10-33.

136. It is not certain who renamed Goose Creek. It was called the Tiber for at least a century before the founding of Washington, D.C., deriving the name from a plantation called "Rome." Frederick Gutheim and Wilcomb E. Washburn, *The Federal City: Plans & Realities* (Washington, D.C.: Smithsonian Institution, 1976) 4.

137. Boyd 20: 83.

138. Caemmerer 151.

139. Quoted in Pamela Scott, "This Vast Empire': The Iconography of the Mall, 1791-1848," Richard Longstreth, ed., *The Mall in Washington, 1791-1991* (Washington, D.C.: National Gallery, 1991) 38 and n7.

140. Jackson and Twohig 6: 164-5.

141. Washington to Stuart, March 18, 1792, Fitzpatrick 32: 506.

142. Caemmerer 152.

143. Jefferson used the term "Capitol" for his statehouse at Richmond of 1786. His source was the Capitol at Williamsburg.

144. In *The Federalist* 39: 244-245, Madison states that a republic is "administered by persons holding their offices during pleasure, for a limited period, and during good behavior." In *The Federalist* 37: 227-228 he discusses the importance of short terms of office.

145. William T. Partridge, "L'Enfant's Methods and Features of His Plan for the Federal City," in National Capital Park and Planning Code Revision, *Reports and Plans, Washington Region,* Supplementary Technical Data to Accompany Annual Report, 1930, 21-33.

146. In Fitzpatrick 35: 228. Montesquieu says that the separation of powers means that one branch cannot assume all of another's functions. Thus the President's veto power allows the executive to share, albeit indirectly, in the legislative function.

147. James Sterling Young, *The Washington Community* 1800-1828 (New York: Columbia University Press, 1966) 8.

148. L'Enfant to Washington, August 19,1791, Caemmerer 158.

149. Caemmerer 153.

150. The siting is difficult to explain. Pamela Scott found no evidence that the location of the Washington Monument was determined by the poor quality of the sub-soil for foundations at the crossing of the Mall's axes. She postulates, instead, that 1) the Meridian Stone erected by Jefferson at the center of the Mall in 1804 was too important to be moved; 2) any determination of the Mall's center was ambiguous in relation to the Capitol, and depended on whether the canal (built in 1804 and widened in 1832) was included in the measurement; and 3) the Monument was built in the center of the Mall, excluding the widened canal, and that it was to be balanced by the Smithsonian Institution building as they were seen from the Capitol terrace. Pamela Scott, "Robert Mills and American Monuments," John M. Bryan, Ed., *Robert Mills, Architect* (Washington, D.C.: AIA Press, 1989) 168.

151. Caemmerer 165.

152. Caemmerer 152-153.

153. Montesquieu, *The Spirit of Laws*, XI.6 and *The Federalist* 81: 522-533.

154. Caemmerer 164.

155. Kite 70.

156. Fitzpatrick 32: 299-230.

157. Julian P. Boyd, "On the Need for 'Frequent Recurrence to Fundamental Principles,'" *Virginia Law Review* 62: 859.

158. Madison's comment was made at the Constitutional Convention during a debate on the best location for the "Seat of Govt." Max Ferrand, ed., *The Records of the Federal Convention of 1787*, Rev. ed. (New Haven: Yale University Press, 1937) 2: 261.

159. Padover 471.

160. Benjamin Henry Latrobe, "Plan of the Principal Story of the Capitol," 1808-1809, presentation drawing. Library of Congress 270/B3.

161. John Adams to John Taylor, 1814, in George Seldes, *The Great Quotations* (Secaucus, N.J.: Carol Publishing Group, 1983) 43.

162. I am indebted to William Allen, former Historian of the Capitol, for this information.

163. One such fort, Fort Washington, was designed by L'Enfant. It guards the entrance to the harbors of Alexandria and Washington. The text of L'Enfant's memorandum to Congress on defense is in Kite 7-8. The letter to Washington is in Caemmerer 127-30.

164. Carroll William Westfall, "Adam and Eve in Post Modern Chicago," *Threshold: Journal of the School of Architecture, University of Illinois at Chicago* Spring 1982: 102.

165. Caemmerer 152.

166. The most recent examples are Norma Evanson, "Monumental Spaces," in Longstreth 21, 43-46; Reps 252; Reps 5; and Vincent Scully, *Architecture: The Natural and the Man Made* (New York: St. Martin's, 1991) 292-293.

167. Scully 221-310.

168. Scott in Longstreth 43.

169. The pertinent data on the engraving matter is contained in the following correspondence: L'Enfant to Tobias Lear, October 6, 1791, Caemmerer 169-171; L'Enfant Memorial to Congress, Caemmerer 171-172; L'Enfant to Lear, October 19, 1791, Caemmerer 173-174; Washington to Stuart, November 20, 1791, discusses Ellicott's opinion that the map was not accurate enough for use at the site. Washington to Stuart, November 20, 1791, Fitzpatrick 31: 421-422.

170. The details of the demolition of Daniel Carroll's house are in Kite 180-82 and in Caemmerer 176-187. Washington informed the commissioners that "I think Mr. Carroll . . . is equally to blame." Washington to Commissioners, Fitzpatrick 31: 446.

171. The controversy about the removal of stakes is discussed in Caemmerer 202-203.

172. The accusation of slander is discussed in Caemmerer 202-203, and Kite 137.

173. For details of the issue of lack of cooperation involving L'Enfant's assistants Isaac Roberdeau and Balentine Baraof, see Caemmerer 199-201.

174. All of the incidents referred to in notes 167-170, above, fall under the rubric of L'Enfant not acknowledging the commissioners' authority. The meat of this accusation was L'Enfant's direct access to the President, which undercut their authority.

175. Washington laid blame for the first delay in securing the engraving on the engraver: see Washington to David Stuart, November 20, 1791, Caemmerer 176. With respect to the Carroll house, Kite states that L'Enfant acted within the law: Kite 80-82; further, the President wrote to the commissioners that after a visit to Georgetown, where he obtained additional information "not only from Majr. L'Enfant but from another on whom I could depend . . . I think Mr. Carroll of Duddington is equally to blame": Washington to Commissioners of the District of Columbia, December 18, 1791, Fitzpatrick 31: 446. Daniel Carroll did not proceed against L'Enfant with his charge of slander and we may surmise that he had no grounds: see Kite 135-138. Many of the local landowners were ardent in their support of L'Enfant and untiring in their efforts to secure a reconciliation between him and the commissioners: Kite 168-179 and Caemmerer 217-218. See also L'Enfant to Jefferson, February 26, 1792, for L'Enfant's reply to his accusers. Caemmerer 210-211.

176. Stuart to Washington, Caemmerer 204. Washington's reply to one point raised in this letter was dated March 18, 1792. Stuart's letter was written earlier.

177. Washington was sympathetic to Jefferson's belief that the United States should remain an agricultural nation that exported food and imported industrial products. In 1788 he wrote that "the introduction of anything which will divert our attention from agriculture must be extremely prejudicial if not ruinous to us." His view of the future was more optimistic and realistic, however, for he understood that the well-being of the nation depended on encouraging industry and developing a sound fiscal policy. Fitzpatrick 29: 351, 30: 45; and Flexner 165-166.

178. L'Enfant described the grid of Jefferson's plan as "tiresome and insipid, and it could never be in its origin but a mean continuance of some cool imagination wanting a sense of the real grand and truly beautiful." Kite 47-48. L'Enfant later described Jefferson as wishing to have as capital a "seat of government stand a mere contemptible hamlet." Flexner 335, and Caemmerer 377.

179. Jefferson to Washington, November 6, 1791, Boyd 22: 263, and Padover 76.

180. That L'Enfant appeared contented with the status quo is implied by Washington's November 20, 1791 letter to Commissioner David Stuart that "you may not infer . . . he [L'Enfant] has expressed any dissatisfaction at the conduct of the Commissioners towards him," Fitzpatrick 31: 421. In the same vein, Commissioner Daniel Carroll,

soon to become his enemy, wrote to Madison on November 29, 1791 of L'Enfant's "very polite" letter to his nephew, whose house stood in a right of way: Carroll to Madison, November 29, 1791, Kite 80-81 n49. Even after L'Enfant authorized the demolition of this house and the affair became explosive, the President wrote to Jefferson, "I am glad to find that matters, after all that has happened, stand so well between the Commrs. and Major L'Enfant": Washington to Jefferson, December 14, 1791, Fitzpatrick 31: 445.

181. Kenneth R. Bowling, *Creating the Federal City, 1774-1800: Potomac Fever* (Washington, D.C.: AIA Press, 1988) 79.

182. Jefferson to Johnson, March 8, 1791, Padover 109.

183. *Benjamin Perley Poore's Reminiscences* 1: 54, quoted in Caemmerer 281.

184. A recommendation from Hamilton led to L'Enfant's appointment to plan Patterson, New Jersey. Hamilton to Governor and Directors of Society for Establishing Useful Manufactures, August 16, 1792, Syrett 12: 217.

185. Washington, "Errors of Government Towards the Indians," February 1792, Fitzpatrick 31: 492.

186. Forrest McDonald, *Alexander Hamilton: A Biography* (New York: Norton, 1979) 23-24.

187. Flexner 327 notes that "the existence of these subordinates (the Commissioners) did not at the start keep Washington from running everything himself."

188. Washington to Jefferson, February 22, 1792, Fitzpatrick 31: 482-483.

189. Washington to Commissioners of the District of Columbia, December 18, 1791, Fitzpatrick 31: 446.

190. Washington to David Stuart, November 30, 1792, Fitzpatrick 32: 244.

191. Washington to David Stuart, November 20, 1791, Fitzpatrick 31: 419-420 and Caemmerer 28. I have not been able to find the source of the last phrase of this quotation. It is not part of the November 20, 1791 letter to David Stuart and Caemmerer does not cite his source.

192. Peets 61-66, 79-87.

193. *The Federalist* 34: 204.

194. Washington to Sarah Cary Fairfax, May 16, 1798, Fitzpatrick 36: 264.